JESUS IS GOD IN THE QUR'AN

The Qur'an states that Jesus is Allah's *"word which he cast into Mary, and a 'spirit' from him"* (Surah 4:171). Jesus is also called a word from Allah in Surah 3:39, 45.
Is the word of Allah eternal or created?

DR. MAXWELL SHIMBA

Published in Manhattan, New York by Shimba Publishing, LLC.

Printed in the United States of America

Shimba Publishing LLC
Printed in the United States of America

First Printing Edition, 2021

Contents

Table of Contents

DR. MAXWELL SHIMBA

NOTE

Authoritative Islamic texts are the Qur'an and Hadith. Muslims believe that the Qur'an is the revealed word of Allah (verse numbers differ slightly in different versions). Surah always stands for a chapter in the Qur'an. Islamic belief is that Muhammad is the perfect example to be followed by all Muslims. Whatever he said, practiced or approved is called Hadith. There are six different sets of authentic ahadith (Hadiths): Bukhari, Muslim, Abu Dawud, Tirmizi, Tabari, Sunnan Ibn Majah and Sunnan Nasa'i. This book is intended to show the teachings and examples of Muhammad, and is not intended to be offensive to Muslims; many Muslims may have little real knowledge of what their god, Allah and their prophet has said on this topic.

INTRODUCTION

Let us start by reading the Holy Quran.

Surah Az-Zukhruf 43:63

فِيهِ تَخْتَلِفُونَ ٱلَّذِى بَعْضَ لَكُم وَلِأُبَيِّنَ بِٱلْحِكْمَةِ جِئْتُكُم قَدْ قَالَ بِٱلْبَيِّنَـٰتِ عِيسَىٰ جَآءَ وَلَمَّا
وَأَطِيعُونِ ٱللَّهَ فَٱتَّقُوا۟

Wa lammaa jaaa'a 'Eesaa bilbaiyinaati qaala qad ji'tukum
bil Hikmati wa li-ubaiyina lakum ba'dal lazee takhtalifoona feehi
fattaqul laaha wa atee'oon

SAHIH INTERNATIONAL:

*And when Jesus brought clear proofs, he said, "I have come to
you with wisdom and to make clear to you some of that over which you
differ, so fear Allah and obey me.*

Since the Qur'an records that Jesus told people to fear
Allah and obey him [Jesus] (Surah 43:63), and that in Surah 7:158
Muslims are told to believe in Jesus and His Scriptures [Torah and
Gospels], it is important for Muslims to know this unique person.
Allah teaches that Jesus not only performed miracles but, being
the Word of God, raised the dead and created birds (Surah 5:110;
4:171; 3:45, 49). Furthermore, Muhammad looked up to Him as a
sinless one, Surah 19:19; 3:36; Bukhari, vol. 4, Hadith No. 651-652.

So, who is Jesus?

The Qur'an states that Jesus is Allah's *"word which he cast
into Mary, and a 'spirit' from him"* (Surah 4:171). Jesus is also called
a word from Allah in Surah 3:39, 45. One question one should ask
is this: Is the Word of Allah eternal or created?

In the same token, Jesus the Word of God in the Bible.

John 1: 1 *In the beginning was the Word, and the Word was with
God, and the Word was God. ² The same was in the beginning with God.
³ All things were made by him; and without him was not anything made
that was made.*

John1: ¹⁴ *And the Word was made flesh, and dwelt among us, (and
we beheld his glory, the glory as of the only begotten of the Father,) full
of grace and truth.*

Jesus is revealed as the "Word of God", and everything was
created by that Word (John 1:1-3, 14). It is obvious that the Word
of any person is uniquely related to that person. In daily life we
express ourselves by our words in joy, sorrow or hurt, and by our

approval or disapproval of things. Our words show our true self which people cannot know by any other means. Similarly, God expresses Himself by His Word. He created and sustains the whole universe by His Word (Hebrews 1:1-3).

To believe that there was any time when God was without His Word suggests that God was ignorant! God does everything by His Word and the Bible teaches that the Word of God is eternal and has always existed with God. In this way, Jesus is Eternal (Isaiah 9:6) and through Him all things were created *(Colossians 1:15-17).* *¹⁵Who is the image of the invisible God, the firstborn of every creature: ¹⁶For by him were all things created, that are in heaven, and that are in earth, visible and invisible, whether they be thrones, or dominions, or principalities, or powers: all things were created by him, and for him: ¹⁷And he is before all things, and by him all things consist.*
Pre-existence of Jesus Christ

Jesus Christ, the eternal Word of God, not only existed before He was born as a human but also appeared to many people in Old Testament (O.T.) times. Jesus Himself speaks of His glory with the Father before the creation of the world *(John 17:5) ⁵And now, O Father, glorify thou me with thine own self with the glory which I had with thee before the world was.,* and He told the Jews that "before Abraham was, I am" and that Abraham was glad to see Him, (John 8:52-59; see Genesis 18:1-33). The Apostle John also records that the Prophet Isaiah saw His glory and wrote about Him (John 12:41; Isaiah 6:1-13). These are what are known as *theophanies* (God manifesting Himself) or *epiphanies* (the glory of God manifested) and there are numerous accounts of these manifestations to people, such as:

1. Genesis 2:18-22; 3:8, 9, 21 - to Adam and Eve.
2. Genesis 32:28, 30 - Jacob wrestled with the Lord!
3. Exodus 3:2-6 - The Angel of the LORD appeared to Moses and said: "I am the God of your father - the God of Abraham, the God of Isaac, and the God of Jacob"
4. Joshua 5:14 - Joshua worshiped the captain of the host of the Lord;
5. Isaiah 6:5; John 12:41 - Isaiah saw Him
6. Ezekiel 1:25-28 - Ezekiel worshiped the Son of Man
7. Daniel 3:24-5 - King Nebuchadnezzar saw the Fourth Man like the Son of God.

As impeccably construed above, Jesus was indeed known to Abraham and Isaiah, it is reasonable to assume that these theophanies were visitations of the Jesus who was Deity.

The Attributes of Jesus Christ

We learn from the Scriptures that all God the Father has belongs to Jesus as well, and that He therefore deserves the same honor as the Father (John 5:23;16:15). There are many characteristics and attributes the deity of Jesus Christ which can be associated with God alone characteristics such as:

The Creator of heaven, the earth and human beings

GOD - Psalm 102:24-27; Malachi 2:10; Proverbs 16:4

JESUS - John 1:1-2; Hebrews 1:10-12; Colossians 1:16

The Mighty God

GOD - Habakkuk 1:12-13; Isaiah 10:20-21

JESUS - Isaiah 9:6

The First and the Last

GOD - Isaiah 44:6; 41:4; 48:12

JESUS - Revelation 1:7-8; 22:13-16

The Everlasting God

GOD - Psalm 90:2; Habakkuk 1:12

JESUS - Micah 5:2

The Unchangeable God

GOD - Malachi 3:6

JESUS - Hebrews 13:8

The Omnipresent - present everywhere

GOD - Psalm 139:7; Jeremiah 23:24

JESUS - Matthew 18:20; 28:20; John 3:13; Ephesians 4:10

The Omniscient - the all seeing

GOD - Psalm 147:5; Proverbs 15:3

JESUS - John 21:17; 16:30; Colossians 2:3)

The Omnipotent - the all powerful

GOD - Genesis 17:1; Jeremiah 32:17; Matthew 19:26; JESUS - Matthew 28:18; Hebrews 1:3; Revelation 1:8)

Worship of Christ Jesus the Messiah

In Jewish religion, the True God and none else can be worshipped. However, a study of the New Testament (N.T.) reveals that many devout Jews who realized that Jesus was the Messiah worshiped Him - as did many gentiles (non-Jews). The

Scriptures also declare that at the end of the ages every human being will worship Him. We need also to note that Jesus never ever forbade anyone from worshiping Him. Following is a list of *some* of the incidents in the Scriptures where Jesus is worshiped as God:

The Messiah as Son of God	The Messiah as Man
Eternal Father or Father of eternity -Isaiah 9:6; Micah 5:2; John 1:1-2).	Was born as a baby -Matthew 1:21-2:11; Luke 2:1-15
He is always the same - Hebrews 13:8	Grew physically and spiritually - Luke 2:52
He was able to feed 5,000 men plus women and children with five loaves and two fish - Matthew 14:15-21	Was hungry - Matthew 4:2
He gives living water - John 4:14	Was thirsty - John 19:28
He was able to still the storm - Luke 8:22-25	Was tired and was sleeping during a sea storm - Mark 4:36-41
He raised the dead after four days by commanding the dead to come out of the grave - John 11:43-44	Wept at the death of a friend - John 11:35
He answers prayers - John 14:13-14	Prayed - Luke 22:41
He gives rest to all who come to Him - Matthew 11:28-29	Was exhausted - John 4:6
He forgave sins - Matthew 9:2; Mark 2:5; Luke 5:20, 23-24	Offered Himself as the sacrifice for sins - Ephesians 5:2; Hebrews 7:27; 9:14
He is the King of kings and the Lord of lords - Revelations 19:6	Was a Servant - Philippians 2:7-8

Wise men - Matthew 2:1-2, 11; A leper - Matthew 8:1-2
A ruler - Matthew 9:18ff; Disciples - Matthew 14:30f
A Canaanite woman - Matthew 15:22-25

A man with an unclean spirit - Mark 5:1-6
After resurrection, the disciples - Luke 24:50-52

Jesus -The Son of God

There are many people who consider only some aspects of Jesus' life and neglect others, and thereby conclude that this Man cannot also be God. For this reason, we ask you to consider the following carefully.

Jesus - The Savior/Redeemer Messiah

Sin causes separation between God and Man; sin is the cause of all evil, of all suffering and of all problems in this world. The first step toward solving these problems is restoration of a right relationship with God. The Bible teaches that people who have not repented of their sins and accepted Jesus Christ as their Lord and Savior are God's enemies and spiritually dead. Without realizing this, all religions try to bridge the gap between man and God. One of the very major differences between the God of the Bible and other gods is His claims to be the only Savior of humankind. Isaiah 43:11 says, "I, *even* I, *am* the LORD; and beside me *there is* no Savior." Isaiah 53 tells us that the Messiah will redeem mankind by His own Holy blood! So, the God who claims to be the only Savior saves His people by the atoning sacrifice of His Son, because there was no other means of paying the price of rebelling against the Almighty God, who is absolutely Holy and absolutely Just. This Holy and Just God always takes sin very seriously and also knows that no sinner can save him/herself. For that reason, He sent Jesus the Messiah, the Holy Word of God Himself of infinite value, to save mankind.

Jesus came to save sinners such as you and me. God has promised that all who call on the name of the Lord shall be saved (Acts 2:21; Romans 10:9). To receive this salvation, you must confess Jesus as Lord and agree with God that you are a sinner who deserves death; and that Jesus the Messiah paid the price for your sins on the cross and bought you with His holy precious blood.

Now you have a further opportunity to find out more, as God has given you the means and the ability to search for the truth.

CHAPTER
I

IS JESUS MENTIONED IN THE QUR'AN?

Is Jesus mentioned in the Quran?

Surah Maryam 19:19

زَكِيًّا غُلَـٰمًا لَكِ لِأَهَبَ رَبِّكِ رَسُولُ أَنَا إِنَّمَآ قَالَ

Qaala innamaa ana rasoolu Rabbiki li ahaba laki ghulaaman zakiyyaa

SAHIH INTERNATIONAL:

He said, "I am only the messenger of your Lord to give you [news of] a pure boy."

Among the non-Christian faith, Islam is the only religion that recognizes the person of Jesus Christ. The Qur'an mentions a great deal about Jesus Christ. In fact, Jesus is mentioned in over ninety verses in the Qur'an. Islam confirms that Jesus was born to a virgin, was sinless, performed miracles, and was superior to other prophets, in contrast, Islam denies the Sonship of Jesus Christ in no uncertain terms. This is one of the strongest doctrinal distinct were Christianity and Islam part ways. Which one of these two has the correct understanding of Jesus? Is it Islam or Christianity? Two opposing views cannot be equally true. Our salvation depends very much on knowing the right answer.

Whereas, Jesus is regarded as a highly respected prophet in Islam, it nevertheless considers Him as no more than a prophet of God. However, for Christians it is an uncompromising truth that Jesus is the begotten Son of God. While the Qur'an denies his Sonship openly, there are numerous internal evidences in the Qur'an itself that testify to the Biblical truth that Jesus is indeed the Son of God. The testimonies regarding Jesus Christ clearly show that He is more than a prophet. In fact, most Muslims are unaware that the Qur'an confirms the following magnificent truths regarding the person of Jesus Christ:

1. *He was born of a Virgin – Surah 3:45-47; Surah 19:17-21.*
2. *He was the Word of God – Surah 4:171.*
3. *He was a Spirit from God – Surah 4:171.*
4. *He was Faultless (Sinless) – Surah 19:19.*
5. *He was the Messiah – Surah 4:171.*
6. *He was Illustrious in this World and would continue to be so in the Hereafter – Surah 3:45.*
7. *He was taken to Heaven by God – Surah 4:158.*
8. *He will come back as a Sign of the Hour of Judgment – Surah 43:61.*

We will now go into the comprehensive details. What is vital for Muslims to note is that the Qur'an will be used extensively to validate the veracity of our argument that Jesus Christ is indeed the idiosyncratic Son of God and God.

The Only Prophet who was conceived without sexual involvement

One of the most important and impeccable points of agreement between Islam and Christianity concerns the conception of Jesus. Both the Infallible Word, the Bible and the Qur'an teach that He was conceived by Mary without the sexual involvement of any man. The virgin-birth of Jesus, taught so plainly in the Holy Bible, is also clearly taught in the Qur'an. The Bible states that Jesus was conceived miraculously with the aid of

God's Holy Spirit. By means of His miraculous power, God transferred the life of Jesus to the womb of a Jewish virgin in order for him to be born as a human. This miraculous conception was not a random act of God. It took place in fulfillment of a divine prophecy foretold centuries in advance in the Bible before actual birth of Jesus. The Book of Isaiah prophesized about the virgin-birth of Jesus more than 700 years before his actual birth: "704-701 BC"

Isaiah 7:14: "Therefore the Lord himself will give you a sign: behold, a virgin shall conceive, and bear a son, and shall call his name Immanuel."

Both the gospel according to Luke and Matthew record this remarkable conception in the Holy Bible. The record states clearly that Mary was a virgin whom no man had touched when Jesus was conceived by the power of the Holy Spirit:

Luke 1:30-35: And the angel said to her: "Do not be afraid, Mary, for you have found favor with God. Behold! You will conceive in your womb and bear a son, and you are to call his name Jesus. This one will be great and will be called Son of the Most High; and the Lord God will give him the throne of David his father, and he will rule as king over the house of Jacob forever, and there will be no end of his kingdom." But Mary said to the angel: "How is this to be, since I am a virgin?" In answer the angel said to her: "Holy spirit will come upon you and power of the Most High will overshadow you. Therefore, the child to be born will be called holy — the Son of God."

Matthew 1:22-23: All this actually came about for that to be fulfilled which was spoken by the Lord God through his prophet, saying: "Look! The virgin will become pregnant and will give birth to a son and they will call his name Immanuel ..."

This distinctive and peculiar feature regarding the conception of Jesus is one of the most clear and unambiguous teachings of both the Bible and the Qur'an. And this truth is fundamentally upheld by both Scriptures. It is referred to more than once in the Qur'an. We will now look at two examples in the Qur'an:

Surah 3:45-47: Behold! The angels said: "O Mary! God giveth thee glad tidings of a Word from Him: his name will be Christ Jesus, the son of Mary, held in honour in this world and the Hereafter and of (the company of) those nearest to God..., She said: "O my Lord! How shall I have a son when no man hath touched me?" He said: "Even so: God createth what He willeth: When He hath decreed a plan, He but saith to it, 'Be,' and it is! (Yusuf Ali)

وَجِيهًا مَرْيَمَ ٱبْنُ عِيسَى ٱلْمَسِيحُ ٱسْمُهُ مِنْهُ بِكَلِمَةٍ يُبَشِّرُكِ ٱللَّهَ إِنَّ يَمَرْيَمُ ٱلْمَلَـٰٓئِكَةُ قَالَتِ إِذْ ٱلْمُقَرَّبِينَ وَمِنَ وَٱلْـَٔاخِرَةِ ٱلدُّنْيَا فِى

3:45

Iz qaalatil malaaa'ikatu yaa Maryamu innal laaha yubashshiruki bi Kalimatim minhus muhul Maseehu 'Eesab nu Maryama wajeehan fid dunyaa wal Aakhirati wa minal muqarrabeen

SAHIH INTERNATIONAL:

[And mention] when the angels said, "O Mary, indeed Allah gives you good tidings of a word from Him, whose name will be the Messiah, Jesus, the son of Mary – distinguished in this world and the Hereafter and among those brought near [to Allah].

ٱلصَّـٰلِحِينَ وَمِنَ وَكَهْلًا ٱلْمَهْدِ فِى ٱلنَّاسَ وَيُكَلِّمُ

3:46

Wa yukallimun naasa filmahdi wa kahlanw wa minassaaliheen

SAHIH INTERNATIONAL:

He will speak to the people in the cradle and in maturity and will be of the righteous."

يَشَآءُ مَا يَخْلُقُ ٱللَّهُ كَذَٰلِكِ قَالَ بَشَرٌ يَمْسَسْنِى وَلَمْ وَلَدٌ لِى يَكُونُ أَنَّىٰ رَبِّ قَالَتْ فَيَكُونُ كُن لَهُ يَقُولُ فَإِنَّمَا أَمْرًا قَضَىٰٓ إِذَا

3:47

Qaalat Rabbi annaa yakoonu lee waladunw wa lam yamsasnee basharun qaala kazaalikil laahu yakhluqu maa yashaaa'; izaa qadaaa amran fa innamaa yaqoolu lahoo kun fayakoon

SAHIH INTERNATIONAL:

She said, "My Lord, how will I have a child when no man has touched me?" [The angel] said, "Such is Allah; He creates what He wills. When He decrees a matter, He only says to it, 'Be,' and it is.

The following is another passage in the Qur'an that records the visitation of Gabriel "Jibril" to Mary announcing the phenomenal conception of Jesus:

Surah 19:17-21: She placed a screen (to screen herself) from them; then We sent her our angel, and he appeared before her as a man

in all respects. She said: "I seek refuge from thee to (God) Most Gracious: (come not near) if thou dost fear God." He said: "Nay, I am only an apostle from thy Lord, (to announce) to thee the gift of a holy son. She said: "How shall I have a son, seeing that no man has touched me, and I am not unchaste?" He said: "So (it will be): Thy Lord saith, 'that is easy for Me: and (We wish) to appoint him as a Sign unto men and a Mercy from Us': It is a matter (so) decreed." (Yusuf Ali)

سَوِيًّا بَشَرًا لَهَا فَتَمَثَّلَ رُوحَنَا إِلَيْهَا فَأَرْسَلْنَا حِجَابًا دُونِهِم مِن فَٱتَّخَذَتْ

19:17

Fattakhazat min doonihim hijaaban fa arsalnaaa ilaihaa roohanaa fatamassala lahaa basharan sawiyyaa

SAHIH INTERNATIONAL:

And she took, in seclusion from them, a screen. Then We sent to her Our Angel, and he represented himself to her as a well-proportioned man.

تَقِيًّا كُنتَ إِن مِنكَ بِٱلرَّحْمَـٰنِ أَعُوذُ إِنِّى قَالَتْ

19:18

Qaalat ineee a'oozu bir Rahmaani minka in kunta taqiyyaa

SAHIH INTERNATIONAL:

She said, "Indeed, I seek refuge in the Most Merciful from you, [so leave me], if you should be fearing of Allah."

زَكِيًّا غُلَـٰمًا لَكِ لِأَهَبَ رَبِّكِ رَسُولُ أَنَا إِنَّمَا قَالَ

19:19

Qaala innamaa ana rasoolu Rabbiki li ahaba laki ghulaaman zakiyyaa

SAHIH INTERNATIONAL:

He said, "I am only the messenger of your Lord to give you [news of] a pure boy."

بَغِيًّا أَكُ وَلَمْ بَشَرٌ يَمْسَسْنِى وَلَمْ غُلَـٰمٌ لِى يَكُونُ أَنَّىٰ قَالَتْ

19:20

Qaalat anna yakoonu lee ghulaamunw wa lam yamsasnee basharunw wa lam aku baghiyyaa

SAHIH INTERNATIONAL:

She said, "How can I have a boy while no man has touched me and I have not been unchaste?"

مَّقْضِيًّا أَمْرًا وَكَانَ مِّنَّا وَرَحْمَةً لِّلنَّاسِ ءَايَةً وَلِنَجْعَلَهُ هَيِّنٌ عَلَىَّ هُوَ رَبُّكِ قَالَ كَذَٰلِكِ قَالَ

19:21

Qaala kazaaliki qaala Rabbuki huwa 'alaiya haiyimunw wa linaj 'alahooo Aayatal linnaasi wa rahmatam minnaa; wa kaana amram maqdiyyaa

SAHIH INTERNATIONAL:

He said, "Thus [it will be]; your Lord says, 'It is easy for Me, and We will make him a sign to the people and a mercy from Us. And it is a matter [already] decreed.' "

If Mary had conceived Jesus through normal sexual intercourse, it would hardly have been necessary for Gabriel to explain the conception she was about to experience. The emphasis of the virgin-birth in the Qur'an can be seen by the title it consistently gives to Jesus, namely *"ibn Maryam" – "the son of Mary." (Surah 3:45).* The regular occurrence of this title in the Qur'an strongly validates the conclusion that she must have conceived Jesus without the agency of a human father. In historical times, children were almost always named after their fathers. There are also other passages in the Qur'an which stress this fact with equal force:

Surah 21:91: "And (remember) her who guarded her chastity: We breathed into her of Our spirit, and We made her and her son a sign for all peoples." (Yusuf Ali)

لِّلْعَٰلَمِينَ ءَايَةً وَٱبْنَهَآ وَجَعَلْنَٰهَا رُوحِنَا مِن فِيهَا فَنَفَخْنَا فَرْجَهَا أَحْصَنَتْ وَٱلَّتِي

Wallateee ahsanat farjahaa fanafakhnaa feehaa min roohinaa wa ja'alnaahaa wabnahaaa Aayatan lil'aalameen.

This Qur'anic ayat "verse" clearly tells us that the conception of Jesus took place through the aid of God's spirit. It states: *"We breathed into her of Our spirit."* The manner by which *"her son"* was brought into existence within her, without any reference to a human father, re-emphasizes the miraculous conception of Jesus Christ. Centuries before the Qur'an even came into existence the Holy Bible affirmed to this truth:

Matthew 1:18: "This is how the birth of Jesus Christ took place..., she was found to be pregnant by holy spirit."

It is also most significant to find that Mary is the sole woman mentioned by name in the entire Qur'an – Surah Maryam. In fact, a whole Surah is named after her – Surah Maryam – Quran Surah 19. Not even Eve – the mother of the human race – is mentioned by name. What is the reason for such exultation of

Mary in the Qur'an? It is because of her significant place in human history as the only woman who conceived a son while still a virgin. And she mothered the greatest among God's prophets.

Surah 3:42: Behold! The angels said: "O Mary! God hath chosen thee and purified thee – chosen thee above the women of all nations." (Yusuf Ali)

The exultation of Mary in the above Qur'anic verse is a reiteration of what was written centuries ago in the Holy Bible:

Luke 1:42: "Blessed are you among women, and blessed is the fruit of your womb."

Reason for His unique conception

Adam as the first man on earth, was created without the agency of a human father or mother. It is logically impossible for him to have earthly parents. Therefore, such an act of creation was necessary at the beginning of the world of mankind. Someone had to be created first. However, in the case of Jesus, we find that he was conceived without the aid of a human father when God's natural process of procreation had already been in existence since the beginning of the human race. Here we find God interrupting the course of nature and overriding the very laws of procreation that He had himself established. God interrupted the very course of nature in order to facilitate the virgin-birth of Jesus Christ. Why would God do that? Surely, such an act could not have been without meaning. Jesus must have held a very special relationship with the One who was the architect of this miraculous conception – a relationship that is shared by no other prophet. The birth of no other prophet has been anything as remotely close as the miraculous conception of Jesus Christ.

To deny that God does anything without a purpose behind it amounts to a denial of God himself. In the Qur'an, we cannot find a clearly defined purpose for the unique conception of Jesus. It is this very absence of purpose in the Qur'an which confounds the seeker of truth as to the meaning behind the miraculous birth of Jesus. Being born of a virgin-woman, Jesus had an exceptional and unique beginning to his life on earth. He was the only man in all human history to come into the world in this remarkable manner. As such, we cannot be satisfied with the Qur'an's declaration that the virgin-birth was simply a demonstration of God's power.

It is an undeniable fact that the virgin-birth of Jesus Christ was brought on by the power of God. However, this in itself does not explain its meaning or purpose. The miraculous conception of Jesus could not have been simply for the purpose of demonstrating the power of God. Why do we say that? The reason is because there was simply no visible manifestation of God's power for humans to behold when God caused the conception to take place. The miraculous conception could not be physically seen as there was no visible evidence of it. Since no one could actually see the miraculous power at work at the time of conception, it would certainly be futile for God to use it as a means to demonstrate his power. Therefore, the virgin-birth could not have been for the purpose to demonstrate the power of God as the Qur'an claims. The Qur'an is clearly in error. Thus, there must be another reason for it.

Why then was the virgin-birth absolutely necessary in the case of Jesus?

Surely, such an extraordinary act by God cannot be without a valid reason or purpose. He would not violate his own perfect laws to cause the virgin-birth if it is not absolutely necessary for him to do so. Something must have required that Jesus be born in this way. The virgin-birth is an article of faith, which is repeatedly upheld in the Qur'an. Yet, we find that there is no explanation for the miraculous birth of Jesus. In the Qur'an we are assured that it took place but we are not told why.

However, the answer is provided in the Holy Bible. Only in the Bible we can find the reason for the unique conception of Jesus. It tells us that unlike all other prophets, Jesus is the unique Son of God. As the unique Son of God, it was not possible for him to be born of a human father when the time arrived for him to come into the world in the likeness of men. Therefore, it was absolutely necessary for Jesus to be born of a virgin-woman. The Bible also tells us that Jesus was with his Father in the heavens before coming to earth as a human. (John 6:38: 8:23). And the Bible directly identifies Jesus as the only-begotten Son of God. (John 3:16). Thus, Jesus could not be procreated by means of a human father since he is already the unique Son of a heavenly Father. Therefore, only God can be the Father of the Son of God.

Only by accepting Jesus as the Son of God, one can understand the significance of the virgin-birth. Thus, the reason for the exceptional birth of Jesus is made clear only in the Bible. He was born in this unique way by the special involvement and intervention of God. That is why every single descendant of Adam came into the world by means of natural procreation – the only exception being Jesus. All other men are made out of the same dust that Adam was created. But only Jesus was conceived solely by the spirit of God. That is why he had this unique beginning to his life on earth – because he himself is unique. He is the unique Son of God.

The Son of God

Christians have no problem regarding the identity of Jesus Christ as the Son of God. This is indeed what the angel informed Mary when he came to explain the miraculous conception:

Luke 1:35: "In answer the angel said to her: "Holy spirit will come upon you and power of the Most High will overshadow you. And for that reason, the one who is born will be called holy, God's Son."

Muslims deny the Sonship of Jesus. Even so, both the Qur'an and the Bible agree on the fact that Jesus had no human father. Now let's at look at the parallel account of the above narration in the Qur'an. In Surah 19:19, the angel Gabriel made the following announcement to Mary:

"Nay, I am only a messenger of thy Lord, to announce to thee the gift of a holy son." (Yusuf Ali)

Since the angel refers to Jesus as a *"holy son"* in Surah 19:19, we would like ask the Muslims whose *"son"* is he? Is it Mary's? Let us carefully analyze this Qur'anic verse step by step to arrive at the correct answer.

In Surah 19:19, the angel announces "the gift of a holy son." This Qur'anic verse makes it clear that the holy son was a gift from God to Mary. Therefore, Mary was only the recipient of that gift. She is not the source of that gift but God. The gift was a son. The gift belongs to God. Therefore, the son belongs to God. The son was His. Or to put it even more clearly, His son. In other words, God's son. This testifies to the Gospel truth that Jesus is the Son of God.

Surah 19:19 is one of the strongest pieces of evidence in the Qur'an which proves that Jesus Christ is indeed the Son of God. Muslims have a great misunderstanding about what Christians mean by calling Jesus the Son of God. To Muslims, it means that Christians believe that God performed a physical sexual act to conceive his son. And most Muslims presume that Christians believe that God committed a sexual act with Mary to conceive Jesus. How disgusting! This is an abhorrent blasphemy. No Christian would ever imagine such a blasphemous concept regarding the true God. It is absolutely not possible for God to beget a son as a man begets a son. This could never be. God is incapable of such a physical act and we must never think of God in this way. Christians do not believe that Jesus is the Son of God in the physical concept of its meaning but absolutely in a spiritual sense.

The Qur'an raises the following objection:

Surah 6:101: "How could He have a son when He has no wife?" (A. Bewley)

Observe carefully how Islam attributes the carnal and physical traits of humans to God in this Qur'anic verse. No consideration whatsoever is given for the divinely infinite nature of the holiness of God. Just because men on earth cannot have sons unless they cohabit with their wives, so the Qur'an blasphemously concludes that God, too, cannot have a son unless he cohabits with a woman. Muhammad could not see beyond the carnal. He could not see beyond the temporal to understand the divine nature of God. Muhammad could not see the utter debased profanity of Allah in this Qur'anic verse. The reason for his failure to understand the deep spiritual things of God is explained for us in the Holy Bible:

1 Corinthians 2:14: But a physical man does not receive the things of the spirit of God, for they are foolishness to him; and he cannot get to know them, because they are examined spiritually.

It is absolutely important for us to note that the words "spiritual" and "spirituality" cannot be found in the entire Qur'an. Can a book that does not contain the word "spiritual" comprehend the deep spiritual things of God? We do not think so.

1 Corinthians 2:10-13: For it is to us God has revealed them through his spirit, for the spirit searches into all things, even the deep things of God. For who among men knows the things of a man except the spirit of man that is in him? So, too, no one has come to know the things of God, except the spirit of God. Now we received, not the spirit of the world, but the spirit which is from God, that we might know the things that have been kindly given us by God. These things we also speak, not with words taught by human wisdom, but with those taught by the spirit, as we combine spiritual matters with spiritual words.

Surah 6:101 raises the question: *"How could He have a son when He has no wife?"* Before we answer this question, we would like to draw attention to the fact that the Qur'an itself answers this question:

Surah 39:4: "If Allah had willed to choose a son, He could have chosen what He would of that which He hath created. Be He Glorified! He is Allah, the One, the Absolute." (Pickthall)

Well, does not this Qur'anic verse prove that Allah could have a son if he wants to? We will now address the question raised in Surah 6:101. This Qur'anic verse raises the question: *"How can God have a son without a wife?"* Try to comprehend the absolute absurdity of Allah's question for a moment. According to the absurd logic of this Qur'anic verse, although God Almighty was able to create the vast universe and every living thing in it *out of nothing,* he is unable to produce a son for himself *"without a wife."*

Furthermore, if God could actually cause Mary to supernaturally bring forth a son without a husband, why would it be impossible for him to similarly produce a son without a wife? Why is Mary capable of doing something that Allah cannot? If Muslims can accept the fact that it was possible for Mary to conceive a son without a husband, why do they then find it difficult to accept the fact that the Almighty Creator could likewise have a son without a wife? Yes, if Mary can beget a son without the sexual involvement of a husband, surely the Almighty God can have a son without the sexual involvement of a wife. It would be very foolish for anyone to limit the power of God by saying, *"God cannot have a son."* The Qur'an itself proclaims:

Surah 2:20: "Surely Allah is powerful to do anything." (Usmani)

Imagine! Allah is powerful to do anything except have a son. Jehovah God is the Almighty Creator of the heavens and the earth and every living thing in them. And God asked Abraham the following question:

Genesis 18:14: "Is anything too extraordinary for the Almighty?" And Jesus Christ, the greatest Prophet of the true God, gives us the answer:

Matthew 19:26: "With God all things are possible."

It is an undeniable truth that God created humans equipping them with procreative powers to bear sons and daughters. Yes, God created Adam with power to have sons and daughters. In the Book of Psalms, God reasons with those who foolishly belittle his power:

Psalms 94:8-9: "Pay attention, you foolish unreasoning people! When will you become wise, you fool? He who planted the ear, can he not hear? He who formed the eye, can he not see?"

And to these thought-provoking questions, we can add, *"He who gave mankind the power to have sons, can he not have a son?"* The logical answer to this question is obvious. With just elementary insight, a reasoning person will agree that God *can* have a son.

The word *"Son"* simply means *"a male offspring"* or *"a male descendant."* Every male child has to be the son of a father who produced or generated his life. Adam had no *human* father, but still he had to be the son of someone. Of whom then was he a son of? It is obvious that Adam is the son of God because God was the originator of his life. God was his father. The Bible, which contains the most ancient recorded history of the human race, testifies to this fundamental truth when it traces the genealogy of the human race:

Luke 3:38: "...son of Enosh, son of Seth, son of Adam, son of God."

A divine act of God's creative powers resulted in the life of Adam – the earthly son of God. Concerning Jesus, it is interesting to note this admission in the Qur'an:

Surah 3:59: "Lo! The likeness of Jesus with Allah is as the likeness of Adam." (Pickthall)

Neither of them had a human father. Hence, in as much as Adam was the son of God, so is Jesus. However, the similitude stops here. This does not in any way equate Adam with Jesus, the glorious first-born Son who lived with his heavenly Father before even Adam or anything or anyone else was ever created. (See Colossians 1:15). Jesus was and is the unique Son of God.

Some Muslims believe that because Jesus was born without a human father, the Christian doctrine of Jesus as the Son of God was automatically established from this point in time onwards. In reality, it must be emphasized that it is the other way around. It is because he was the pre-existing Son of God, it was not possible for him to be born in any other way. Muslims need to appreciate that the only reason that Jesus was born in this supernatural manner was because there was no other way that he, as the pre-existing Son of God could be born. If he had been conceived by ordinary means, there would be little to argue for his pre-human heavenly existence as the Son of God. The doctrine of the virgin-birth is crucial to the Christian belief that Jesus is the Son of God. The very uniqueness of his birth is vital to the Christian belief in Jesus as the unique Son of God.

Once the Qur'an denies the fact that Jesus is the Son of God, it can find no meaning for this phenomenon. On the contrary, the Bible gives an absolutely necessary purpose for it – being the Son of God there was no other way he could have been conceived. It is this phenomenal character of the virgin-birth that hints at its real significance and meaning. It is behind the fact of the virgin-birth that we find its true meaning. It is interesting to see how the Qur'an goes a long way towards recognizing this meaning, only to ultimately stumble at it through its denial of Jesus as the Son of God.

The Bible reveals that the coming of Jesus as a human is crucial in the out-working of God's purpose for the salvation of mankind. It was the very heart of God's divine purpose to redeem fallen mankind who by their sinful nature was subjected to futility. (See Romans 8:20). Therefore, mankind's salvation – your salvation – is essentially linked to the gaining of an accurate knowledge of the divine purpose behind the miraculous birth of Jesus Christ. Let us now look at other evidences in the Qur'an that points to uniqueness of Jesus as the divine Son of God.

The Only Prophet who is called the "Word of God"

The Qur'an testifies very clearly that Jesus is the Word of God.

Surah 3:45: Behold! The angels said: "O Mary! Allah giveth Thee glad tidings of a Word from Him: his name will be Christ Jesus. The son of Mary, held in honor in this world and the Hereafter and of (the company of) those nearest to Allah;" (Yusuf Ali)

وَجِيهًا مَرْيَمَ ٱبْنُ عِيسَى ٱلْمَسِيحُ ٱسْمُهُ مِنْهُ بِكَلِمَةٍ يُبَشِّرُكِ ٱللَّهَ إِنَّ يَـٰمَرْيَمُ ٱلْمَلَـٰئِكَةُ قَالَتِ إِذْ ٱلْمُقَرَّبِينَ وَمِنَ وَٱلْءَاخِرَةِ ٱلدُّنْيَا فِى

Iz qaalatil malaaa'ikatu yaa Maryamu innal laaha yubashshiruki bi Kalimatim minhus muhul Maseehu 'Eesab nu Maryama wajeehan fid dunyaa wal Aakhirati wa minal muqarrabeen

And

Surah 4:171: "The Messiah, Jesus the son of Mary, was but the messenger of Allah and His Word, which He cast into Mary and a Spirit from Him." (H. S. Aziz)

ٱلْحَقَّ إِلَّا ٱللَّهِ عَلَى تَقُولُواْ وَلَا دِينِكُمْ فِى تَغْلُواْ لَا ٱلْكِتَـٰبِ يَـٰأَهْلَ مِّنْهُ وَرُوحٌ مَّرْيَمَ إِلَىٰ أَلْقَىٰهَآ وَكَلِمَتُهُ ٱللَّهِ رَسُولُ مَرْيَمَ ٱبْنُ عِيسَى ٱلْمَسِيحُ إِنَّمَا وَٰحِدٌ إِلَـٰهٌ ٱللَّهُ إِنَّمَا لَّكُمْ خَيْرًا ٱنتَهُواْ ثَلَـٰثَةٌ تَقُولُواْ وَلَا وَرُسُلِهِ بِٱللَّهِ فَـَٔامِنُواْ وَكِيلًا بِٱللَّهِ وَكَفَىٰ ٱلْأَرْضِ فِى وَمَا ٱلسَّمَـٰوَٰتِ فِى مَا لَّهُ وَلَدٌ لَّهُ يَكُونَ أَن سُبْحَـٰنَهُ

Yaaa Ahlal Kitaabi laa taghloo fee deenikum wa laa taqooloo 'alal laahi illalhaqq; innamal Maseehu 'Eesab-nu-Maryama Rasoolul laahi wa Kalimatuhooo alqaahaaa ilaa Maryama wa roohum minhum fa aaminoo billaahi wa Rusulihee wa laa taqooloo salaasah; intahoo khairallakum; innamal laahu Ilaahunw Waahid, Subhaanahooo any yakoona lahoo walad; lahoo maa fissamaawaati wa maa fil ard; wa kafaa billaahi Wakeelaa (section 23)

Surah 3:45 states that Allah gave Mary glad tidings "of a Word from Him." In Arabic, the expression used here is "kalimatim-minhu." It means: kalmia (word) min (from) hu (him). It is of vital importance for Muslims to note that Jesus Christ is the only Prophet who ever lived, who is called a "Word from God." And In Surah 4:171, Jesus is addressed as "His Word." In other words, "God's Word." Centuries before the Qur'an came into existence, this same title was given to Jesus in the Holy Bible:

John 1:14: "And the Word became flesh and made is dwelling among us. We have seen his glory, the glory of the one and only Son who came from the father, and he was full of undeserved kindness and truth."

Revelation 19:13: "...the name by which he is called is the Word of God."

But why is Jesus distinctively called the *"Word of God"*? In view of the fact that the Qur'an attributes this title to Jesus without explanation, it is in the Bible that we find the ultimate meaning of this term. The Bible reveals that even before Jesus came to the earth, he was known as the *"Word of God"* during his pre-human existence in heaven. (John 1:1). And after he ascended to heaven, this unique title was still applied to him. (Revelation 19:13). Biblical titles often describe the function or the duty performed by the bearer of the title. For instance, it is stated in the Bible that God made Aaron to serve as a *"mouth"* for Moses:

Exodus 4:16: "He must speak for you to the people; and it must occur that he will serve as a mouth to you, and you will serve as God to him."

As we can see, this means that Aaron served as the *"mouth"* or *"spokesman"* for Moses. In a similar way Jesus served as the *"Word"* or *"Spokesman"* for God. When God communicated with humans, he used Jesus as his angelic mouthpiece. God used Jesus as his *"Word"* or *"Spokesman"* to communicate his divine messages to his servants here on earth. Thus, Jesus served in the exalted capacity of being the *"Word"* or *"Spokesman"* of God. He was and still is the special *"Spokesman"* of God. That is why Jesus alone is honored with this unique title – a title that is shared by no other prophet. Jesus is Jehovah's communicator par excellence. As the *"Word"* or *"Spokesman"* for his Father, Jesus stated the following:

John 12:49-50: "I have not spoken out of my own impulse, but the Father himself who sent me has given me a commandment as to what to tell and what to speak..., Therefore the things I speak, just as the Father has told me them, so I speak them."

The ascriptions *"His Word"* and *"a Word from Him"* are unique in the Qur'an. No other prophets are described as such. In spite of all appearances of reverence towards the person of Christ, Muslim apologists secretly view him as a rival to the grandeur of Muhammad. Therefore, it should not surprise us when they try to simplify the profound and unique titles of Jesus Christ. Consider for example how Muslim scholars try to falsify and undervalue the true meaning of the title of Jesus as *"The Word from God."* One Muslim website states:

"Whenever God decides to do something, like giving life or causing death, He says the word "Be" and it happens. Since Jesus was born without a father, he was not conceived by the male sperm cells. Instead, his creation, similar to Adam, is solely attributed to the Word of God, 'Be.' God says: "Indeed the likeness of Jesus to God is as the likeness of Adam; He created him from dust, then said to him, 'Be,' and he was." (Qur'an 3:59).

In essence, Jesus is God's 'Word' because he came into existence by God's Word – 'Be'.

Most Muslim scholars also give a similar explanation. If their explanation is true, then why is Adam not called the *"Word of God"*? If the title *"Word of God"* is given merely because of Allah's utterance of the word *"Be,"* then is it not more appropriate for Adam to receive this title as he was the first man to be created in this way? The Qur'an identifies only two persons by name who were brought into existence in this manner. The only two persons who were brought into existence by the utterance of the word, *"Be"* was Adam and Jesus. Yet, Adam was not called the *"Word of God"* in the Qur'an. Like Jesus, Adam had no human father. Yet, he is never described as the *"Word of God."* Neither the angels nor any other creatures are given this unique title in the Qur'an. Jesus alone is called the *"Word of God."* The title applies to Jesus alone.

This tendency to falsify the truth rather than to honestly investigate the reasons for the grandeur and the supernatural phenomenon involving Jesus can only lead to the path of error for Muslims. The act of insincerely concealing the uniqueness of Jesus Christ by Muslim scholars should serve as a warning to sincere Muslims. It should awaken them to the dangers of the lies they are being fed. In fact, obedience to Jesus Christ is an important requirement for all true worshippers of God. This is clearly expressed in the Qur'an. The Qur'an records the following instruction of Jesus:

Surah 3:50: "I have come to you, to attest the Law which was before me. And to make lawful to you part of what was before forbidden to you; I have come to you with a Sign from your Lord. So fear God, and obey me." (Yusuf Ali)

عَلَيْكُمْ حُرِّمَ ٱلَّذِى بَعْضَ لَكُم وَلِأُحِلَّ ٱلتَّوْرَٰلةِ مِنَ يَدَىَّ بَيْنَ لِّمَا وَمُصَدِّقًا وَأُطِيعُونِ ٱللَّهَ فَٱتَّقُواْ رَّبِّكُمْ مِّن بِـَٔايَةٍ وَجِنْتُكُم

Wa musaddiqal limaa baina yadaiya minat Tawraati wa liuhilla lakum ba'dal lazee hurrima 'alaikum; wa ji'tukum bi Aayatim mir Rabbikum fattaqul laaha wa atee'oon

And the Holy Bible confirms this truth:

John 3:16-18: "For God so loved the world, that he gave his only begotten Son, that whoever believes in him should not perish but have eternal life. For God did not send his Son into the world to condemn the world, but in order that the world might be saved through him. Whoever believes in him is not condemned, but whoever does not believe is condemned already, because he has not believed in the name of the only Son of God."

We will now move on to another unique descriptive title of Jesus in the Qur'an.

The Only Prophet who is described as a "Spirit from God"

In Islam, Jesus is given the unique title, Ruhullah, meaning *"Spirit of God."*

Surah 4:171: "The Messiah, Jesus the son of Mary, was but the messenger of Allah and His Word, which He cast into Mary and a Spirit from Him." (H. S. Aziz)

ٱلْحَقَّ إِلَّا ٱللَّهِ عَلَى تَقُولُواْ وَلَا دِينِكُمْ فِى تَغْلُواْ لَا ٱلْكِتَٰبِ يَٰٓأَهْلَ مِنْهُ وَرُوحٌ مَّرْيَمَ إِلَىٰ أَلْقَٰهَآ وَكَلِمَتُهُۥٓ ٱللَّهِ رَسُولُ مَرْيَمَ ٱبْنُ عِيسَى ٱلْمَسِيحُ إِنَّمَا وَٰحِدٌ إِلَٰهٌ ٱللَّهُ إِنَّمَا لَّكُمْ خَيْرًا ٱنتَهُواْ ثَلَٰثَةٌ تَقُولُواْ وَلَا وَرُسُلِهِ بِٱللَّهِ فَـَٔامِنُواْ وَكِيلًا بِٱللَّهِ وَكَفَىٰ ٱلْأَرْضِ فِى وَمَا ٱلسَّمَٰوَٰتِ فِى مَا لَّهُ وَلَدٌ لَهُۥ يَكُونَ أَن سُبْحَٰنَهُۥٓ

Yaaa Ahlal Kitaabi laa taghloo fee deenikum wa laa taqooloo 'alal laahi illalhaqq; innamal Maseehu 'Eesab-nu-Maryama Rasoolul laahi wa Kalimatuhooo alqaahaaa ilaa Maryama wa roohum minhum fa aaminoo billaahi wa Rusulihee wa laa taqooloo salaasah; intahoo khairallakum; innamal laahu Ilaahunw Waahid, Subhaanahooo any yakoona lahoo walad; lahoo maa fissamaawaati wa maa fil ard; wa kafaa billaahi Wakeelaa (section 23)

In Surah 4:171 Jesus is described *ruhun-minhu* which means *"a Spirit from Him."* Thus, the Qur'an describes Jesus, as a Spirit from God. With Jesus being the only exception, no other humans are ever described as such – not even Muhammad. Once again, we find that no attempt is made to explain this absolutely unique title of Jesus in the Qur'an. Interestingly, this verse strongly supports the Christian belief that Jesus was a pre-existing *"Spirit"* who took on a human form when he came to earth. In fact, Surah 4:171 presupposes that Jesus existed as a *"Spirit"* before he was conceived by a virgin-woman.

The Qur'an identifies Jesus as a *"Spirit from God"* who was *"cast into Mary."* This proves that Jesus was with God before he was conceived by Mary. This is the strongest admission in the Qur'an that Jesus had a pre-human existence before he was sent to earth. The total absence of any clarification in the Qur'an regarding the unique status and titles of Jesus shows that Muhammad never knew or understood their significance. He could not see their significance in the light of God's Word. He failed to understand that all these extraordinary characteristics of Jesus testify to the truth that he was more than a prophet. Unlike any prophet, Jesus is the unique Son of God. Yes! The Son of God who existed as a *"Spirit"* in the heavens before he came to earth as a human. The Bible, in no uncertain term, testifies to this divine truth. It testifies that the Jesus was transferred from the spirit realm and *"came to be in the likeness of men."*

Philippians 2:5-8: Keep this mental attitude in you that was also in Christ Jesus, who, although he was existing in God's form, gave no consideration to a seizure, namely, that he should be equal to God. No, but he emptied himself and took a slave's form and came to be in the likeness of men. More than that, when he found himself in fashion as a man, he humbled himself and became obedient as far as death, yes, death on a torture stake.

And

John 16:28: "I came out from the Father and have come into the world. Further, I am leaving the world and am going my way to the Father."

As we have noted, Jesus Christ is identified as the *"Word of God"* and as a *"Spirit from God"* in the Qur'an. Since no other prophet has been called or can be called by such titles, then this would essentially make Jesus more than a prophet. Such titles would be appropriate only for the one who is the unique Son of

God. Thus, Muslims are forced to acknowledge that the unique titles given to Jesus elevate him to a far superior position – into heaven itself. And this provides the clear reason why he was taken up there following his death on earth. In contrast, the status of Muhammad, as nothing more than a prophet of Allah, explains why he returned to very dust from where he had come from.

The Only Prophet called "Holy" in the Quran

The Holy Bible records the angelic announcement of the birth of Jesus to Mary:

Luke 1:35: In answer the angel said to her: "Holy spirit will come upon you, and power of the Most High will overshadow you. And for that reason, the one who is born will be called holy, God's Son.

And the Qur'an confirms the truthfulness of this angelic announcement:

Surah 19:19: "He said: Nay, I am only a messenger of thy Lord, to announce to thee the gift of a holy son." (Yusuf Ali)

"He said: I am only a messenger of thy Lord, that I may bestow on thee a faultless son." (Pickthall)

زَكِيًّا غُلَٰمًا لَكِ لِأَهَبَ رَبِّكِ رَسُولُ أَنَا إِنَّمَآ قَالَ

Qaala innamaa ana rasoolu Rabbiki li ahaba laki ghulaaman zakiyyaa

The Arabic word, "zakiyya" which means "faultless" implies that Jesus was totally without sin. Among mankind, only Jesus Christ is described as faultless or sinless in both the Qur'an and the Bible. While Jesus is emphatically described as such in both Scriptures, no other prophets are ever portrayed as such – not even Muhammad. While both the Qur'an and the Bible confirm the sinful state of all other prophets, yet both these Scriptures leave us with the firm conviction that Jesus alone was without sin. In the above Qur'anic verse, the holiness of Jesus is shown to be the reason for his unique birth. This means that a man cannot be born of a virgin-woman unless he is faultless. Therefore, since Jesus Christ is the only man to be born in this way, it proves that he must also be the only sinless man who ever lived.

Having come from God and not from the seed of man, the life of Jesus was untouched by the effects of sin. Contrary to the claim made by Muslims that all prophets are sinless, it is evident in the Qur'an itself that even the greatest of the prophets of God prayed for His forgiveness. Unlike Jesus, they too, like all other men were born from the seed of Adam. Muslims should carefully reflect on this acknowledgement in the Qur'an that even the great prophets sinned against God and required his forgiveness. Let us look at some examples in the Qur'an:

ADAM: Surah 7:23: Both of them cried out, "Our Lord, we committed a sin against ourselves! Now, if You did not forgive us, and have mercy on us, we would surely be the losers." (Munir Munshey)

ٱلْخَـٰسِرِينَ مِنَ لَنَكُونَنَّ وَتَرْحَمْنَا لَنَا تَغْفِرْ لَّمْ وَإِن أَنفُسَنَا ظَلَمْنَا رَبَّنَا قَالَا

Qaalaa Rabbanaa zalamnaaa anfusanaa wa illam taghfir lanaa wa tarhamnaa lanakoonanna minal khaasireen

ABRAHAM: Surah 26:82: "It is He whom I expect to forgive my sins on the Day of Judgment." (Muhammad Sarwar)

ٱلدِّينِ يَوْمَ خَطِيٓـَٔتِى لِى يَغْفِرَ أَن أَطْمَعُ وَٱلَّذِى

Wallazeee atma'u ai yaghfira lee khateee' atee Yawmad Deen

MOSES: Surah 28:16: "He prayed, 'Forgive me Lord, for I have sinned against my soul.' God forgave him; for He is the Forgiving One, the Merciful." (W. Khan)

ٱلرَّحِيمُ ٱلْغَفُورُ هُوَ إِنَّهُۥ لَهُۥ فَغَفَرَ لِى فَٱغْفِرْ نَفْسِى ظَلَمْتُ إِنِّى رَبِّ قَالَ

Qaala Rabbi innee zalamtu nafsee faghfir lee faghafaralah; innahoo Huwal Ghafoorur Raheem

DAVID: Surah 38:24: "And David gathered that We had tried him; he asked forgiveness of His Lord, fell down, bowing in prostration, and turned to God in repentance." (Yusuf Ali)

نِعَاجِهِۦ إِلَىٰ نَعْجَتِكَ بِسُؤَالِ ظَلَمَكَ لَقَدْ قَالَ

ٱلصَّـٰلِحَـٰتِ وَعَمِلُوا۟ ءَامَنُوا۟ ٱلَّذِينَ إِلَّا بَعْضٍ عَلَىٰ بَعْضُهُمْ لَيَبْغِى ٱلْخُلَطَآءِ مِّنَ كَثِيرًا وَإِنَّ

وَأَنَابَ رَاكِعًا وَخَرَّ رَبَّهُۥ فَٱسْتَغْفَرَ فَتَنَّـٰهُ أَنَّمَا دَاوُۥدُ وَظَنَّ هُم مَّا وَقَلِيلٌ تِ

Qaala laqad zalamaka bisu 'aali na'jatika ilaa ni'aajih; wa inna kaseeran minal khulataaa'i la-yabghee ba'duhum 'alaa ba'din illal lazeena aamanoo wa 'amilus saalihaati wa qaleelun maa hum; wa zanna Daawoodu annamaa fatannaahu fastaghfara Rabbahoo wa kharra raaki'anw wa anaab (make sajdah)

SOLOMON: Surah 38:35: "He said, 'O my Lord! Forgive me.'" (Yusuf Ali)

ٱلْوَهَّابُ أَنتَ إِنَّكَ بَعْدِىٓ مِّنۢ لِّأَحَدٍ يَنۢبَغِى لَّا مُلْكًا لِى وَهَبْ لِى ٱغْفِرْ رَبِّ قَالَ

Qaala Rabbigh fir lee wa hab lee mulkal laa yambaghee li ahadin min ba'dee innaka Antal Wahhaab

JONAH: Surah 37:142-144: "Then the big Fish did swallow him, and he had done acts worthy of blame. Had it not been that he repented and glorified God, he would certainly have remained inside the fish." (Yusuf Ali)

مُلِيمٌ وَهُوَ ٱلْحُوتُ فَٱلْتَقَمَهُ

37:142

Faltaqamahul hootu wa huwa muleem

SAHIH INTERNATIONAL:

Then the fish swallowed him, while he was blameworthy.

ٱلْمُسَبِّحِينَ مِنَ كَانَ أَنَّهُ فَلَوْلَآ

37:143

Falaw laaa annahoo kaana minal musabbiheen

SAHIH INTERNATIONAL:

And had he not been of those who exalt Allah,

يُبْعَثُونَ يَوْمِ إِلَىٰ بَطْنِهِ فِى لَلَبِثَ

37:144

Lalabisa fee batniheee ilaa Yawmi yub'asoon

SAHIH INTERNATIONAL:

He would have remained inside its belly until the Day they are resurrected.

The Qur'an also testifies that even Muhammad was a sinner and needed God's forgiveness:

MUHAMMAD: Surah 48:1-2: "Lo! We have given thee O Muhammad a signal victory, That Allah may forgive thee of thy sin that which is past and that which is to come." (Pickthall)

مُّبِينًا فَتْحًا لَكَ فَتَحْنَا إِنَّا

48:1

Innaa fatahnaa laka Fatham Mubeenaa

SAHIH INTERNATIONAL:

Indeed, We have given you, [O Muhammad], a clear conquest

مُّسْتَقِيمًا صِرَٰطًا وَيَهْدِيَكَ عَلَيْكَ نِعْمَتَهُ وَيُتِمَّ تَأَخَّرَ وَمَا ذَنْبِكَ مِن تَقَدَّمَ مَا ٱللَّهُ لَكَ لِّيَغْفِرَ

48:2

Liyaghfira lakal laahu maa taqaddama min zanbika wa maa ta akhkhara wa yutimma ni'matahoo 'alaika wa yahdiyaka siraatan mustaqeema

SAHIH INTERNATIONAL:

That Allah may forgive for you what preceded of your sin and what will follow and complete His favor upon you and guide you to a straight path

Surah 47:19: "So know (O Muhammad) that there is no God save Allah, and ask forgiveness for thy sin and for believing men and believing women. Allah knoweth (both) your place of turmoil and your place of rest." (Pickthall)

وَٱلْمُؤْمِنَـٰتِ وَلِلْمُؤْمِنِينَ لِذَنۢبِكَ وَٱسْتَغْفِرْ ٱللَّهُ إِلَّا إِلَـٰهَ لَآ أَنَّهُ فَٱعْلَمْ
وَمَثْوَىٰكُمْ مُتَقَلَّبَكُمْ يَعْلَمُ وَٱللَّهُ

Fa'lam annahoo laaa ilaaha illal laahu wastaghfir lizambika wa lilmu'mineena walmu'minaat; wallaahu ya'lamu mutaqallabakum wa maswaakum (section 2)

Muhammad was commanded by Allah to *"ask forgiveness"* for both his and the sins of his followers. This conclusively proves that just like any ordinary Muslim, Muhammad was also in need of forgiveness. All men, prophets or not, are sinners. Centuries before the Qur'an came into existence, the Holy Bible attested to this undeniable truth:

Romans 3:23: "For all have sinned and fall short of the glory of God."

The only exception – Jesus Christ

1 Peter 2:22: "He (Jesus) committed no sin, and no deceit was found in his mouth."

Concerning Jesus, the Book of Hebrews states:

Hebrews 4:15: "For we do not have a high priest who cannot sympathize with our weaknesses, but one who has been tempted in every way, like ourselves, but without sin."

As we have noted, Islam also acknowledges that Jesus was sinless. Besides the Qur'an, the Hadith also records the sinlessness of Jesus. It states that he was untouched by Satan. And Muhammad himself believed this to be true.

Sahih Muslim, Volume 4, page 1261:

Abu Huraira reported Allah's Messenger (saw) as saying: The Satan touches every son of Adam on the day when his mother gives birth to him with the exception of Mary and her son.

Notice carefully, this Hadith states that *"Satan touches every son of Adam on the day when his mother gives birth to him."* Therefore, it shows that the subject of this Hadith is Jesus, not Mary. Why then was Mary also spoken of being protected from Satan? It is because of the child she was carrying in her womb. Only Jesus is spoken of as a *"holy son"* in the Qur'an.

Nowhere in the Qur'an it is stated that Mary is the *"holy mother"* of Jesus. Neither is she addressed in the Qur'an as a *"holy daughter."* However, since she was privileged to become the instrument of God to deliver his Son as a human on earth, it also necessitated the protection of her. It is for this reason alone; Mary was protected during her delivery of Jesus. To protect the *"holy son,"* Mary had to be protected.

Yes! Jesus Christ committed no sin. What kind of man must he be that he has never sinned? There is not a single verse in either the Qur'an or the Bible saying that Jesus asked God for forgiveness of his sins. The reason for this is absolutely clear. It is because Jesus is the Son of God. As such, he was Sinless, Holy, and Pure. He was the only human who came from the realms above. That is why the Qur'an acknowledges Jesus as a "Spirit from God." And Jesus himself testified to this truth in the following Biblical verse.

John 8:23: "So he went on to say to them: 'You are from the realms below; I am from the realms above. You are from this world; I am not from this world.'"

Why is Jesus the only man without sin among mankind? The Qur'an admits his sinlessness but gives no reason for it. Saying that Jesus was a prophet of God does not provide the answer. If this assertion is true, then why are the other prophets not described equally as sinless? In fact, quite a few, including Muhammad, are shown to be sinners. But we must ask again, *"Why was Jesus the only one among mankind who is sinless?"* Only by acknowledging the unique status of Jesus as the Son of God, Muslims can understand the reason why both the Qur'an and the Bible speak of Jesus as the only one who is without sin.

Muslims must also know the full significance of his role in God's purpose. And they must ask themselves: *"Why are all these unique features vested in one man and no one else?"* It is also important for Muslims to realize that all these unique features of Jesus strongly support the Christian belief that he is the Son of God. And these unique features are absolutely necessary for the defense of the Christian position regarding the Sonship of Jesus Christ. Thus, the Christian conviction is based solidly on evidences and not on emotions. Since the Qur'an does not provide the reason for the uniqueness of Jesus, Muslims need to go to the Bible for the answer.

An issue that confronts all Muslims

The Gospel of Matthew recorded an incident that took place about two days before the death of Jesus. Jesus was engaged in a lengthy debate with the Jewish religious leaders. Initially the Pharisees and then the Sadducees tried to trap him in his talk. At the end of the day, when their efforts were exhausted and they were all standing before him, Jesus finally put a question to them. It was to be the last time he would engage in debate with them. He asked the Pharisees:

Matthew 22:42: "What do you think of the Messiah? Whose son is he?"

They promptly answered, *"The Son of David."* And turning to them, Jesus replied:

Matthew 22: 43-46: "How, then, is it that David by inspiration calls him 'Lord,' saying, 'Jehovah said to my Lord: "Sit at my right hand until I put your enemies beneath your feet"'? If, therefore, David calls him 'Lord,' how is he his son?" And nobody was able to say a word in reply to him, nor did anyone dare from that day on to question him any further.

Jesus was quoting from the Book of Psalms (Zabur):

Psalms 110:1: The utterance of Jehovah to my Lord is: "Sit at my right hand until I place your enemies as a stool for your feet."

Using the Book of Psalms, Jesus pointed out to them that since David called the Messiah his Lord, how could he then be David's son? This momentous question by Jesus ended all debate between him and the Jewish leaders.

"What do you think of the Messiah, whose son is he?" was the climactic charge Jesus set before the Jewish religious leaders. With this, his public confrontation with them finally came to an end. Let us now turn our attention to the Muslims. The Qur'an identifies Jesus Christ as *"the Messiah."*

Surah 3:59: And remember when the angels said: O Mary! Allah giveth thee glad tidings of a word from Him, whose name is the Messiah, Jesus, son of Mary, illustrious in the world and the Hereafter, and one of those brought near (unto Allah). (Pickthall)

إِنَّ مَثَلَ عِيسَىٰ عِندَ ٱللَّهِ كَمَثَلِ ءَادَمَ ۖ خَلَقَهُ مِن تُرَابٍ ثُمَّ قَالَ لَهُ كُن فَيَكُونُ

Inna masala 'Eesaa 'indal laahi kamasali Aadama khalaqahoo min turaabin summa qaala lahoo kun fayakoon

Well Muslims, what do you think of *"the Messiah?"* Whose Son, is he? This very charge is set before each and every one of you. Your eternal salvation depends on knowing who really Jesus is.

1 John 4:9: By this the love of God was made manifest in our case, because God sent forth his only-begotten Son into the world that we might gain life through him.

For Muslims who are adamant that Christians are wrong in their understanding of Jesus as the Son of God, it is good for them to reflect on the following Qur'anic verse. Two different translations of this verse are provided here:

Surah 3:55: When Allah said: O Jesus, I will cause thee to die and exalt thee in My presence and clear thee of those who disbelieve and make those who follow thee above those who disbelieve to the day of Resurrection. (Maulana Ali)

اَتَّبَعُو ٱلَّذِينَ وَجَاعِلُ كَفَرُواْ ٱلَّذِينَ مِنَ وَمُطَهِّرُكَ إِلَىَّ وَرَافِعُكَ مُتَوَفِّيكَ إِنِّى يَٰعِيسَىٰٓ ٱللَّهُ قَالَ إِذْ
تَخْتَلِفُونَ فِيهِ كُنتُمْ فِيمَا بَيْنَكُمْ فَأَحْكُمُ مَرْجِعُكُمْ إِلَىَّ ثُمَّ ٱلْقِيَٰمَةِ يَوْمِ إِلَىٰ كَفَرُوٓاْ ٱلَّذِينَ فَوْقَ كَ

Iz qaalal laahu yaa 'Eesaaa innee mutawaffeeka wa raafi'uka ilaiya wa mutah hiruka minal lazeena kafaroo wa jaa'ilul lazeenattaba ooka fawqal lazeena kafarooo ilaa Yawmil Qiyaamati summa ilaiya marji'ukum fa ahkumu bainakum feemaa kuntum feehi takhtaliifoon

I will make those who follow thee superior to those who disbelieve until the Day of Resurrection. (Yusuf Ali)

Those who follow Jesus are Christians. According to the above Qur'anic verse, Christians will be made *"superior"* over the disbelievers *"until the Day of Resurrection."* The *"Day of Resurrection"* or *Qiyamah* will occur at the *"time of the end."* Therefore, until the time of the end, true Christians will be made superior over the unbelievers. Since the Qur'an contrasts the followers of Jesus with the unbelievers, this in itself proves that Christians are true believers. Can you imagine Christians being judged as true believers *"until the Day of Resurrection"* by Allah himself when Muslims believe that Christians are in error regarding their understanding of Jesus as the unique Son of God.

John 14:6: Jesus said: "I am the way and the truth and the life. No one comes to the Father except through me."

And the Qur'an agrees. Muslims need to "*follow*" Jesus Christ in order to be on the "*straight way*" leading to God. The Qur'an testifies to this indisputable truth:

Surah 43:63-64: When Jesus came with clear signs he said, "Now have I come to you with wisdom, and to make clear to you some of that which you dispute. Therefore be aware of God and follow me. For God, He is my Lord and your Lord. So worship Him. This is a straight way." (Bilal Muhammad)

فِيهِ تَخْتَلِفُونَ ٱلَّذِى بَعْضَ لَكُم وَلِأُبَيِّنَ بِٱلْحِكْمَةِ جِئْتُكُم قَدْ قَالَ بِٱلْبَيِّنَـٰتِ عِيسَىٰ جَآءَ وَلَمَّا وَأَطِيعُونِ ٱللَّهَ فَٱتَّقُوا۟ ۖ

43:63

Wa lammaa jaaa'a 'Eesaa bilbaiyinaati qaala qad ji'tukum bil Hikmati wa li-ubaiyina lakum ba'dal lazee takhtalifoona feehi fattaqul laaha wa atee'oon

SAHIH INTERNATIONAL:

And when Jesus brought clear proofs, he said, "I have come to you with wisdom and to make clear to you some of that over which you differ, so fear Allah and obey me.

مُّسْتَقِيمٌ صِرَٰطٌ هَـٰذَا ۚ فَٱعْبُدُوهُ وَرَبُّكُمْ رَبِّى هُوَ ٱللَّهَ إِنَّ

43:64

Innal laaha Huwa Rabbee wa Rabbukum fa'budooh; haaza Siraatum Mustaqeem

SAHIH INTERNATIONAL:

Indeed, Allah is my Lord and your Lord, so worship Him. This is a straight path."

And the invitation that Jesus extended at beginning of his ministry centuries ago is still open to Muslims today:

John 1:43: "Be my follower.

CHAPTER

II

WHO IS THE FATHER OF JESUS?

Who is the Father of Jesus?

Is Jesus the Son of Allah? The Qur'an says no. Yet it is also entirely consistent with the Qur'an to consider Allah the Father of Jesus for the following reasons:
1) Allah caused Mary to become pregnant with Jesus.
2) Allah determined some of the physical characteristics of Jesus.
3) All of the genetic characteristics of Jesus were determined by just two parties: Allah and Mary.

A Muslim might argue "Being a father implies having sex", and therefore Allah cannot be the father. Not necessarily so. Modern science has brought us "test tube babies", which are conceived without any sex. There is nothing to support the idea that if Allah wants a baby, he must resort to normal human means to have one.

Again, a Muslim may say that if we are going to call Jesus the son of Allah, then we should say that Adam is the son of Allah too. No, we cannot compare Adam to Jesus this way because Adam came into existence without a mother.

Let us first review some background material. What does the Qur'an say about how Mary became pregnant with Jesus? In Surah 3:45-49 we read:

The angels said to Mary: "Allah bids you rejoice in a word from him. His name is the Messiah, Jesus the son of Mary. He shall be noble in this world and the hereafter, and shall be favored by Allah. He shall preach to men in his cradle and the prime of manhood, and shall lead a righteous life."

"Lord", she said, "how can I bear a child when no man has touched me?"

He replied: "Such is the will of Allah. He creates whom He will. When He decrees a thing, He need only say: 'Be' and it is. He will instruct him in the Scriptures and in wisdom, in the Torah and in the Gospel, and send him forth as an apostle to the Israelites..."

From this passage we can draw the conclusions presented above:

1) Allah caused Mary to become pregnant with Jesus. Muslims infer from this passage and others like it that Jesus was conceived while Mary was a virgin by the word spoken by Allah, and not by a man.

Not that this in itself implies that Allah is the father. When a doctor causes a woman to become pregnant by artificial insemination, he is not considered the father. Hence the following two points:

2) Allah determined some of the physical characteristics of Jesus.

When Allah said "Be", did he have something specific in mind? Certainly! Allah had a very detailed plan in mind for Jesus. In particular, Allah decided that Jesus would be male. Normally, it is the sperm that decides the gender of the baby. Here Allah made the choice instead.

3) All of the genetic characteristics of Jesus were determined by precisely two parties: Allah and Mary.

This is clear because they were the only two parties involved. So, we conclude that Allah and Mary are the only two possible candidates for the title "Father".

Hence it appears legitimate to call Allah the father of Jesus, *at least in a figurative sense.* Therefore, we are at a loss to explain why the Qur'an spends so much space arguing against this. Certainly, more and better justification is needed than what appears in these passages:

Surely, they lie when they declare: "Allah has begotten children".

-- Sura 37:151

Where is the "lie" in our reasoning above?

They say: "Allah has begotten a Son". Glory be to Him! His is what the heavens and the earth contain; all things are obedient to Him. Creator of the heavens and the earth! When he decrees a thing, He need only say "Be", and it is.

-- Sura 2:116

Allah made Mary pregnant. What more would Allah have to do if he wanted a legitimate son?

Allah forbid that He Himself should beget a son! When He decrees a thing He need only say "Be," and it is. -- Sura 19:35

So *is Allah unable* to beget a son by saying "Be"?

Say: "If the Lord of Mercy had a son, I would be the first to worship him".
-- Sura 43:82

We would prefer something more convincing from the Qur'an than this.

CHAPTER

III

DOES THE QURAN RECOGNIZE JESUS
AS GOD OR NOT?

Does the Quran recognize Jesus as God or Not?

The Quran presents criteria to distinguish the true God from false gods.

Is He then Who creates like him who does not create? Do you not then mind?... And those whom they call on besides Allah have not created anything while they are themselves created; Dead (are they), not living, and they know not when they shall be raised. S. 16:17, 20-21 Shakir

And they have taken besides Him gods, who do not create anything while they are themselves created, and they control not for themselves any harm or profit, and they control not death nor life, nor raising (the dead) to life. S. 25:3 Shakir

These preceding passages state that:

1. The objects which others call upon besides God (i.e., whether other gods, angels, and/or individuals) have not created anything.
2. These objects cannot bring death, cause life, or resurrect.
3. These objects of worship are dead.

Which implies that:

1. God is the Creator.
2. God is the Source of Life.
3. God is ever-Living.

It is no secret that the Holy Bible states that the Lord Jesus created the cosmos and was called upon in worship by the first Christians:

"Through him all things were made; without him nothing was made that has been made... He was in the world, and though the world was made through him, the world did not recognize him." John 1:3, 10

"In Damascus there was a disciple named Ananias. The Lord called to him in a vision, 'Ananias!' 'Yes, Lord,' he answered. The Lord told him, 'Go to the house of Judas on Straight Street and ask for a man from Tarsus named Saul, for he is praying. In a vision he has seen a man named Ananias come and place his hands on him to restore his sight.' 'Lord,' Ananias answered, 'I have heard many reports about this man and all the harm he has done to your saints in Jerusalem. And he has come here with authority from the chief priests to arrest all who call on your name.' But the Lord said to Ananias, 'Go! This man is my chosen instrument to carry my name before the Gentiles and their kings and before the people of Israel. I will show him how much he must suffer for my name.' Then Ananias went to the house and entered it. Placing his hands on Saul, he said, 'Brother Saul, the Lord-Jesus, who appeared to you on the road as you were coming here--has sent me so that you may see again and be filled with the Holy Spirit'... All those who heard him were astonished and asked, 'Isn't he the man who raised havoc in Jerusalem among those who call on this name? And hasn't he come here to take them as prisoners to the chief priests?'" Acts 9:10-17, 21

"To the church of God in Corinth, to those sanctified in Christ Jesus and called to be holy, together with all those everywhere who call on the name of our Lord Jesus Christ-their Lord and ours:" 1 Corinthians 1:2

"He is the image of the invisible God, the firstborn over all creation. For BY HIM all things were created: things in heaven and on earth, visible and invisible, whether thrones or powers or rulers or authorities; all things were created BY HIM and FOR HIM. He is before all things, and IN HIM all things hold together. And he is the head of the body, the church; he is the beginning and the firstborn from among the dead, so that in everything he might have the supremacy." Colossians 1:15-18

"but in these last days he has spoken to us by his Son, whom he appointed heir of all things, and through whom he made the universe. The Son is the radiance of God's glory and the exact representation of his being, sustaining all things by his powerful word. After he had provided purification for sins, he sat down at the right hand of the Majesty in heaven... And again, when God brings his firstborn into the world, he says, 'Let all God's angels worship him'... But about the Son he says... 'In the beginning, O Lord, you laid the foundations of the earth, and the heavens are the work of your hands. They will perish, but you remain; they will all wear out like a garment. You will roll them up like a robe; like a garment they will be changed. But you remain the same, and your years will never end.'" Hebrews 1:2-3, 6, 8a, 10-12

According to the same Holy Bible, the Lord Jesus is alive forever and ever, having conquered death and ushering in glorious immortality:

"So do not be ashamed to testify about our Lord, or ashamed of me his prisoner. But join with me in suffering for the gospel, by the power of God, who has saved us and called us to a holy life-not because of anything we have done but because of his own purpose and grace. This grace was given us in Christ Jesus before the beginning of time, but it has now been revealed through the appearing of our Savior, Christ Jesus, who has destroyed death and has brought life and immortality to light through the gospel." 2 Timothy 1:8-10

"When I saw him, I fell at his feet as though dead. Then he placed his right hand on me and said: 'Do not be afraid. I am the First and the Last. I am the Living One; I was dead, and behold I am alive for ever and ever! And I hold the keys of death and Hades.'" Revelation 1:17-18

"To the angel of the church in Smyrna write: These are the words of him who is the First and the Last, who died and came to life again." Revelation 2:8

By conquering death, Christ demonstrated that he is truly the source of life for all:

"In him was life, and that life was the light of men." John 1:4

"For just as the Father raises the dead and gives them life, even so the Son gives life to whom he is pleased to give it... I tell you the truth, a time is coming and has now come when the dead will hear THE VOICE OF THE SON OF GOD and those who hear will live... Do not be amazed at this, for a time is coming when all who are in their graves will hear HIS VOICE and come out-those who have done good will rise to live, and those who have done evil will rise to be condemned." John 5:21, 25, 28-29

"Jesus said to her, 'I AM THE RESURRECTION AND THE LIFE. He who believes in me will live, even though he dies; and whoever lives and believes in me will never die. Do you believe this?' 'Yes, Lord,' she told him, 'I believe that you are the Christ, the Son of God, who was to come into the world.'" John 11:25-27

"Jesus answered, 'I am the way and the truth and THE LIFE. No one comes to the Father except through me.'" John 14:6

"But our citizenship is in heaven. And we eagerly await a Savior from there, the Lord Jesus Christ, who, by the power that enables him to bring everything under his control, will transform our lowly bodies so that they will be like his glorious body." Philippians 3:20-21

"For you died, and your life is now hidden with Christ in God. When Christ, who is your life, appears, then you also will appear with him in glory." Colossians 3:3-4

The Lord Jesus fits the criteria given in the Quran which demonstrates true Deity (i.e., the Creator, the Source of Life, and ever-Living). Christians are therefore justified in worshiping him as their sovereign Lord.

Now the Muslim will definitely object to our appeal to the Holy Bible on the grounds that it doesn't accurately reflect the life and teachings of the historical Jesus, and as such it cannot be used to prove that Jesus and his original followers truly believed that Christ was God.

It is not the object of this present paper to provide the evidence which establishes the historical veracity of the NT documents, or to demonstrate that the first followers of Christ confessed their belief in the absolute Deity of the Lord Jesus, or in his death and resurrection.

What we would like to do here is to show that even according to the testimony of the Quran, the Lord Jesus perfectly fulfills the criteria of being Deity.

and he shall be a prophet to the people of Israel (saying), that I have come to you, with a sign from God, namely, that I will CREATE for you out of clay (annee AKHLUQU lakum mina ALTTEENI) as though it were the form of a bird, and I will blow thereon and it shall become a bird by God's permission; and I will heal the blind from birth, and lepers; and I will bring the dead to life by God's permission; and I will tell you what you eat and what ye store up in your houses. Verily, in that is a sign for you if ye be believers. S. 3:49 Palmer

When God shall say, O Jesus son of Mary, remember my favor towards thee, and towards thy mother; when I strengthened thee with the holy spirit, that thou shouldest speak unto men in the cradle, and when thou wast grown up; and when I taught thee the scripture, and wisdom, and the law, and the gospel; and when thou didst CREATE of clay (*wa-ith TAKHLUQU mina ALTTEENI*) as it were the figure of a bird, by my permission, and didst breathe thereon, and it became a bird by my permission; and thou didst heal one blind from his birth, and the leper, by my permission; and when thou didst bring forth the dead [from their graves], by my permission; and when I with-held the children of Israel from [killing] thee, when thou hadst come unto them with evident [miracles], and such of them as believed not, said, this is nothing but manifest sorcery. S. 5:110 Sale

These two passages demonstrate that Christ has the breath of life and can create in exactly the same way God creates:

HE it is Who created you from clay (*Huwa allathee KHALAQAKUM min TEENIN*) and then HE decreed a term. And there is another term fixed with HIM. Yet you doubt. S. 6:2 Y. Ali

Behold, thy Lord said to the angels: "I am about to create man from clay (*innee KHALIQUN basharan min TEENIN*): When I have fashioned him (in due proportion) and breathed into him of My spirit, fall ye down in obeisance unto him." S. 38:71-72 Y. Ali

Note the connection between God breathing his Spirit into man with Christ being strengthened with the Holy Spirit, breathing life into clay birds and resurrecting the dead. And also notice that Christ created a living bird from clay just as God created man from clay. These passages therefore teach that Christ had the same life-giving Spirit of God!

The Quran says by way of mocking the gods of the people:

"O mankind! A similitude has been coined, so listen to it (carefully): verily! Those on whom you call besides Allah cannot create (even) a fly, even though they combine together for the purpose. And if the fly snatched away a thing from them, they would have no power to release it from the fly. So weak are (both) the seeker and the sought." S. 22:73

Even though Jesus didn't create a fly, he did create a bird and breathed life into it just as Allah did to Adam!

In fact, according to one Salafi Muslim site the word for create (*khalaqa*) refers to creating something from nothing, an act which only God can perform:

Imam al-Bukhari reported in his Saheeh from Abu Sa`eed (may Allah be pleased with him) that the Prophet (Peace & Blessings of Allah be upon Him) said: "There is no created being but Allah created it." In Arabic, the word "khalaqa" means to make out of nothing, which is something that ONLY ALLAH CAN DO; it is impossible for anyone except Allah to do this. It also carries the meaning of decreeing or foreordaining.

See Fath al-Bari Sharh Saheeh al-Bukhari, 13/390. (439: Evidence that only Allah is the Creator of life; bold and capital emphasis ours)

But this very same word is applied to Christ which means, at least according to the above position, that Jesus must be God! Note how this works out logically:

1. God alone can create out of nothing (i.e., the literal meaning of *khalaqa*).
2. *Khalaqa* is applied to Jesus.
3. Therefore, Jesus must be God according to Islam.

The Quran also implies that Christ is alive in heaven:
And when Allah said: O Isa, I am going to terminate the period of your stay (on earth) and cause you to ascend unto Me and purify you of those who disbelieve and make those who follow you above those who disbelieve to the day of resurrection; then to Me shall be your return, so I will decide between you concerning that in which you differed. S. 3:55 Shakir

That they said (in boast), "We killed Christ Jesus the son of Mary, the Apostle of God"; - but they killed him not, nor crucified him, but so it was made to appear to them, and those who differ therein are full of doubts, with no (certain) knowledge, but only conjecture to follow, for of a surety they killed him not:- Nay, God raised him up unto Himself; and God is Exalted in Power, Wise; - S. 4:157-158 Y. Ali

Orthodox Islam has generally understood these passages to mean that Christ was taken alive into heaven, into the very presence of God himself.
Moreover, specific Islamic narrations teach that Jesus will be an intercessor for his people:

... "Surely! Allah wrongs not even of the weight of an atom (or a smallest ant) but if there is any good (done) He doubles it." (4.40) The Prophet added, "Then THE PROPHETS and Angels and the believers will intercede, and (last of all) the Almighty (Allah) will say, 'Now remains My Intercession. He will then hold a handful of the Fire from which He will take out some people whose bodies have been burnt, and they will be thrown into a river at the entrance of Paradise, called the water of life. ..." (*Sahih al-Bukhari*, Volume 9, Book 93, Number 532s)
Ibn Kathir wrote in reference to Sura 3:45 that:

Held in honor in this world and in the Hereafter, and will be one of those who are near to Allah.> meaning, he will be a leader and honored by Allah in this life, because of the Law that Allah will reveal to him, sending down the Scripture to him, along with the other bounties that Allah will grant him with. `Isa will be honored in the Hereafter and will intercede with Allah, by His leave, on behalf of some people, just as is the case with his brethren the mighty Messengers of Allah, peace be upon them all. (Source: Al Tafsir)

The next text supports the interpretation that Jesus may intercede:

And We did not send before you any apostle but We revealed to him that there is no god but Me, therefore serve Me. And they say: The Beneficent God has taken to Himself a son. Glory be to Him. Nay! they are honored servants. They do not precede Him in speech and (only) according to His commandment do they act. He knows what is before them and what is behind them, and they do not intercede *except for him whom He approves and for fear of Him they tremble.* And whoever of them should say: Surely, I am a god besides Him, such a one does We recompense with hell; thus do, We recompense the unjust. S. 21:25-29 Shakir

This reference says that at least some of those honored servants who were wrongly worshiped as gods or considered children of God will indeed intercede. And since according to the Quran Jesus is an honored servant who was wrongly worshiped as God and as the Son of God this therefore means that he may well be one of those interceding.

But this directly conflicts with the following text:

And those whom they invoke besides God HAVE NO POWER OF INTERCESSION; - only he who bears witness to the Truth, and they know (him). If thou ask them, who created them, they will certainly say, God: How then are they deluded away (from the Truth)? (God has knowledge) of the (Prophet's) cry, "O my Lord! Truly these are people who will not believe!" S. 43:86-88 No intercessor will they have from those whom they made equal with Allah (partners i.e., their so-called associate gods), and they will (themselves) reject and deny their partners. S. 30:13 Hilali-Khan

The above references claim that those invoked by the unbelievers have no power to intercede. Jesus happens to be one of those very beings that so-called unbelieving Christians invoked and continue to invoke in their prayers. Thus, either Jesus can intercede which means that the Quran is wrong; or he cannot intercede which means that the Islamic tradition is wrong.

In light of the aforementioned citations, we are left with the conclusion that:

1. Jesus creates in the same way God creates.
2. Jesus gives life in the same way God gives life.

3. Jesus is alive in heaven.

Therefore, the Quran clearly shows that the Lord Jesus fits the description of God, fulfilling the very criteria which demonstrates that Christ is indeed very God of very God.

Yet, it is at this precise point that we have a contradiction within the Quran itself. There is no denying that the Quran rejects the Deity of Jesus (cf. 4:171; 5:17, 70-75; 9:30). But, as we just saw, the Quran attributes titles, qualities and functions to Christ which shows that he is indeed God. Other titles given to Christ which affirm his essential Deity include the Word of God and a Spirit from God (cf. 3:39, 45; 4:171).

A Muslim may say that Jesus was given the ability to create and give life by God, just as the passages themselves state. He didn't have this ability within himself. This response doesn't solve the contradiction, but only pushes it a step further.

Why would God grant Jesus the abilities and characteristics of Deity? Why is God permitting Jesus to perfectly fit the description and fulfill the criteria which places one within the category of God?

Second, the expression "by God's permission" doesn't necessarily mean that Christ was given abilities he did not already have. The statements can be understood in light of the biblical teaching that Christ did nothing on his own initiative, but did everything in perfect union with his Father's will. (cf. John 5:16-30)

In other words, the Quranic expression simply implies that Christ only exercised his divine prerogatives in accordance with the decree of God, never acting on his own behest or initiative. It need not deny that Christ always had these divine attributes and characteristics. This becomes all the more likely when we recall that the Quran describes Christ as God's Word and a Spirit proceeding from God, titles which point to Christ's divinity and pre-existence.

CHAPTER

IV

JESUS IS AL MALIK-KING

The Qur'an which was revealed more than 632 years after the Bible, says that one of God's Attributes is the "Al-Malik" meaning Allah is the King. Let us first verify this through the words of Allah.

God is referred to as "King" five times in the Quran.

He is Allah, other than whom there is no deity, the Sovereign King, the Pure, the Perfection, the Bestower of Faith, the Overseer, the Exalted in Might, the Compeller, the Superior. Exalted is Allah above whatever they associate with Him. (Quran 59:23)

If Allah is the King, where is his Kingdom and who will be there?

"So exalted be Allah (God), the True King!" (Quran 20:114)

"...the King of humanity, the God of humanity." (Quran 114:2)

"Lo! the righteous will dwell among gardens and rivers, in the seat of honor with a Mighty King." (Quran 54:54-55)

In Arabic, the word for "owner" (mālik) is closely related to the word "king" (malik), the only difference being that "owner" is pronounced with an added stress on the letter a. God is referred to by this related name "Owner" in other verses, including:

"Owner of Judgment Day." (Quran 1:4)

(Indeed, in some modes of reciting the Qur'an, the word is pronounced with an unstressed a so the verse reads: "King of Judgment Day.")

Also: "Say: O Allah (God)! Owner of Sovereignty!" (Quran 3:26)

God is "the owner of sovereignty". Indeed, he is the King of Kings, since the lives and destinies of all earthly kings are in His hands. It is as God says: "Blessed is He for whom sovereignty is in His hand." (Quran 67:1) And thus He is the "True King" who has "sovereignty of the heavens and the Earth".

God's sovereignty is absolute. It has no limit. "Human beings can be described as possessing "sovereignty", but theirs is transient and it is limited in scope. We say that someone is the king of a particular country. We likewise say that someone is the owner of a field or a vehicle. These types of sovereignty and ownership are limited in their timeframe – the duration of a person's lifetime at most, often less – as well as in the scope of what is being possessed or being ruled.

All over the world, we can see artifacts and monuments left behind by past civilizations: mighty castles, great estates, the ruins of Egypt, Greece, and Rome. They attest to those who once possessed great power but then passed on into the annals of history. They held sway for a period of time over a part of the globe. Then God decreed that their rule would come to an end. Thus, it becomes clear to us that true sovereignty belongs to God alone, whereas human sovereignty is fleeting and capricious, restricted and incomplete.

Ahmad Zaky has written a series of moving articles entitled Civilizations Which Have Come and Gone. How accurate this title is.

Who has ever possessed the entire world? People talk about people like Pharaoh, Nimrod, Alexander the Great, Nebuchadnezzar, or Hitler, but none of them were able to take possession of the whole world or bring all of humanity under their sway. All who rule do so over a limited domain for a limited time. God has made it the norm throughout the ages that nations, kings, and powers would contend with one another. He says: "And if not, God did not check one set of people by means of another, the Earth would indeed be full of mischief: But God is full of bounty to all the worlds." (Quran 2:251)

No human being has ever possessed the whole of the Earth or has been able to govern all of its affairs. Consider, then, how small a part the Earth is of God's vast universe.

'God, indeed, is the True King in every way. He gives to His servants when they beseech Him, and Prophet Muhammad, may the mercy and blessings of God be upon him, informs us that in Paradise, God will bestow "what no eye has yet seen, no ear ever heard, and no mind ever imagined."

Now, let us verify "Al-Malik" the attribute of God through the Bible. Who is Al-Malik and when was this title claimed?

632 years before the Qur'an was revealed, one of the grandest name descriptions of our God in the Bible is "King of Kings and Lord of Lords." This position is used to declare God's authority over all creation and reminds believers of His power and might.

While exploring this phrase, I found that this term has been used in both secular and Christian ways. For instance, Merriam-Webster's definition says, "An earthly sovereign," and then "God; Christ." And the Oxford English Dictionary refers to both God and Jesus with the term.

"King of Kings and Lord of Lords" has been used to describe a grand ruler in the Middle East, as recently as the early 20th century. It applied to a Pharaoh or a monarch who held a higher position than any other kings in a region. But Scripture makes it clear that only our Lord is truly worthy of the title.

Approximately 632 years prior to the birth of Muhammad and the Quran revealed Jesus called Himself KING OF KINGS which is Exhibited in the Bible.

1 Timothy 6: 14 to keep this command without spot or blame until the appearing of our Lord Jesus Christ, which God will bring about in his own time—God, the blessed and only Ruler, the King of kings and Lord of lords...

Revelations 17:14 They will wage war against the Lamb, but the Lamb will triumph over them because he is Lord of lords and King of kings—and with him will be his called, chosen and faithful followers."

In the verses we have just read, we have seen that Jesus is called King of kings, which is a unique Attribute of God in both the Bible and Qur'an pursuant to Surah 59 verse 23. Wherefore, Allah and Quran have consented that Jesus is God by both verifying that Jesus owns the Attribute of the KING OF KINGS many years before Quran was revealed to Muhammad. Revelations 17 verse 14.

Why is Allah using the Name of Jesus as his name?

Though Old Testament books may not use the exact phrase "King of Kings and Lord of Lords," there are many declarations of God's supreme rule:

"Do you not know? Have you not heard? Has it not been told to you from the beginning? Have you not understood since the earth was founded? He sits enthroned above the circle of the earth, and its people are like grasshoppers. He stretches out the heavens like a canopy and spreads them out like a tent to live in. He brings princes to naught and reduces the rulers of this world to nothing" (Isaiah 40:21-23).

"The Lord has established his throne in heaven, and his kingdom rules over all" (Psalm 103:19).

"David praised the Lord in the presence of the whole assembly, saying, 'Praise be to you, Lord, the God of our father Israel, from everlasting to everlasting. Yours, Lord, is the greatness and the power and the glory and the majesty and the splendor, for everything in heaven and earth is yours. Yours, Lord, is the kingdom; you are exalted as head over all. Wealth and honor come from you; you are the ruler of all things" (1 Chronicles 29:10-12).

In the New Testament, this attribute is bestowed on Jesus as well. "Christ," which means "anointed king," was part of His name. And He proved Himself to be a member of what we now call the Trinity - God the Father, Christ the Son, and the Holy Spirit.

When Jesus rose from the dead, He appeared to the disciples, revealing that God had given Him dominion.

"Then Jesus came to them and said, 'All authority in heaven and on earth has been given to me'" (Matthew 28:18).

Years later in his letters, the Apostle Paul openly echoes Jesus' claims during and after His earthly ministry.

"When he has done this, then the Son himself will be made subject to him who put everything under him, so that God may be all in all" (1 Corinthians 15:28).

"In the sight of God, who gives life to everything, and of Christ Jesus, who while testifying before Pontius Pilate made the good confession, I charge you to keep this command without spot or blame until the appearing of our Lord Jesus Christ, which God will bring about in his own time—God, the blessed and only Ruler, the King of kings and Lord of lords, who alone is immortal and who lives in unapproachable light, whom no one has seen or can see. To him be honor and might forever. Amen" (1 Timothy 6:13-16).

The book of Revelation recounts a vision given to the Apostle John in his old age. It includes several mentions of the risen Christ as the victorious King.

"...and from Jesus Christ, who is the faithful witness, the firstborn from the dead, and the ruler of the kings of the earth" Revelation 1:5.

"They will wage war against the Lamb, but the Lamb will triumph over them because he is Lord of lords and King of kings—and with him will be his called, chosen and faithful followers" Revelation 17:14.

"On his robe and on His thigh, he has this name written: King of kings and Lord of lords" Revelations 19:16.

When we see God as the King of Kings, we are agreeing that He has absolute dominion. The title ought to stir up a sense of respect, worship, and even wonder within us.

Giving God rule over our lives is not meant to be a fearful thing, though. In fact, letting God take His rightful place in our hearts is the beginning of a wonderful new life. For this King longs to be in close relationship with each of His people.

Since He created us, He knows us intimately. And our Lord desires for us to grow in character so that we become more like him. As we let Him change us, we'll be more aware of His power working in and through us, for good.

Reflecting on God this way will actually impact our character:

God is Omnipotent

He invites us to bring our burdens to Him and release our need to take care of ourselves. Then, humility before God and gratitude for His blessings will take hold.

"Humble yourselves, therefore, under God's mighty hand, that he may lift you up in due time. Cast all your anxiety on him because he cares for you" 1 Peter 5:6-7.

Superiority over the world

"In this world you will have trouble. But take heart! I have overcome the world" John 16:33.

The very beginning of the Bible gives a detailed account of God creating the heavens and earth. All of nature, animals, birds and other creatures – and finally mankind – came to life at His command. Scripture goes on to celebrate the wonderful fact that nothing God created can ever be greater than He is. "But I tell you, in this, you are not right, for God is greater than any mortal" Job 33:12.

"As the heavens are higher than the earth, so are my ways higher than your ways and my thoughts than your thoughts" Isaiah 55:9.

"My sheep listen to my voice; I know them, and they follow me. I give them eternal life, and they shall never perish; no one will snatch them out of my hand. My Father, who has given them to me, is greater than all..." John 10: 27-29.

"You, dear children, are from God and have overcome them because the one who is in you is greater than the one who is in the world" 1 John 4:4.

Phrases like King of Kings and Lord of Lords are called "double titles," which some Biblical authors used to highlight God's supremacy.

Why is Allah scared of the Malik Al-Amlak – The King of kings?

Sahih Al Bukhari: Volume 8, Book 73, Number 224: Narrated by Abu Huraira

Allah's Apostle said, "The most awful name in Allah's sight on the Day of Resurrection, will be (that of) a man calling himself Malik Al-Amlak (the king of kings)."

Sahih Al Bukhari: Volume 8, Book 73, Number 225: Narrated by Abu Huraira

The Prophet said, "The most awful (meanest) name in Allah's sight." Sufyan said more than once, "The most awful (meanest) name in Allah's sight is (that of) a man calling himself king of kings." Sufyan said, "Somebody else (i.e. other than Abu Az-Zinad, a sub-narrator) says: What is meant by 'The king of kings' is 'Shahan Shah.

Sahih Bukhari: Book of "Good Manners" (sahih-bukhari.com)

If Allah is Al Malik, why is he scared of Jesus?

Al Malik: King (الملك) - Jesus is the King (Revelation 17:14)

CHAPTER

V

JESUS IS AL AWWAL AND AL AKHIR
ALPHA AND OMEGA

One of the Attribute of God is Al Awwal and Al Akhir– Alpha and Omega– The First and Last in both the Bible and the Qur'an. Al Awwal means the FIRST, ALPHA, and Al Akhir means the LAST, OMEGA.

The Attribute al-Awwal means the One on Whom all others rely, the One who advances all others. Applied only to the Almighty, it means: He was never preceded in existence by anyone at all; He does not need anyone else at all; He is Independent of everything and everyone. He is a self-existing Elohim.

As Allah's names are mentioned in the Qur'an, similarly the Bible mentions the same names referring to Jesus as God approximately 632 years before the Qur'an was given to

Muhammad: 1. The Truth is al-Haq 2. The Resurrection is al-Baith 3. The Alpha and the Omega is al-Awal and al-Akhir, the first and the last 4. King of Kings is al-Malik 5. "I am the door" is al-Hadi. 6. I am the light is al-Noor. In this chapter, we will discuss the name of Alpha and Omega.

عَلِيمٌ شَيْءٍ بِكُلِّ وَهُوَ وَٱلْبَاطِنُ وَٱلظَّٰهِرُ وَٱلْءَاخِرُ ٱلْأَوَّلُ وُ

57:3 Surah Hadid

Huwal Awwalu wal'Aakhiru waz Zaahiru wal Baatinu wa huwa bikulli shai'in Aleem

SAHIH INTERNATIONAL:

He is the First and the Last, the Ascendant and the Intimate, and He is, of all things, Knowing.

Al-Awwal is the first of anything different from Him, what about his WORD, is Allah's word eternal or Allah's word is a CREATION?

How can we reconcile between the name of Allah al-Aakhir (the Last) and the fact that the people of Paradise will be in Paradise forever and the people of Hell will be in Hell forever?

If we will live forever in Paradise, and there will be no death there, does that not contradict the fact that nothing is eternal except Allah?

In Christianity, we are the image of God, we are the spirit living in the body and having soul, in contrast, in Islam, humans are not spirits.

According to the Qur'an, Allah has the upper hand over His foes, an advancement due neither to time nor to place nor to anything else that can be conceived by mind or acquired by knowledge. Al-Awwal means the timeless, the perpetual, the One Who has neither a beginning nor an end. He is the First without a beginning; He exists on His own even before His creatures were ever there.

In the last book of the Bible, Jesus reveals himself as "the Alpha and the Omega, the First and the Last, the Beginning and the End." Present at the world's beginning, Jesus will also be present at its end, when He and His work are finally and fully revealed. When you pray to Christ as the Alpha and the Omega, you are praying to the One who is, who was, and who is to come. He is our all-sufficient Lord, who will not fail to complete the good work he has begun in us.

Key Scripture: "I am the Alpha and the Omega, the First and the Last, the Beginning and the End." Revelation 22:13

What Does it Mean that God is Alpha?

Revelations 1:8, (NIV) tells us, "I am the Alpha and Omega," says the Lord God, "who is, and who was, and who is to come, the Almighty."

The Merriam-Webster Online Dictionary defines Alpha this way: something that is first. Other words for Alpha include beginning, creation, and origination.

What a revelatory mystery this is! So much so, that our finite minds sometimes grapple with this grand declaration.

Humans have many of their own "firsts". At conception, human life begins. Life occurs in a linear fashion. Babies achieve important milestones. Toddlers learn. Children grow and achieve. Gangly teenagers transform into educated adults.

Jesus told Nicodemus "Unless one is born again, he cannot see the kingdom of God," (John 3:1-21). Our spiritual transformation happens when a gentle God intersects our human life. God becomes the "Alpha" of our individual lives during our spiritual rebirth.

What Does it Mean that God is Omega?

When we revisit Revelations 1:8, we are reminded that God is also our Omega: "Who is to come." These awe-inspiring words delight me, but in all honesty, these words cause me to feel reverential fear.

As a finite being on earth, I will one day stand before the Alpha and Omega of the galaxies. As a finite being, I admit to compartmentalizing the ultimate Creative visionary of the universe.

I Corinthians 2:7 reveals the beauty of God's wisdom, "We speak God's hidden wisdom in a mystery, a wisdom God predestined before the ages for our glory." (CSB).

The Merriam-Webster Online Dictionary defines Omega as the extreme of the final part. Other words for Omega are the last, conclusion, and perfection.

Author of the classic book, The Pursuit of God, A.W. Tozer wrote this on the concept of Alpha and Omega:

"If we grope back to the farthest limits of thought where imagination touches the pre-creation void, we shall find God there.

In one unified present glance, He comprehends all things from everlasting, and the flutter of a seraph's wing a thousand ages hence is seen by Him now without moving His eyes.

Our finite minds were not meant to comprehend the mysterious King who was before the beginnings of earthly time. But because of his mercy and love, God humbled himself and became a man."

Jesus himself embraced his own "Alpha and Omega" story on Earth.

He was born of a virgin. (Luke 1:28)

He entered the temple as a young boy. (Luke 2:41)

Christ began his three-year ministry, sacrificed himself on a cross because he loved us, and cut through His own "time-space" continuum on our behalf. (John 18:37)

As Warren Wiersbe puts it: "If you want to understand God, you have to know Jesus Christ. I have met people who say, "Well, I get so much truth about God from walking in the woods." You can learn some things about God by walking in the woods, but you cannot get the full revelation you have in Christ. Some say, "I love to sit and look at a beautiful sunset; it tells me so much about God." Well, it can; but you will learn much more of God's revelation through His Son, Jesus Christ. God has spoken in Jesus Christ, and this is His last word. Jesus Christ is God's last word, and if you want to know about God, you have to come to Jesus Christ. Jesus Christ is Alpha and Omega; His ministry is the ministry of revelation — He reveals God to us."

Jesus proclaimed Himself to be the "Alpha and Omega" in Revelation 1:8; 21:6; and 22:13. Alpha and omega are the first and last letters of the Greek alphabet. Among the Jewish rabbis, it was common to use the first and the last letters of the Hebrew alphabet to denote the whole of anything, from beginning to end. Jesus as the beginning and end of all things is a reference to no one but the true God. This statement of eternality could apply only to God. It is seen especially in Revelation 22:13, where Jesus proclaims that He is "the Alpha and the Omega, the First and the Last, the Beginning and the End."

One of the biblical meanings of Jesus being the "Alpha and Omega" is that He was at the beginning of all things and will be at the close. It is equivalent to saying He always existed and always will exist. It was Christ, as second Person of the Trinity, who brought about the creation: "Through him all things were made; without him nothing was made that has been made" (John 1:3), and His Second Coming will be the beginning of the end of creation as we know it (2 Peter 3:10). As God incarnate, He has no beginning, nor will He have any end with respect to time, being from everlasting to everlasting.

A second meaning of Jesus as the "Alpha and Omega" is that the phrase identifies Him as the God of the Old Testament. Isaiah ascribes this aspect of Jesus' nature as part of the triune God in several places. "I, the Lord, am the first, and with the last I am He" (41:4). "I am the first, and I am the last; and beside me there is no God" (Isaiah 44:6). "I am he; I am the first, I also am the last" (Isaiah 48:12). These are clear indications of the eternal nature of the Godhead.

Christ, as the Alpha and Omega, is the first and last in so many ways. He is the "author and finisher" of our faith (Hebrews 12:2), signifying that He begins it and carries it through to completion. He is the totality, the sum and substance of the Scriptures, both of the Law and of the Gospel (John 1:1, 14). He is the fulfilling end of the Law (Matthew 5:17), and He is the beginning subject matter of the gospel of grace through faith, not of works (Ephesians 2:8-9). He is found in the first verse of Genesis and in the last verse of Revelation. He is the first and last, the all in all of salvation, from the justification before God to the final sanctification of His people.

Jesus is the Alpha and Omega, the first and last, the beginning and the end. Only God incarnate could make such a statement. Only Jesus Christ is God incarnate.

Al Awwal: the First (الأول) Al Akhir: the Final (الآخر) - Jesus is the First and the Last; alpha & omega (Revelation 22:13,16) (Isaiah 41:4)

CHAPTER VI

JESUS IS AL HADI

One of God's attributes in both the Quran and the Bible is Al Hadi.

The Attribute al-Hadi means: the One who provides guidance to mankind.

Allah وَتَعَلَىٰ سُبْحَنَهُ is Al Haadi (in Arabic: اَلْهَادِي), The One who gives guidance to His believers. His Guidance is beneficial and protects them from whatever may be harmful. He is The One who sent prophets (may peace be upon them) as the deliverers of His message to ensure mankind is guided on the right path.

The Guidance of Muhammad ﷺ

بِٱلْمُهْتَدِينَ أَعْلَمُ وَهُوَ يَشَآءُ مَن يَهْدِي ٱللَّهَ وَلَٰكِنَّ أَحْبَبْتَ مَن تَهْدِي لَا إِنَّكَ

Innaka laa tahdee man ahbabta wa laakinn Allaha yahdee mai yashaaa'; wa huwa a'lamu bil muhtadeen

English Translation:

"Indeed, [O Muhammad], you do not guide whom you like, but Allah guides whom He wills. And He is most knowing of the [rightly] guided."— (Qur'an 28:56)

Divine Guidance:

The second interpretation of what it means for Allah سُبْحَٰنَهُ وَتَعَٰلَىٰ to be referred to as Al-Hadi is expanded with the understanding of this ayah.

هَدَىٰ ثُمَّ خَلْقَهُ شَيْءٍ كُلَّ أَعْطَىٰ ٱلَّذِيَ رَبُّنَا قَالَ

Qaala Rabbunal lazeee a'taa kulla shai'in khalqahoo summa hadaa

English Translation:

"He said, 'Our Lord is He who gave each thing its form and then guided [it].'"— (Qur'an 20:50)

From this ayah, we can infer that Allah's guidance is not just an attribute of showing people the path of faith. It is more encompassing than that. Each creation has been divinely guided to what is required to satisfy its needs.

Imam al-Ghazali writes of how an infant knows how to crawl up to the mother's breast and take milk without any intervention (a phenomenon known as "the breast crawl"). It's also why bees build their hives in a hexagonal pattern. It's the most efficient use of space. This shape is better than all others as it requires the least amount of wax to build, creates a compact structure, and leaves the most space for honey and rearing larvae. Everything has been perfectly guided and accounted for.

فَهَدَىٰ قَدَّرَ وَٱلَّذِى

Wallazee qaddara fahadaa

English Translation:

"And who destined and [then] guided"— (Qur'an 87:3)

JESUS IS OUR GUIDE!

What do you think of when you hear the word "guide?" Do you think of someone who blazes a trail before you? Do you think of someone who has already been where you are going, and therefore someone who can lead you there safely? THAT'S JESUS!

There is only one person who could have been our guide. Jesus has already experienced death, and when He was raised from the dead, He demonstrated that He had blazed the trail for us and that He knows how to get us from HERE to ETERNITY in perfect fellowship with God in heaven. Jesus told us that He was our guide when He said John 14:6, "I am the way–and the truth and the life. No one comes to the Father except through me." Jesus is the WAY from HERE to ETERNITY!

Therefore, it is so important that we keep our eyes glued to Jesus and follow Him all of our lives. The book of Hebrews says in Hebrews 12:1-3,

"Let us throw off everything that hinders and the sin that so easily entangles, and let us run with perseverance the race marked out for us. Let us fix our eyes on Jesus, the Pioneer and Perfecter of our faith, who for the joy set before Him endured the cross, scorning its shame, ad sat down at the right hand of the throne of God. Consider Him who endured such opposition from sinful men, so that you will not grow weary and lose heart."

Psalm 23:1-6 ESV

A Psalm of David. The Lord is my shepherd; I shall not want. He makes me lie down in green pastures. He leads me beside still waters. He restores my soul. He leads me in paths of righteousness for his name's sake. Even though I walk through the valley of the shadow of death, I will fear no evil, for you are with me; your rod and your staff, they comfort me. You prepare a table before me in the presence of my enemies; you anoint my head with oil; my cup overflows.

Philippians 4:6 ESV

Do not be anxious about anything, but in everything by prayer and supplication with thanksgiving let your requests be made known to God.

John 11:25 ESV

Jesus said to her, "I am the resurrection and the life. Whoever believes in me, though he dies, yet shall he live,

In John 13:33, Jesus said, "My children, I will be with you only a little longer. You will look for me, and just as I told the Jews, so I tell you now: Where I am going, you cannot come." This prompted Peter to ask where He was going (verse 36). Peter and the others did not understand that Jesus was speaking of His death and ascension to heaven. Jesus' response was, "Where I am going, you cannot follow now, but you will follow later." Peter was still misunderstanding and declared that he would follow Jesus anywhere and even lay down His life if necessary. As Jesus patiently continued to teach His disciples, He began speaking more plainly about heaven, describing the place He was going to prepare for them (John 14:2–3). Then Jesus said, "You know the way to the place where I am going" (verse 4). Speaking for the others, Thomas said they did not know where He was going, so how could they know how to follow Him there? It was in answer to this question that Jesus uttered one of the seven famous "I am" statements.

I am – In the Greek language, "I am" is a very intense way of referring to oneself. It would be comparable to saying, "I myself, and only I, am." Several other times in the Gospels we find Jesus using these words. In Matthew 22:32 Jesus quotes Exodus 3:6, where God uses the same intensive form to say, "I am the God of Abraham, and the God of Isaac, and the God of Jacob." In John 8:58, Jesus said, "Truly, truly I say unto you, before Abraham was, I am." The Jews clearly understood Jesus to be calling Himself God because they took up stones to stone Him for committing blasphemy in equating Himself with God. In Matthew 28:20, as Jesus gave the Great Commission, He gave it emphasis by saying, "I am with you always, to the end of the age." When the soldiers came seeking Jesus in the garden the night before His crucifixion, He told them, "I am he," and His words were so powerful that the soldiers fell to the ground (John 18:4–6). These words reflect the very name of God in Hebrew, *Yahweh*, which means "to be" or "the self-existing one." It is the name of power and authority, and Jesus claimed it as His own.

The way – Jesus used the definite article to distinguish Himself as "the only way." A way is a path or route, and the disciples had expressed their confusion about where He was going and how they could follow. As He had told them from the beginning, Jesus was again telling them (and us) "follow me." There is no other path to heaven, no other way to the Father. Peter reiterated this same truth years later to the rulers in Jerusalem, saying about Jesus, "Salvation is found in no one else, for there is no other name under heaven given to men by which we must be saved" (Acts 4:12). The exclusive nature of the only path to salvation is expressed in the words "I am the way."

The truth – Again Jesus used the definite article to emphasize Himself as "the only truth." Psalm 119:142 says, "Your law is the truth." In the Sermon on the Mount, Jesus reminded His listeners of several points of the Law, then said, "But I say unto you . . ." (Matthew 5:22, 28, 32, 34, 39, 44), thereby equating Himself with the Law of God as the authoritative standard of righteousness. In fact, Jesus said that He came to fulfill the Law and the prophets (Matthew 5:17). Jesus, as the incarnate Word of God (John 1:1) is the source of all truth.

The life – Jesus had just been telling His disciples about His impending death, and now He was claiming to be the source of all life. In John 10:17–18, Jesus declared that He was going to lay down His life for His sheep, and then take it back again. He spoke of His authority over life and death as being granted to Him by the Father. In John 14:19, He gave the promise that "because I live, you also will live." The deliverance He was about to provide was not a political or social deliverance (which most of the Jews were seeking), but a true deliverance from a life of bondage to sin and death to a life of freedom in eternity.

In these words, Jesus was declaring Himself the great "I Am," the only path to heaven, the only true measure of righteousness, and the source of both physical and spiritual life. He was staking His claim as the very God of Creation, the Lord who blessed Abraham, and the Holy One who inhabits eternity. He did this so the disciples would be able to face the dark days ahead and carry on the mission of declaring the gospel to the world. Of course, we know from Scripture that they still didn't understand, and it took several visits from their risen Lord to shake them out of their disbelief. Once they understood the truth of His words, they became changed people, and the world has never been the same.

If Allah is God because he is Al Hadi, what do you think of Jesus who confessed that 632 years before the birth of Muhammad and the revelation of the Quran?

Qur'an confirmed to us that Jesus is God – Al Hadi.

Al Hadi: Guide (الهادي) - Jesus is Guide (John 10:9, 14:6)

CHAPTER VII

JESUS IS AL HAQQ-THE TRUTH

One of God's attributes in both the Bible and the Quran is Al Haqq. Al Haqq means the TRUTH.

This is one of the unique attributes of God that represents either Allah or Jesus. In this chapter, we will learn, through Bible and Quran verses that Jesus is the TRUE AL HAQQ and not Allah. According to philosopher and logician Aristotle (384-322 BC): The meaning of the TRUTH is to say of what is that it is, or of what is not that it is not, ...

Truth is the self-expression of God. That is the biblical meaning of truth. Because the definition of truth flows from God, truth is theological. Truth is also ontological —which is a fancy way of saying it is the way things really are.

قَدِيرٌ شَيْءٍ كُلِّ عَلَىٰ وَأَنَّهُ ٱلْمَوْتَىٰ يُحْيِ وَأَنَّهُ ٱلْحَقُّ هُوَ ٱللَّهَ بِأَنَّ لِكَ ذَٰ

22:6 Surat Al Hajj

Zaalika bi annal laaha Huwal haqqu wa annahoo yuhyil mawtaa wa annahoo 'alaakulli shai'in Qadeer

SAHIH INTERNATIONAL:

That is because Allah is the Truth and because He gives life to the dead and because He is over all things competent.

ثُمَّ عَلَقَةٍ مِن ثُمَّ نُطْفَةٍ مِن ثُمَّ تُرَابٍ مِّن خَلَقْنَـٰكُم فَإِنَّا ٱلْبَعْثِ مِّنَ رَيْبٍ فِي كُنتُمْ إِن ٱلنَّاسُ يَـٰٓأَيُّهَا ثُمَّ مُسَمًّى أَجَلٍ إِلَىٰ نَشَآءُ مَا ٱلْأَرْحَامِ فِي وَنُقِرُّ لَكُمْ لِّنُبَيِّنَ مُخَلَّقَةٍ وَغَيْرِ مُّخَلَّقَةٍ مُّضْغَةٍ مِن يَعْلَمَ لِكَيْلَا ٱلْعُمُرِ أَرْذَلِ إِلَىٰ يُرَدُّ مَّن وَمِنكُم يُتَوَفَّىٰ مَّن وَمِنكُم أَشُدَّكُمْ لِتَبْلُغُوٓا۟ ثُمَّ طِفْلًا نُخْرِجُكُم مِن وَأَنبَتَتْ وَرَبَتْ ٱهْتَزَّتْ ٱلْمَآءَ عَلَيْهَا أَنزَلْنَا فَإِذَآ هَامِدَةً ٱلْأَرْضَ وَتَرَى شَيْئًا عِلْمٍ بَعْدِ مِنْ بَهِيجٍ زَوْجٍ كُلِّ

22:5 SAHIH INTERNATIONAL:

O People, if you should be in doubt about the Resurrection, then [consider that] indeed, We created you from dust, then from a sperm-drop, then from a clinging clot, and then from a lump of flesh, formed and unformed – that We may show you. And We settle in the wombs whom We will for a specified term, then We bring you out as a child, and then [We develop you] that you may reach your [time of] maturity. And among you is he who is taken in [early] death, and among you is he who is returned to the most decrepit [old] age so that he knows, after [once having] knowledge, nothing. And you see the earth barren, but when We send down upon it rain, it quivers and swells and grows [something] of every beautiful kind.

Allah calls Himself Al-Haqq— The Absolute Truth, The Reality— on nine occasions in the Quran. Al-Haqq is true in and of Himself and in His attributes; His existence is undeniable and nothing else can exist except through Him. His words are truth; the meeting with Him is truth; His Messengers are truth; His Books are truth; His religion is the Truth; the worship of Him Alone, with no partners or associates, is the Truth; everything that has to do with Him is truth! [Tayseer al-Kareem al-Rahmaan fi Tafseer Kalaam al-Mannaan, Shaykh 'Abd al-Rahmaan al-Sa'di]

The Truth, the Reality, the Just and Correct

Haqq comes from the root haa-qaaf-qaaf, which points to three main meanings. The first meaning is to be true, genuine, substantial and real. The second main meaning is to be right and to be suitable to the requirements of wisdom and justice. The third is to be established as fact, to be unavoidable and to happen without doubt. The forth main meaning is to be proper and to be in accord with the needs of the situation.

This root appears 287 times in the Quran in seven derived forms. Examples of these forms include haqqa ("proved true"), ahaqqu ("more right"), al haqq ("the truth") and al haqqatu ("the inevitable reality").

The truth is a value, whereas justice means the truth being put into action. Haqq refers to the One He acts in accord with the needs of every situation. He cannot but exist and His essence is unavoidable, every truth comes from Al-Haqq!

Al-Haqq Himself says: And say: 'The Truth is from your Lord.' Then whosoever wills, let him believe, and whosoever wills, let him disbelieve... [Quran, 18:29] ... So, after the truth, what else can there be, save error? ... [Quran, 10:32].. And say: 'Truth has come and falsehood has vanished. Surely, falsehood is ever bound to vanish. [Quran, 17:81]

Accordingly, if Allah is Al Haqq, why is he lying in the same Qur'an?

The Quran describes Allah as the best deceiver there is, a liar who is not above using the same evil and wicked schemes of his opponents.

For example, the Quran calls Allah a makr, in fact the best makr there is:

But they (the Jews) were deceptive, and Allah was deceptive, for Allah is the best of deceivers (Wamakaroo wamakara Allahu waAllahu khayru al-makireena)! S. 3:54; cf. 8:30

Other texts that identify Allah as a makr include:

Are they then securing from Allah's deception (makra Allahi)? None deemeth himself secure from Allah's deception (makra Allahi) save folk that perish. S. 7:99

So, they schemed a scheme: and We schemed a scheme (Wamakaroo makran wamakarna makran), while they perceived not. S. 27:50

The word for deception/deceiver/scheme is makr. The lexical sources define the term as:

Miim-Kaf-Ra = To practice deceit or guile or circumvention, practice evasion or elusion, to plot, to exercise art or craft or cunning, act with policy, practice stratagem.

makara vb. (1)

     perf. act. 3:54, 3:54, 7:123, 13:42, 14:46, 16:26, 16:45, 27:50, 40:45, 71:22

     impf. act. 6:123, 6:123, 6:124, 8:30, 8:30, 8:30, 10:21, 12:102, 16:127, 27:70, 35:10

     n.vb. 7:99, 7:99, 7:123, 10:21, 10:21, 12:31, 13:33, 13:42, 14:46, 14:46, 14:46, 27:50, 27:50, 27:51, 34:33, 35:10, 35:43, 35:43, 71:22

     pcple. act. 3:54, 8:30 LL, V7, p: 256 (Al Tafsir)

And:

He practiced DECEIT, GUILE, or CIRCUMVENTION, desiring to do another a foul, an abominable, or an evil action, clandestinely or without his knowing whence it proceeded. (Lane's Arabic-English Lexicon; source)

Lest Muslims accuse these lexicons of bias or distortion notice what Muslim scholar Dr. Mahmoud M. Ayoub says when he asks,

"how the word makr (scheming or plotting), which implies deceitfulness or dishonesty, could be attributed to God." (The Quran and Its Interpreters – The House of Imran [State University of New York Press [SUNY], Albany 1992], Volume II, p. 165; italic emphasis ours)

Is Jesus Al Haqq?

More than 76 times in the Bible Jesus declares that He is the Truth – Al Haqq, or that He is on the side of Truth.

The Greek word for "truth" is aletheia, which refers to "divine revelation" and is related to a word that literally means "what can't be hidden." It conveys the thought that truth is always there, always open and available for all to see, with nothing being hidden or obscured. The Hebrew word for "truth" is emeth, which means "firmness," "constancy" and "duration." Such a definition implies an everlasting substance and something that can be relied upon.

John 14:6 NIV

Jesus answered, "I am the way and the truth and the life. No one comes to the Father except through me. (Jesus is the only way, this way was never changed to Muhammad or Islam. The way to heaven is the same from the beginning of time until now. Jesus

is the ONLY way. If someone comes after Jesus and say there is another way, that person or god is a LIAR)
John 18:37

"You are a king, then!" said Pilate. Jesus answered, "You say that I am a king. In fact, the reason I was born and came into the world is to testify to the truth. Everyone on the side of truth listens to me."

During the six trials of Jesus, the contrast between the truth (righteousness) and lies (unrighteousness) was unmistakable. There stood Jesus, the Truth, being judged by those whose every action was bathed in lies. The Jewish leaders broke nearly every law designed to protect a defendant from wrongful conviction. They fervently worked to find any testimony that would incriminate Jesus, and in their frustration, they turned to false evidence brought forward by liars. But even that could not help them reach their goal. So, they broke another law and forced Jesus to implicate Himself.

Once in front of Pilate, the Jewish leaders lied again. They convicted Jesus of blasphemy, but since they knew that wouldn't be enough to coax Pilate to kill Jesus, they claimed Jesus was challenging Caesar and was breaking Roman law by encouraging the crowds to not pay taxes. Pilate quickly detected their superficial deception, and he never even addressed the charge. Jesus the Righteous was being judged by the unrighteous. The sad fact is that the latter always persecutes the former. It's why Cain killed Abel. The link between truth and righteousness and between falsehood and unrighteousness is demonstrated by a number of examples in the New Testament:

• For this reason, God will send upon them a deluding influence so that they will believe what is false, in order that they all may be judged who did not believe the truth, but took pleasure in wickedness" (2 Thessalonians 2:11–12, emphasis added).

• "For the wrath of God is revealed from heaven against all ungodliness and unrighteousness of men who suppress the truth in unrighteousness" (Romans 1:18, emphasis added).

• "who will render to each person according to his deeds; to those who by perseverance in doing good seek for glory and honor and immortality, eternal life; but to those who are selfishly ambitious and do not obey the truth, but obey unrighteousness, wrath and indignation" (Romans 2:6–8, emphasis added).

• "[love] does not act unbecomingly; it does not seek its own, is not provoked, does not take into account a wrong suffered, does not rejoice in unrighteousness, but rejoices with the truth" (1 Corinthians 13:5–6, emphasis added).

The truth – Again Jesus used the definite article to emphasize Himself as "the only truth." Psalm 119:142 says, "Your law is the truth." In the Sermon on the Mount, Jesus reminded His listeners of several points of the Law, then said, "But I say unto you . . ." (Matthew 5:22, 28, 32, 34, 39, 44), thereby equating Himself with the Law of God as the authoritative standard of righteousness. In fact, Jesus said that He came to fulfill the Law and the prophets (Matthew 5:17). Jesus, as the incarnate Word of God (John 1:1) is the source of all truth.

Al Haqq: truth (الحق) - Jesus is the truth (John 14:6)

CHAPTER VIII

JESUS IS AL WARITH – ULTIMATE INHERITOR

One of God's attributes in both the Bible and the Quran is Al Warith. Al Warith means the ultimate inheritor.

This is one of the unique attributes of God that represents either Allah or Jesus. In this subject, we will learn, through Bible and Quran verses that Jesus is the TRUE AL WARITH and not Allah.

نَحْنُ نَرِثُ ٱلْأَرْضَ وَمَنْ عَلَيْهَا وَإِلَيْنَا يُرْجَعُونَ

19:40 Surat Al Maryam

Innaa nahnu narisul arda wa man 'alaihaa wa ilainaa yurja'oon (section 2)

SAHIH INTERNATIONAL:

Indeed, it is We who will inherit the earth and whoever is on it, and to Us they will be returned.

ن Allah calls Himself Al-Waarith—The Inheritor, the Heir— on one occasion in the Quran. Al-Waarith is the One who remains after the extinction of everyone and everything. He is the only One to whom all will return; He is the sole inheritor and owner of the whole creation!

The Inheritor, The Supreme Heir

Waarith comes from the root waaw-raa-thaa, which points to four main meanings. The first meaning is to inherit. The second main meaning is to be an heir or survivor, and the third is to be the owner or maintainer after one has passed.

This root appears 35 times in the Quran in five derived forms. Examples of these forms are narithu ("we will inherit"), meeraathu ("(the) heritage"), and al waaritheena ("the inheritors").

Linguistically, waratha refers to the action of inheriting whereas waarith is the one doing the action, the inheritor and al-meeraath is the inheritance. Even though there is the concept of heirs and inheritance of worldly possessions in this world, Al-Waarith is the supreme Heir to whom the heritage of the heavens and earth belongs.

Al-Waarith Himself says: . . . And indeed, it is We who give life and cause death, and We are the Inheritor [Quran, 15:23] ...And to Allah belongs the heritage of the heavens and the earth. And Allah, with what you do, is [fully] Acquainted. [Quran, 3:180]

Why is Allah calling himself Al Warith? What is he inheriting?

Can you inherit what you worked for? I mean, why is Allah inheriting what he has created?

Hebrews 1:2 King James Version 2 Hath in these last days spoken unto us by his Son, whom he hath appointed heir of all things, by whom also he made the worlds;

Verses 1 and 2 of Hebrews emphasize the fact that Christ is the latest part of God's continuous, consistent message. Where God had spoken through the prophets of the Old Testament, He now speaks through the person of Jesus Christ. These are not contradictory messages. Jesus is the Messiah of whom those prophets spoke. Since this is a message from God, it stands to reason that those who love God ought to listen. Knowing that Jesus is a message from God, and is God, and is the ultimate truth sets the table for this letter's many warnings against rejecting the gospel.

The end of verse 2 also introduces an idea which is fundamental to the Christian faith: Jesus Christ is God. The first four verses of this book establish that Jesus is not some created being or a higher form of angel. According to verse 3, Jesus is the "exact imprint" of the nature of God. This is the consistent teaching of the Bible, that Christ is both fully God and fully man.

The words of this verse echo the Gospel of John, which notes that "all things were made through [Christ], and without [Christ] was not anything made that was made" (John 1:3). This establishes that Jesus is, in fact, part of the un-created and eternal God. All things which "were made" were made by God; the only thing not "made" is the eternal Creator.

Matthew 11:27 New King James Version 27 All things have been delivered "given" to Me by My Father, and no one knows the Son except the Father. Nor does anyone know the Father except the Son, and the one to whom the Son wills to reveal Him.

This is Divine Inheritance

Jesus Al-Warith- The heir, inheritor (Hebrews 1:2; Matthew 28:18)

CHAPTER

IX

JESUS IS AL BAITH

One of the names of Allah of Islam is Al Baith which means RESURRECTION. Note that the name of Allah is Allah. The name carries Allah's attributes which is Allah. In short, the 99 names of Allah are Allah. Allah = Al Baith.

Between Jesus and Allah, who do you think deserved to be called AL BAETH?

Approximately 632 years prior to the birth of Muhammad and the revelations of the Quran and Islam, Jesus called himself Al Baith and raised the dead. Did Allah ever raise anyone from the dead?

Surat Al-Haj 22: 5. SAHIH INTERNATIONAL: O People, if you should be in doubt about the Resurrection, then [consider that] indeed, We created you from dust, then from a sperm-drop, then from a clinging clot, and then from a lump of flesh, formed and unformed – that We may show you. And We settle in the wombs whom We will for a specified term, then We bring you out as a child, and then [We develop you] that you may reach your [time of] maturity. And among you is he who is taken in [early] death, and among you is he who is returned to the most decrepit [old] age so that he knows, after [once having] knowledge, nothing. And you see the earth barren, but when We send down upon its rain, it quivers and swells and grows [something] of every beautiful kind.

Why are people doubting Allah that he will be able to resurrect them on the last day? The main reason for their doubt is simple. They have never seen Allah or his prophet Muhammad raising the dead.

Now, why is Allah calling himself Al Baith without raising anybody?

All Allah did was to give vain words to the Ummah of Islam, that he will raise them on the last day.
Jesus is Al Baith:

John 11:23-25 New International Version 23 Jesus said to her, "Your brother "Lazarus" will rise again." 24 Martha answered, "I know he will rise again in the resurrection at the last day." 25 Jesus said to her, "I am the resurrection and the life.
43 When he had said this, Jesus called in a loud voice, "Lazarus, come out!" 44 The dead man came out, his hands and feet wrapped with strips of linen, and a cloth around his face. Jesus said to them, "Take off the grave clothes and let him go."

Jesus spoke. 'I am the resurrection and the life.' He shared these words with Martha, as she grieved the loss of her brother Lazarus. Reading or hearing the words Jesus spoke can bring comfort and peace. The book of John shares how when Martha heard that Jesus was coming, she went to meet him. The brother of Martha and Mary had died. Lazarus had been in the tomb for four days. After Lazarus died, people had come to visit the mourning family. Jesus waited to visit, and Martha wondered why the delay.

As Jesus spoke this profound and important statement of 'I am the resurrection and the life', Martha had yet to understand the meaning.

Do we read that Scripture and understand? Are we filled with faith in our Lord or are we filled with doubt? The Word of God is the same yesterday, today, and tomorrow. Yes, He is the light of the world.

What Does I am the Resurrection and the Life Mean? As sisters Martha and Mary sent word to Jesus that their brother Lazarus had died, perhaps they thought Jesus would drop whatever He was doing and start the journey to get to them immediately. In Scripture, we read Jesus shared with his disciples that he was going there to wake Lazarus (John 11:11). Jesus stayed two more days before leaving to go to his friend Lazarus. Jesus shares that what He is doing is for the glory of God, not man. Even then, the disciples did not fully know the meaning of death. They thought Jesus meant Lazarus was asleep.

Jesus spoke 'I am' statements. 'I am the resurrection and the life' is one of those statements (John 11:25).

Jesus shares with Martha that her brother Lazarus will rise again. She responds by saying she knows he will rise on the last day. Martha doesn't understand the true depth of what Jesus is telling her. Martha is referring to a day in the future.

Jesus tells Martha that He is the resurrection and the life. He explains that anyone who believes in Him will live and never die. Jesus is referring to life eternal with God, not the earthly life. Jesus showed His power over earthly death as He called for Lazarus to come out of the tomb (John 11:43). Jesus asked for the stone to be taken away. Then, Jesus thanked God for hearing his prayers. What lessons we can learn from this Scripture. Jesus thanked His Father for hearing his prayers. Lazarus came out of the tomb and was released from bindings.

In Scripture, we read that no one comes to the Father except through Jesus Christ (John 14:6). Without Jesus, we have no hope for eternal life with God. When we seek a relationship with God, our faith and hope can grow. Perhaps you have read "Jesus is the way, the truth, and the life." on a t-shirt or billboard or maybe a bumper sticker. Knowing Jesus and growing closer to God in each moment gives us the strength, stamina, and hope to journey through good times and bad times. We are sinners and fall short of how we should treat each other. Yet, through believing Christ and growing that special relationship, we are more prepared to share His love with others.

If someone asks, "Who is this Jesus you speak about?" or "Why do you believe?", how will you respond? Do you have an answer? Are you ready to share your faith journey? Are you ready to share how you came to know Christ?

Al Ba'ith: resurrection (الباعث) - Jesus is resurrection (Jonh 11:25-26)

CHAPTER
X

JESUS WAS SINLESS

Jesus was sinless

Romans 3:23: "For all have sinned and fall short of the glory of God."

The only exception – Jesus Christ

1 Peter 2:22: "He (Jesus) committed no sin, and no deceit was found in his mouth."

Concerning Jesus, the Book of Hebrews states:

Hebrews 4:15: "For we do not have a high priest who cannot sympathize with our weaknesses, but one who has been tempted in every way, like ourselves, but without sin."

As we have noted, Islam also acknowledges that Jesus was sinless. Besides the Qur'an, the Hadith also records the sinlessness of Jesus. It states that he was untouched by Satan. And Muhammad himself believed this to be true.

Sahih Muslim, Volume 4, page 1261:

Abu Huraira reported Allah's Messenger (saw) as saying: The Satan touches every son of Adam on the day when his mother gives birth to him with the exception of Mary and her son.

Notice carefully, this Hadith states that ***"*Satan touches every son of Adam on the day when his mother gives birth to him.*" ***

Therefore, it shows that the subject of this Hadith is Jesus, not Mary.   Why then was Mary also spoken of being protected from Satan? It is because of the child she was carrying in her womb. Only Jesus is spoken of as a "holy son" in the Qur'an. Nowhere in the Qur'an it is stated that Mary is the "holy mother" of Jesus. Neither is she addressed in the Qur'an as a "holy daughter." However, since she was privileged to become the instrument of God to deliver his Son as a human on earth, it also necessitated the protection of her. It is for this reason alone; Mary was protected during her delivery of Jesus. To protect the "holy son," Mary had to be protected.

Yes! Jesus Christ committed no sin. What kind of man must he be that he has never sinned? There is not a single verse in either the Qur'an or the Bible saying that Jesus asked God for forgiveness of his sins. The reason for this is absolutely clear. It is because Jesus is the Son of God. As such, he was Sinless, **Holy, **and **Pure. **He was the only human who came from the realms above. That is why the Qur'an acknowledges Jesus as a "Spirit from God." And Jesus himself testified to this truth in the following Biblical verse.

John 8:23: "So he went on to say to them: 'You are from the realms below; I am from the realms above. You are from this world; I am not from this world.'"

Why is Jesus the only man without sin among mankind? The Qur'an admits his sinlessness but gives no reason for it. Saying that Jesus was a prophet of God does not provide the answer. If this assertion is true, then why are the other prophets not described equally as sinless? In fact, quite a few, including Muhammad, are shown to be sinners. But we must ask again, "Why was Jesus the only one among mankind who is sinless?" Only by acknowledging the unique status of Jesus as the Son of God, Muslims can understand the reason why both the Qur'an and the Bible speak of Jesus as the only one who is without sin.

CHAPTER XI

THE QURAN PROVES ONLY JESUS CAN BEAR OUR SINS

The Quran proves only Jesus can bear our sins.

One Muslim objection which is so often raised against Christianity is the sacrificial death of Jesus Christ for our sins. This fundamental Christian doctrine is well-known as the *"Ransom Sacrifice of Jesus Christ."* Provided below is an example of the typical argument used by   Muslims against the doctrine of the *Ransom Sacrifice*:

How can God punish an innocent man for the sins of other people? That is like saying that God punishes an innocent person for the sins of a murderer and then forgives the murderer. In Islam each person pays for his own sins. When Allah wants to forgive people, he does not need to punish an innocent man for what they have done. He can just forgive them. The Christian view is unfair and unjust.

Does it sound familiar? Of course, we can easily refute this argument by simply quoting what the Bible says about Jesus Christ dying for our sins and then quoting what the Qur'an says about the Bible being the authoritative incorruptible *Word of God.* This would leave Muslims with just two options. They must either *submit* to the Qur'an's testimony regarding the authenticity of the Bible and *accept* the *Ransom Sacrifice of Jesus Christ* or *reject* the Qur'an's testimony regarding the authenticity of the Bible and *deny* the *Ransom Sacrifice of Jesus Christ.* Either option means a denial of Islam for Muslims.

However, we intend to provide more than a quick refutation to the Muslim objection. In the interest of both Muslims and Christians, we are determined to deal directly and extensively with the objection itself. This will help Christians understand that they have nothing to fear from the objections raised against Christianity. Every objection raised against Christianity opens the door of opportunity to engage in conversation with Muslims. In fact, there are devastating responses to the most common Muslim objections. If Christians would simply take the time to learn how to counter these objections, it would fortify and strengthen their faith tremendously. By the end of this article, you will learn how the denial of the sacrificial death of Jesus actually spells disaster for the Muslims. We will now prove the following facts:

One: The Qur'an contradicts itself on this issue.

Two: Muhammad was a false prophet.

Three: The Qur'an proves that only Jesus is qualified to bear our sins.

To begin, why do Muslims so strongly believe that no one can redeem the sins of another? This is because several verses of the Qur'an teach that *"no bearer of burdens shall bear the burden of another."* Let's read one such verse:

Surah 6:164: Say: What! Shall I seek the Lord other than Allah? And he is the lord of all things and no soul earns (evil) but against itself, and no bearer of burdens shall bear the burden of another. (Shakir)

عَلَيْهَا إِلَّا نَفْسٍ كُلُّ تَكْسِبُ وَلَا ۚ   شَىْءٍ كُلِّ رَبٌّ وَهُوَ رَبًّا أَبْغِى ٱللَّهِ أَغَيْرَ قُلْ

تَخْتَلِفُونَ فِيهِ كُنتُمْ بِمَا فَيُنَبِّئُكُم مَّرْجِعُكُمْ رَبِّكُم إِلَىٰ ثُمَّ ۚ أُخْرَىٰ وِزْرَ وَازِرَةٌ تَزِرُ وَلَا ۚ

Qul aghairal laahi abghee Rabbanw wa Huwa Rabbu kulli
shaiyy'; wa laa taksibu kullu nafsin illaa 'alaihaa; wa laa taziru
waaziratunw wizra ukhraa; summa ilaa Rabbikum marji'ukum fa
yunabbi'ukum bimaa kuntum feehi takhtalifoon

SAHIH INTERNATIONAL:

*Say, "Is it other than Allah I should desire as a lord while He is
the Lord of all things? And every soul earns not [blame] except against
itself, and no bearer of burdens will bear the burden of another. Then to
your Lord is your return, and He will inform you concerning that over
which you used to differ."*

The term *"burden"* used here refers to the *burden of
sin.* Other Qur'anic verses also contain similar teachings.
See *Surah 17:15, Surah 35:18, Surah 39:7* and *Surah 53:38.* Muslims
who read these Qur'anic verses are convinced that Islam teaches
that *no one* can bear the burdens of others. Unfortunately for
Muslims, there are serious problems with this claim. We will now
discuss these problems.

The Quran contradicts itself on these issue

There are several verses in the Qur'an which state that
some people will bear the burdens of others. We will cite just one
example to prove our point. Absurdly, Allah even changes his
mind immediately from one Qur'anic verse to the next. Allah
states in *Surah 29:12* that the *unbelievers* will never bear the *sins* of
others:

*Surah 29:12: Those who deny the truth say to the faithful, follow
our way, and we will bear the burden of your sins. But they will bear none
of their sins. They are surely lying. (W. Khan)*

خَطَـٰيَـٰهُ مِنْ بِحَـٰمِلِينَ هُم وَمَا خَطَـٰيَـٰكُمْ وَلْنَحْمِلْ سَبِيلَنَا ٱتَّبِعُوا۟ ءَامَنُوا۟ لِلَّذِينَ كَفَرُوا۟ ٱلَّذِينَ وَقَالَ

لَكَـٰذِبُونَ إِنَّهُمْ ۖ شَىْءٍ مِّن م

Wa qaalal lazeena kafaroo lillazeena aamanut tabi'oo
sabeelanaa walnahmil khataayaakum wa maa hum bihaamileena
min khataa yaahum min shai'in innahum lakaaziboon

However, in the very next verse Allah contradicts himself
and states that *unbelievers* will bear their own burdens and the
burdens of others:

*Surah 29:13: And most certainly they shall carry their own
burdens, and other burdens with their own burdens, and most certainly*

*they shall be questioned on the resurrection day as to what they forged.
(Shakir)*

يَفْتَرُونَ كَانُوا عَمَّا ٱلْقِيَـٰمَةِ يَوْمَ وَلَيُسْئَلُنَّ ۙ أَثْقَالِهِمْ مَّعَ وَأَثْقَالًا أَثْقَالَهُمْ وَلَيَحْمِلُنَّ

Wa la yahmilunna asqaa lahum wa asqaalam ma'a
asqaalihim wa la yus'alunna Yawmal Qiyaamati 'ammaa kaanoo
yaftaroon (section 1)

As we can see, the Qur'an contradicts itself on this issue.
This means the Qur'an also contradicts the objection raised by the
Muslims. So apparently some people can bear the burdens of
others. Thus, the Qur'an contradicts its own ruling that *"no bearer
of burdens shall bear the burden of others."*

Muhammad contradicts the Muslims claim.

Muslims are commanded not only to believe in *Allah* but
also to believe in *Muhammad.* This means that Muslims must
accept both the *teachings of Allah* and the *teachings of
Muhammad.* And Muslims are not authorized to dispute with any
of their teachings:

*Surah 33:36: It is not for a believing man or believing woman,
if Allah and His Messenger issue any command, that they have any
choice in their decision. And anyone who disobeys Allah and
His Messenger, he has gone far astray. (The Monotheist Group)*

أَمْرِهِمْ مِنْ ٱلْخِيَرَةُ لَهُمُ يَكُونَ أَن أَمْرًا وَرَسُولُهُ ٱللَّهُ قَضَى إِذَا مُؤْمِنَةٍ وَلَا لِمُؤْمِنٍ كَانَ وَمَا
مُبِينًا ضَلَـٰلًا ضَلَّ فَقَدْ وَرَسُولَهُ ٱللَّهَ يَعْصِ وَمَن ۚ

Wa maa kaana limu'mininw wa laa mu'minatin izaa qadal
laahu wa Rasooluhooo amran ai yakoona lahumul khiyaratu min
amrihim; wa mai ya'sil laaha wa Rasoolahoo faqad dalla dalaalam
mubeenaa

SAHIH INTERNATIONAL:

*It is not for a believing man or a believing woman, when Allah
and His Messenger have decided a matter, that they should [thereafter]
have any choice about their affair. And whoever disobeys Allah and His
Messenger has certainly strayed into clear error.*

The Qur'an clearly teaches that no Muslim can disobey
the *"command/decision"* of *Allah* or *Muhammad* and remain a
Muslim. In fact, the Qur'an teaches that obeying Muhammad is
the same as obeying Allah:

*Surah 4:79-80: We have sent you to mankind as a Messenger.
Allah suffices as a Witness. Whoever obeys the Messenger has obeyed*

Allah. If anyone turns away, We did not send you to them as their keeper. (A. Bewley)

رَسُولًا لِلنَّاسِ وَأَرْسَلْنَاكَ ۚ نَّفْسِكَ فَمِن سَيِّئَةٍ مِنْ أَصَابَكَ وَمَآ ۚ اللَّهِ فَمِنْ حَسَنَةٍ مِنْ أَصَابَكَ مَّآ شَهِيدًا بِاللَّهِ وَكَفَىٰ ۚ

4:79

Maaa asaabaka min hasanatin faminal laahi wa maaa asaaabaka min saiyi'atin famin nafsik; wa arsalnaaka linnaasi Rasoolaa; wa kafaa billaahi Shaheedaa

SAHIH INTERNATIONAL:

What comes to you of good is from Allah, but what comes to you of evil, [O man], is from yourself. And We have sent you, [O Muhammad], to the people as a messenger, and sufficient is Allah as Witness.

حَفِيظًا عَلَيْهِمْ أَرْسَلْنَاكَ فَمَآ تَوَلَّىٰ وَمَن ۚ اللَّهَ أَطَاعَ فَقَدْ الرَّسُولَ يُطِعِ مَّن

4:80

Many yuti'ir Rasoola faqad ataa'al laaha wa man tawallaa famaaa arsalnaaka 'alaihim hafeezaa

SAHIH INTERNATIONAL:

He who obeys the Messenger has obeyed Allah; but those who turn away – We have not sent you over them as a guardian.

This means that Muslims must believe in the *teachings of Allah* which state:

1. *No bearer of burdens shall bear the burdens of others.*
2. *Some people will bear the burdens of others.*

And they must also believe in the *teachings of Muhammad* which states that Allah will punish the Christians and the Jews in Hell for the sins of the Muslims. Let's read four important narrations from Muhammad.

Sahih Muslim, Book 37, Hadith 6665:

Allah's Messenger said: When it will be the Day of Resurrection Allah would deliver to every Muslim a Jew or a Christian and say: That is your rescue from Hell-Fire.

Well, how is a Jew or a Christian going to rescue a Muslim from Hell-Fire? By taking the place of that Muslim in Hell.

Sahih Muslim, Book 37, Hadith 6666:

Allah's Apostle said: No Muslim would die but Allah would admit in his stead a Jew or a Christian in Hell-fire.

Muhammad clearly taught that Allah will deliver the Jews and the Christians into Hell-fire to redeem the Muslims. But it gets even worse. It does not matter to Allah how heavy the sins of the Muslims are, Allah will just transfer their sins upon the Jews and the Christians and make them carry the burden of the sins of the Muslims.

Sahih Muslim, Book 37, Hadith 6668:

Allah's Messenger said: There would come people amongst the Muslims on the Day of Resurrection with his heavy sins as a mountain, and Allah would forgive them and He would place in their stead the Jews and the Christians.

Muslims who are loaded with sins as heavy as mountains have nothing to worry. Allah will punish the Jews and the Christians for their mountain load of sins.

110 Ahadith Qudsi, Hadith Number 8:

Allah's Messenger said: On the Day of Resurrection, my Ummah (nation) will be gathered into three groups. One sort will enter Paradise without rendering an account (of their deeds). Another sort will be reckoned an easy account and admitted into Paradise. Yet another sort will come bearing on their backs heaps of sins like great mountains...Allah we'll ask the angels though He knows best about them: Who are these people? They will reply: They are humble slaves of yours. He will say: Unload the sins from them and put the same over the Jews and Christians: then let the humble slave get into Paradise by virtue of my mercy.

Even though the sins of the Muslims are as massive as great mountains, Allah will order the angels on the *Day of Resurrection* to unload their sins and place them on the Jews and the Christians. Muhammad taught from the Qur'an that *"no bearer of burdens shall bear the burden of others."* Contradicting himself, he also taught from the same Qur'an saying that some people will bear their own burdens and the burdens of others. This proves that Muhammad was inventing revelations as he went along. Muslims argue that it is unjust and unfair for God to punish one person for the sins of others. Yet, we find Muhammad teaching that this is exactly what Allah is going to do. Therefore, according to Muslims, Muhammad must be a false prophet since his teachings accuses Allah of being unjust and unfair.

Muslims, if you are preparing to use the weak Hadith defense, we have news for you. All the Hadiths cited in this article are classified as *Sahih (Authentic)*. Muslims have a habit of deceitfully rejecting any Hadith that does not line up with their watered-down whitewashed version of Islam. If Muslims reject all these *Sahih* narrations, then they are throwing out the best historical information they have on their Prophet. It must be remembered that Muslims who reject the Hadiths are classified as apostates in Islam.

The Quran proved only Jesus can bear our sins

Muslims are known to pick and choose verses of the Qur'an which they want to believe. They will mentally switch off the verses that incriminate Islam. They will pretend that such verses do not exist. They will pretend that the Qur'an does not contradict itself on whether people can bear the burdens of others or not. And Muslims do the same with the teachings of Muhammad. They will pretend that Muhammad did not declare over and over again that Allah will punish the Jews and Christians in Hell for the sins of the Muslims.

There is a reason why Muslims conveniently choose to believe only the verses in the Qur'an which says that *"no bearer of burdens shall bear the burden of others."* The reason is because this is the part Muslims can use to condemn Christianity. Let's do them a favor. Let's focus on the part that Muslims want to believe. We will read once again the Qur'anic verse which Muslims intentionally choose to accept as true while ignoring all the other related verses:

Surah 6:164: Say: What! Shall I seek the Lord other than Allah? And he is the lord of all things and no soul earns (evil) but against itself, and no bearer of burdens shall bear the burden of another. (Shakir)

قُل أَغَيْرَ ٱللَّهِ أَبْغِى رَبًّا وَهُوَ رَبُّ كُلِّ شَىْءٍ إِلَّا نَفْسٍ كُلُّ تَكْسِبُ وَلَا عَلَيْهَا وَلَا تَزِرُ وَازِرَةٌ وِزْرَ أُخْرَىٰ ثُمَّ إِلَىٰ رَبِّكُم مَّرْجِعُكُم فَيُنَبِّئُكُم بِمَا كُنتُمْ فِيهِ تَخْتَلِفُونَ

Qul aghairal laahi abghee Rabbanw wa Huwa Rabbu kulli shaiyy'; wa laa taksibu kullu nafsin illaa 'alaihaa; wa laa taziru waaziratunw wizra ukhraa; summa ilaa Rabbikum marji'ukum fa yunabbi'ukum bimaa kuntum feehi takhtalifoon

Notice carefully what Allah is actually saying in the above Qur'anic verse. This Qur'anic verse does not say *"no one shall bear the burden of another"* but rather it says *"no bearer of burdens shall bear the burden of another."* In other words, *no one* who already has the *burden of sin* can bear the burden of others. Therefore, no sinner can bear the burden of another. Why? This is because a sinner is in no position to bear the sins of others while he has his own sins to deal with. So, no one who has a burden of sin can bear the burdens of others. This is excellent theology and Christians completely agree with this. In fact, centuries before the arrival of the Qur'an, the Bible taught and upheld this fundamental truth: *Psalms 49:7: None of them can ever redeem a brother. Or give to God a ransom for him.*

Therefore, what alternative does both the Bible and the Qur'an leave wide-open? That only someone who is sinless and has no burden of sin can bear the burden of others. Can we think of someone who is sinless and has no burden of sin? Muslims, if you think it is Muhammad, we encourage you to open your Qur'an and read the following verses:

Surah 40:55: (Muhammad), exercise patience. The promise of God is true. Seek forgiveness for your sins and glorify your Lord with His praise in the evenings and in the early mornings. (Sarwar)

Surah 47:19: Know, then, that there is none worthy of worship but Allah. And ask forgiveness for your sins, (O Muhammad) and for the sins of all other believing men and women. (M. Shafi)

Surah 48:2: So Allah may forgive all your sins, the ones in the past as well as those in the future, so He may conclude His blessings upon you and may guide you on to the straight path. (Munir Munshey)

Allah repeatedly commands Muhammad to ask forgiveness for his sins. As a sinner, Muhammad himself needs a redeemer. Having read the above Qur'anic verses, now read the following Hadith where Muhammad confesses:

Sahih Bukhari, Volume 8, Book 75, Hadith Number 319:

"By Allah! I ask for forgiveness from Allah and turn to Him in repentance more than seventy times a day."

More than 70 times a day! That is like asking forgiveness every 20 minutes. What was Muhammad committing? While this certainly proves that Muhammad is a habitual sinner, the Qur'an testifies that Jesus is sinless. The angel announced to Mary:

Surah 19:19: He said: "I am only a messenger of thy Lord, that I may bestow on thee a faultless son." (Pickthall)
"I am only a messenger from thy Lord, to announce to thee the gift of a holy son." (Yusuf Ali)

The Qur'an describes Jesus as *"faultless"* and *"holy."* No one is ever described as such. In fact, Muhammad testifies that with the exception of Jesus, Satan touches every child born into the world. Satan simply could not touch Jesus.

Sahih Bukhari, Volume 4, Book 54, Hadith Number 506:

The Prophet said, "When any human being is born, Satan touches him at both sides of the body with his two fingers, except Jesus, the Son of Mary, whom Satan tried to touch but failed, so he touch the placenta cover instead.

The Bible acknowledges that not only is Jesus unique but it also repeatedly declares that he is sinless:

Hebrews 4:15: For we do not have a high priest who cannot sympathize with our weaknesses, but we have one who has been tested in all respects as we have, but without sin.

I Peter 2:21-22: In fact, to this course you were called, because even Christ suffered for you, leaving a model for you to follow his steps closely. He committed no sin, nor was deception found in his mouth.

1 John 3:5: You know, too, that he was made manifest to take away our sins, and there is no sin in him.

The *Message of Christianity* is that the one person who qualifies to bear our burden of sin did so to save us. The *Message of Islam* is that the one person who qualifies to bear our burden of sin did not do so. And Jesus confirms the *Message of Christianity*:

Matthew 20:28: Just as the Son of man came, not to be ministered to, but to minister and to give his life as a ransom in exchange for many.

Unlike Muhammad, Jesus was not inventing revelations as he went along. Amazingly, *700 years* before the arrival of Jesus, the *Prophet Isaiah* prophesied regarding God's purpose for sending Jesus to earth. Under inspiration, the *Prophet Isaiah* revealed that Jesus was sent to mankind for the purpose of bearing our sins through his death:

Isaiah 53:11: By means of his knowledge the righteous one, my servant, will bring a righteous standing to many people and their sins he will bear.

There is perfect harmony between the divine teachings of the *Old Testament* and the *New Testament Scriptures*. However, Islam denies the salvation work of Jesus. As a result, Muslims are left with a *Book* that contradicts itself and a *Prophet* who blasphemously shifts the sins of his followers to the Jews and

Christians. And Muslims think we are the ones who have a theological problem on this issue.

Sadly, for Muslims, their religious leaders hide what the Qur'an actually teaches. And they conceal what Muhammad actually taught in the Hadith. The reason why the religious leaders of Islam do not reveal what their own Islamic sources teach is because Muslims will soon realize that Muhammad's position on salvation are completely incoherent and contradictory. They are afraid that Muslims will lose their faith in Islam. So, they keep Muslims in a state of ignorance for Islam to flourish. We would like to conclude this article by leaving this thought with Muslims. If your religious leaders conceal what Muhammad really taught about salvation, what else are they hiding from you about Islam?

CHAPTER XII

THE BASIS FOR THE RANSOM SACRIFICE OF JESUS IN THE QURAN

The basis for the ransom sacrifice of Jesus in the Quran.

Islam completely rejects the Biblical doctrine of Substitutionary Atonement, namely the Ransom Sacrifice of Jesus Christ. Yet, it may surprise many to learn that the doctrine of the ransom as a release from death can be found in the teachings of the Qur'an. The Qur'an's clear testimony to the fact that Allah redeemed Abraham's son by means of a Substitutive Sacrifice should awaken Muslims to reconsider their denial of the doctrine of the ransom sacrifice of Jesus. The account of a substitutive sacrifice as a ransom can be found in the following Qur'anic verses:

Surah 37:101-103: So, We gave him the good news of a boy ready to suffer and forbear. Then, when the son reached the age of serious work with him, he said: "O my son! I see in vision that I offer thee in sacrifice: Now see what is thy view!" The son said: "O my father! Do as thou art commanded: thou will find me, if Allah so wills one practicing Patience and Constancy!" So when they had both submitted their wills to Allah, and he had laid him prostrate on his forehead for sacrifice. (Yusuf Ali)

حَلِيمٍ بِغُلَـٰمٍ فَبَشَّرْنَـٰهُ

37:101

Fabashsharnaahu bighulaamin haleem

SAHIH INTERNATIONAL:

So We gave him good tidings of a forbearing boy.

تَرَىٰ مَاذَا فَٱنظُرْ أَذْبَحُكَ أَنِّى ٱلْمَنَامِ فِى أَرَىٰ إِنِّىَ يَـٰبُنَىَّ قَالَ ٱلسَّعْىَ مَعَهُ بَلَغَ فَلَمَّا ٱلصَّـٰبِرِينَ مِنَ ٱللَّهُ شَآءَ إِن سَتَجِدُنِىٓ ۚ تُؤْمَرُ مَا أَفْعَلْ يَـٰٓأَبَتِ قَالَ ۖ

37:102

Falamma balagha ma'a hus sa'ya qaala yaa buniya inneee araa fil manaami anneee azbahuka fanzur maazaa taraa; qaala yaaa abatif 'al maa tu'maru satajidunee in shaaa'allaahu minas saabireen

SAHIH INTERNATIONAL:

And when he reached with him [the age of] exertion, he said, "O my son, indeed I have seen in a dream that I [must] sacrifice you, so see what you think." He said, "O my father, do as you are commanded. You will find me, if Allah wills, of the steadfast."

لِلْجَبِينِ وَتَلَّهُ أَسْلَمَا فَلَمَّا

37:103

Falammaaa aslamaa wa tallahoo liljabeen

SAHIH INTERNATIONAL:

And when they had both submitted and he put him down upon his forehead,

The Qur'anic account then continues with these significant words of Allah:

Surah 37:104-108: We called out to him "O Abraham! Thou hast already fulfilled the vision!" – Thus indeed do We reward those who do right. For this was obviously a trial- And We ransomed him with a <u>momentous</u> sacrifice: And We left this blessing for him among generations to come in later times. (Yusuf Ali)

يَـٰٓإِبْرَٰهِيمُ أَن وَنَـٰدَيْنَـٰهُ

37:104

Wa naadainaahu ai yaaaa Ibraheem

SAHIH INTERNATIONAL:

We called to him, "O Abraham,

ٱلْمُحْسِنِينَ نَجْزِى كَذَٰلِكَ إِنَّا ۚ ٱلرُّءْيَآ صَدَّقْتَ قَدْ

37:105

Qad saddaqtar ru'yaa; innaa kazaalika najzil muhsineen

SAHIH INTERNATIONAL:

You have fulfilled the vision." Indeed, We thus reward the doers of good.

ٱلْمُبِينُ ٱلْبَلَٰٓؤُا۟ لَهُوَ هَٰذَا إِنَّ

37:106

Inna haazaa lahuwal balaaa'ul mubeen

SAHIH INTERNATIONAL:

Indeed, this was the clear trial.

عَظِيمٍ بِذِبْحٍ وَفَدَيْنَٰهُ

37:107

Wa fadainaahu bizibhin 'azeem

SAHIH INTERNATIONAL:

And We ransomed him with a great sacrifice,

ٱلْءَاخِرِينَ فِى عَلَيْهِ وَتَرَكْنَا

37:108

Wa taraknaa 'alaihi fil aakhireen

SAHIH INTERNATIONAL:

And We left for him [favorable mention] among later generations:

The above Qur'anic verses reveal a very important fact. It reveals that Allah ransomed Abraham's son by personally providing "a momentous sacrifice." Note how this phrase is rendered in other translations of the Qur'an:

"We ransomed his son for a great sacrifice." (Malik)

"And We ransomed him with a tremendous sacrifice." (Asad)

"And We ransomed him with a magnificent slain (sacrifice)." (M.M. Ghali)

"And We ransomed him with a mighty sacrifice." (Maududi)

"And We ransomed him with a noble victim." (Sale)

"We have ransomed his son with a great sacrifice." (Sarwar)

Why is the sacrifice, which both Muslims and Christians believe to have been a ram, called "momentous" or "great" in the Qur'an? How can a mere ram be described as "momentous" or "great" in comparison with Abraham's son? Is not a human far greater and more valued than a ram? A ram is a male sheep. While the Bible testifies it was Isaac who was offered as the sacrifice, Muslims have traditionally held that it was Ishmael.

Muslims are taught to believe that the only reason for Allah to command Abraham to sacrifice his son was to test his obedience. While it is true that it served as a test for Abraham, it was however not the primary reason. God had in mind of something far greater in importance than that. Consider this, when Abraham came close to sacrificing his son, Allah intervened and said: *"O Abraham! Thou hast already fulfilled the vision!"* This proves beyond doubt that Abraham passed the test of obedience.

If Allah's purpose was only to test Abraham's obedience, then this raises some very important questions. Since Abraham had already passed the test successfully, why could not Allah then simply allow Abraham to take his son and leave? Why was a ransom needed to free Abraham's son? Allah stated explicitly in the Qur'an: *"We ransomed him."* The payment of a ransom is required only for someone who has to be redeemed from some sort of a captivity. Therefore, by itself, the requirement of a ransom for the son of Abraham does not make any sense at all. So, what is the message that Allah wants us to understand here? To deny that God does anything without a purpose behind it amounts to a denial of God himself.

Surah 38:27: It was not without purpose that We created the heavens and the earth and everything in between. (Abdel Haleem)

If you are a Muslim who is sincerely seeking to know the truth, then ask yourself the following questions:

(1) Why in the first place must a Ransom be paid for Abraham's son?

(2) Why was a Sacrifice required as a Ransom to free Abraham's son?

(3) Why was it absolutely necessary for Allah to provide the ram as a Substitute Sacrificial Offering to redeem Abraham's son?

(4) What legal obligation could there be to enforce the rule that the only justifiable way for Allah to free Abraham's son was by Substituting another Sacrifice in his place?

(5) Allah clearly stated: "We ransomed him." To whom did Allah pay the Ransom price to?

(6) If it is to himself, why could not Allah simply cancel the requirement of the Ransom price?
(7) As Muslims so often like to tease the Christians regarding the doctrine of the Ransom Sacrifice of Jesus, are Muslims now prepared to tease Allah also of taking money from one pocket and putting it into another?
(8) Why was there still a need for Allah to provide a Ransom Sacrifice at all since Abraham had already passed the test successfully?

These are vital questions that Muslims must seek to know the answer. Only by recognizing the full implications of these questions, will Muslims be able to understand why the sacrificial death of Jesus as a ransom is absolutely necessary for the redemption of mankind from sin and death. However, the answers to the above questions cannot be found in the Qur'an. Only in the Bible we can find the answers to these vital questions. The key to finding the answers is in the word, *"Ransom."* Basically, a ransom is the price paid to bring about the release of someone from captivity. It applies to someone or something that is exchanged to take the place of a person in captivity in order to secure his or her release. In this case, a ram was slain in the place of Abraham's son to set him free. The ram served as a means to redeem Abraham's son. This is exactly what is taught in the Biblical doctrine of substitutional sacrifice. While the principal of redemption is stated clearly in the Qur'an, it does not tell us why it was required.

The ransom price demanded is usually equal or close to the value of the person for whom the price for release is paid for. Can a mere ram be equal in value to a human? Should not the value of the ransom price be equivalent to that of a human to take the place of Abraham's son? While the Bible shows that the ram is only a pre-figuration of a greater sacrifice to come, the Qur'an is transfixed with the animal itself. How can it be when the substitute sacrifice is spoken of as being *"greater"* than the son of Abraham himself?

Thus, the sacrifice points to someone *"greater"* than any ordinary human. Who could that be?

As a Muslim, ask yourself:

"Why did Allah describe the substitutive sacrifice as "Azzim" which means "Momentous" "Tremendous" "Mighty" or "Great" means when it was just a ram. By no means can the slaughtering of a mere ram be considered as a *"momentous sacrifice"* especially in comparison with Abraham's son. The ram by itself is by no means special. Therefore, how could a mere ram be greater than a human being?

It will rationally make sense to describe the sacrificial ram as such only when it goes beyond itself to represent an altogether greater sacrifice – a greater sacrifice yet to come.

It is vital for Muslims to note that the Arabic term *"al-Azzim"* is one of the ninety-nine names of Allah in the Qur'an. Therefore, the Arabic term *"Azzim"* makes it highly impossible for the sacrifice of Allah to refer to a mere ram which Abraham subsequently found and slaughtered in his son's stead. (See *Genesis 22:13*).

Thus, the greatness of the sacrificial ram lies not within itself but somewhere else. The ram symbolically represented something far more significant in terms of its redeeming value. The sacrificial ram pointed to an ultimate sacrifice that was yet to come. A sacrifice that will be presented by God himself. As God is the one who ransomed Abraham's son by providing the alternate sacrifice, it will be God who will once again prepare the greater sacrifice prefigured by the ram. Redemption was God's arrangement, not Abraham's. A ram was slain to redeem Abraham's son. And that redemption required the shedding of blood.

The principle of animal life for human life as an offering to God pointed beyond itself. As God provided a ram to atone for Abraham's son, he has likewise provided a perfect, spotless lamb to atone for the sins of all those who turn to Him in true repentance. Therefore, the ram was only a symbol of the greater sacrifice to come in the person of Christ Jesus. God's provision of a substitute sacrifice to redeem Abraham's son on Mount Moriah served as a demonstration of the legal basis for the redemption of mankind through the ransom sacrifice of Jesus. In the Biblical account of this event, we find an interesting conversation that took place between Abraham and his son. As Abraham and his son were walking to the hill where the sacrifice is to take place, the boy notices that they had everything except an animal to sacrifice. And so he asks his father:

Genesis 22:7-8: "My father!" In turn he said: "Here I am, my son!" So he continued: "Here are the fire and the wood, but where is the sheep for the burnt offering?" To this Abraham said: "God will provide himself the sheep for the burnt offering, my son."

Notice that both Abraham and his son considered that the appropriate animal for the sacrifice was a sheep. Under inspiration, centuries before the arrival of Jesus Christ, the prophet Isaiah prophesied about the coming Messiah and recognized him to be the sacrificial lamb/sheep:

Isaiah 53:7: "He was oppressed and afflicted, yet he did not open his mouth; he was led like a lamb to the slaughter, and as a sheep before its shearers is silent, so he did not open his mouth."

And Jesus came to the earth to fulfill this divine prophecy. When John the Baptist saw Jesus coming toward him, John proclaimed:

John 1:29: "Look, the Lamb of God, who takes away the sin of the world!"

And the apostle Peter wrote under inspiration:

1 Peter 1:18-19: For you know that it was not with corruptible things, with silver or gold, that you were delivered from your fruitless form of conduct received by tradition from your forefathers. But it was with precious blood, like that of an unblemished and spotless lamb, even Christ's.

By denying the provision of the ransom sacrifice of Jesus Christ, the prophetic significance of the ransom sacrifice as a means to redeem Abraham's son has no meaning in Islam. According to the Qur'an, Abraham was commanded to show his love for Allah in a way which Allah has never matched Abraham in return. Can this really be true? Can a man's love for God surpass God's love for mankind?

The Muslim festival known as Eid-ul-Adha (Festival of Sacrifice) is a commemoration of an act of love by a man for God which has no parallel in Islam. Has Allah ever done anything for mankind to match Abraham's supreme act of love for God? Can Allah match Abraham's willingness to sacrifice his own son for God? One of the great absurdities of the Eid-ul-Adha festival is that it commemorates an act of love by a man for God which has no parallel from Allah in return. In the Eid-ul-Adha commemoration, we see a man showing love for God in a far more surpassing way than Allah has ever shown for man.

However, in Christianity, the sacrifice of Abraham's son was only a foreshadowing of the supreme manifestation of God's love that was yet to come. It was only a foreshadowing of God's greatest act of love for mankind which he manifested through the ransom sacrifice. Abraham's love was only a reflection of the supreme love that God was determined to show on our behalf through the gift of his only-begotten Son. Ask any Muslim this simple question: If the greatest way a man could show his love for God was by his willingness to sacrifice his son for God, what will be the greatest way God could ever show his love for us? There can only be one obvious answer to this question.

The depth of Jehovah's love for mankind could not be manifested in a way greater than this. While Jehovah halted the sacrificial execution of Abraham's son, he did not spare his own Son. He went right through with his love for us by giving his Son as the ultimate sacrifice to die for our sins. Can a love as great as this be surpassed?

Romans 8:32: "He who did not spare his own Son but gave him for us all, will he not also give us all things with him?"

1 John 4:10: "In this is love, not that we loved God, but that he loved us, and sent his Son to be the expiation of our sins."

The Qur'an's narration of the ram that served as a substitution for Abraham's son should have pointed Islam towards the correct understanding of the concept of the ransom sacrifice. But it did not. Islam misses the point and fails where it matters most. It failed to see the meaning of the prophetic drama which is recorded in Genesis 22. The Qur'an restates this account in Surah 37 without understanding the full significance of its meaning. Islam failed to comprehend that the sacrificial event of Abraham is actually a prophetic drama foreshadowing the greater sacrifice of the Messiah. The failure to understand this simple truth renders this highly significant prophetic drama meaningless in Islam.

The only thing that Islam achieved from this event is the meaningless slaughter of thousands of animals annually which it claims is being done in commemoration of Abraham's love for

Allah. Do such acts by Muslims accurately reflect the love of Abraham? Muslims failed to see that it is not the slaughtering of the ram by Abraham that counted with God but rather his willingness to sacrifice his son. It is only this act by Abraham that proved his obedience and love for God.

Genesis 22:15-17: And God proceeded to call to Abraham the second time out of the heavens and to say: "'By myself I do swear,' is the utterance of Jehovah, 'that by reason of the fact that you have done this thing and you have not withheld your son, your only one, I shall surely bless you and I shall surely multiply your seed like the stars of the heavens and like the grains of sand that are on the seashore."

All sacrifices according to the Law of Moses were based upon the principle of substitutionary atonement. There is however no remission of sins through the blood of sacrificed animals. The principle of animal life for human life as an offering to God pointed beyond itself.

Hebrews 10:3-4: To the contrary, by these sacrifices there is a reminding of sins from year to year, for it is impossible for the blood of bulls and of goats to take sins away.

The animal sacrifices required under the Law of Moses were only a shadow of the realities to come. And the reality belongs to Christ Jesus.

Hebrews 10:1: "The Law of Moses is only a shadow of the good things that are to come, but it is not the actual manifestation of the realities themselves. Therefore, it can never, by means of the same sacrifices repeated endlessly year after year, bring to perfect those who approach the Holy Place to offer them."

The animal sacrifices served as a reminder to the people of Israel of their need for the full forgiveness of their sins. Jesus Christ – the Lamb of God – came to offer the final atonement for our sins. All those who sincerely exercise faith in this loving provision, can experience the personal forgiveness of their sins. Jesus Christ is the one true Sacrifice. Please read the following two Biblical passages carefully:

Hebrews 9:11-14: "However, when Christ came as a high priest of the good things that have come to pass, through the greater and more perfect tent not made with hands, that is, not of this creation, he entered, no, not with the blood of goats and of young bulls, but with his own blood, once for all time into the holy place and obtained an everlasting deliverance for us. For if the blood of goats and of bulls and the ashes of a heifer sprinkled on those who have been defiled sanctifies to the extent of cleanness of the flesh, how much more will the blood of the Christ, who through an everlasting spirit offered himself without blemish to God, cleanse our consciences from dead works that we may render sacred service to the living God?"

Hebrew 10:5-10: Consequently, when Christ came into the world, he said, "Sacrifices and offerings you have not desired, but a body have you prepared for me; in burnt offerings and sin offerings you have taken no pleasure. Then I said, 'Behold, I have come to do your will, O God, as it is written of me in the scroll of the book.'" When he said above, "You have neither desired nor taken pleasure in sacrifices and offerings and burnt offerings and sin offerings" (these are offered according to the law), then he added, "Behold, I have come to do your will." He does away with the first in order to establish the second. And by that will we have been sanctified through the offering of the body of Jesus Christ once for all.

One of the arguments that Muslims use for their rejection of the ransom as a requirement for the forgiveness of sins is that they assert that God could forgive sins without requiring anything in return. If true, why could not Allah release the son of Abraham without requiring a substitute ransom? This proves that, in principle, the Qur'an admits that some sort of payment has to be made. A ransom is defined as the payment paid for the release of a person in captivity. Now let us look at Surah 37:107 once again.

"We have ransomed his son with a great sacrifice." (Sarwar)

When Islam denies the provision of the ultimate ransom in the person Christ Jesus, it shows that the One who actually redeemed Abraham's son by means of a ransom could not be Allah but Jehovah. Only Jehovah knew why Abraham had to be tested this way. The true God tested Abraham to ascertain whether he was worthy to father the nation that would birth his Son – the ultimate Sacrifice. That is why when Abraham proved beyond any doubt that he was willing to sacrifice his son, Jehovah made this profound statement in the Hebrew Scriptures (Torah):

Genesis 22:18: And by means of your seed all nations of the earth will certainly bless themselves due to the fact that you have listened to my voice."

And we find the fulfillment of the above prophetic promise of Jehovah in the Christian Greek Scriptures:

Galatians 3:16: Now the promises were spoken to Abraham and to his seed. It says, not: "And to seeds," as in the case of many such, but as in the case of one: "And to your seed," who is Christ.

Yes! It was Jehovah's purpose to save mankind through the seed of Abraham. Allah had no clue regarding this magnificent purpose of Jehovah. He had no clue whatsoever regarding God's means of redeeming mankind from sin and death. In fact, Islam contradicts itself by denying the reality – the ransom sacrifice of Jesus Christ.

Being illiterate, Muhammad did not have a full comprehension of God's purpose in the outworking of mankind's salvation. He failed to understand that the animal sacrifices that the Jews sacrificed were only a prefiguration of the ransom sacrifice of Jesus Christ. As a result, Muhammad failed to understand the prophetic significance of God's commandment to Abraham. Ironically, Muhammad taught that the sins those who touch or kiss the Black Stone of the Ka'ba would be forgiven on Judgment Day.

Narrated by al-Tirmidhi, 959:

The Messenger of Allah (peace and blessings of Allah be upon him) say:

"Touching them both (the Black Stone and al-Rukn al-Yamani) is an expiation for sins."

While Muslims are taught to reject the atoning value of the ransom sacrifice of Jesus Christ, yet these very same Muslims are taught to believe that a dead stone can achieve the very objective that they deny Jesus could accomplish. Muslims, remember that each time you sacrifice or see an animal being sacrificed on Eid-ul-Adha, that sacrificed animal testifies to a much greater sacrifice – the sacrifice of Jesus Christ, the Lamb of God, who takes away the sins of men.

Hebrews 10:4: It is impossible for the blood of bulls and of goats to take sins away.

John 1:29: "Look, the Lamb of God, who takes away the sin of the world!"

CHAPTER XIII

DOES THE QURAN CONFIRM THE
DEATH OF JESUS AT THE CROSS

Does the Quran confirm the death of Jesus at the Cross?

The Death and Resurrection of Jesus Christ are central to the Christian faith. The Bible attaches great importance to the death of Jesus. One reference work says that the death of Jesus is mentioned some 175 times in the Christian Greek Scriptures (New Testament). On the way to Jerusalem to celebrate his final Passover, Jesus told his disciples:

Mark 10:34-35: The Son of man will be delivered to the chief priests and the scribes, and they will condemn him to death and will deliver him to men of the nations, and they will make fun of him and will spit upon him and scourge him and kill him.

However, Muslims strongly deny that Jesus was put to death by execution on the stake. They believe that God rescued him from death and raised him to heaven – without experiencing death. This discrepancy between Islam and Christianity is crucial to the seeker of truth. Either Islam is true or Christianity is. But certainly not the both. Therefore, if it can be proven beyond doubt that Jesus actually died before his ascension to heaven, then not only will Christianity stand vindicated but Islam will also be proven to be false. What is important for Muslims to note is the fact that while the Qur'an denies the death of Jesus, at the same instance, in numerous verses it proves that Jesus actually died before his ascension to heaven. We will now prove this fact with absolute certainty.

Muslims are taught to believe that Jesus did not die but was bodily raised directly to heaven. The general Islamic view is that someone else was executed in the place of Jesus, with most Muslims believing that it was Judas Iscariot. According to Islam, Judas Iscariot was made to look like Jesus on the night before Christ was executed. And as a result, the unbelieving Jews supposedly thought that they had killed Jesus when it was Judas Iscariot. The idea that Jesus did not die developed from the following Qur'anic verse:

Surah 4:157: And their saying: Surely, we have killed the Messiah, Isa son of Marium, the messenger of Allah; and they did not kill him nor did they crucify him, but it appeared to them so (like Isa) and most surely those who differ therein are only in a doubt about it; they have no knowledge respecting it, but only follow a conjecture, and they killed him not for sure. (Shakir)

And another translation renders it as follows:

And because of their saying: We slew the Messiah Jesus son of Mary, Allah's messenger They slew him not nor crucified, but it appeared so unto them; and lo! those who disagree concerning it are in doubt thereof; they have no knowledge thereof save pursuit of a conjecture; they slew him not for certain. (Pickthall)

لَهُ شُبِّهَ وَلَكِن صَلَبُوهُ وَمَا قَتَلُوهُ وَمَا ٱللَّهِ رَسُولَ ٱبْنَ مَرْيَمَ عِيسَى ٱلْمَسِيحَ قَتَلْنَا إِنَّا وَقَوْلِهِمْ يَقِينًا قَتَلُوهُ وَمَا ٱلظَّنِّ ٱتِّبَاعَ إِلَّا عِلْمٍ مِنْ بِهِ لَهُم مَا مِنْهُ شَكٍّ لَفِى فِيهِ ٱخْتَلَفُوا ٱلَّذِينَ وَإِنَّ مْ

Wa qawlihim innaa qatal nal maseeha 'Eesab-na-Maryama Rasoolal laahi wa maa qataloohu wa maa salaboohu wa laakin shubbiha lahum; wa innal lazeenakh talafoo feehee lafee shakkim minh; maa lahum bihee min 'ilmin illat tibaa'az zann; wa maa qataloohu yaqeenaa

SAHIH INTERNATIONAL:

And [for] their saying, "Indeed, we have killed the Messiah, Jesus, the son of Mary, the messenger of Allah." And they did not kill him, nor did they crucify him; but [another] was made to resemble him to them. And indeed, those who differ over it are in doubt about it. They have no knowledge of it except the following of assumption. And they did not kill him, for certain.

The denial of the execution of Jesus by impalement is based entirely on this single verse in the entire Qur'an. This Qur'anic verse contradicts the Bible's clear testimony regarding the absolute certainty of the death of Jesus.

Muslims willingly accept the teaching of this single Qur'anic verse despite the fact that Muhammad came hundreds of years after the event, lived hundreds of miles away, and did not provide a single piece of evidence to substantiate his claim. The Qur'an is clearly in error for the following valid reasons.

The writings of the Bible were completed some six-hundred years before the arrival of the Qur'an. Since the Qur'an contradicts the essential teachings of the Bible regarding the death of Jesus while at the same instant affirming the authority of the Bible as a reliable guide, the Qur'an is evidently in error. How is it possible for Allah to deny the death of Jesus Christ and at the same instant validate the authority of the Bible? If the Bible is wrong about the death of Jesus, then it surely cannot be a reliable guidance for mankind. As such, would it not be an enormous error for Allah to give Christians the following commandment in the Qur'an? Consider the commandment of Allah in this Qur'anic verse:

Surah 5:68: Say: "O followers of the Bible! You have no valid ground for your beliefs – unless you truly observe the Torah and the Gospel, and all that has been bestowed from on high upon you by your Sustainer!" (Asad)

قُلْ يَٰٓأَهْلَ ٱلْكِتَٰبِ لَسْتُمْ عَلَىٰ شَىْءٍ حَتَّىٰ تُقِيمُوا۟ ٱلتَّوْرَىٰةَ وَٱلْإِنجِيلَ وَمَآ أُنزِلَ إِلَيْكُم مِّن رَّبِّكُمْ وَلَيَزِيدَنَّ كَثِيرًا مِّنْهُم مَّآ أُنزِلَ إِلَيْكَ مِن رَّبِّكَ طُغْيَٰنًا وَكُفْرًا فَلَا تَأْسَ عَلَى ٱلْقَوْمِ ٱلْكَٰفِرِينَ

Qul yaaa Ahlal Kitaabi lastum 'alaa shai'in hattaa tuqeemut Tawraata wal Injeela wa maaa unzila ilaikum mir Rabbikum; wa layazeedanna kaseeram minhum maa unzila ilaika mir Rabbika tugh yaananw wa kufran falaa taasa 'alal qawmil kaafireen

SAHIH INTERNATIONAL:

Say, "O People of the Scripture, you are [standing] on nothing until you uphold [the law of] the Torah, the Gospel, and what has been revealed to you from your Lord." And that which has been revealed to you from your Lord will surely increase many of them in transgression and disbelief. So do not grieve over the disbelieving people.

And Allah even commanded Muhammad to seek guidance from those who studied the Bible:

Surah 10:94: If thou wert in doubt as to what We have revealed unto thee, then ask those who have been reading the Book from before thee: the Truth hath indeed come to thee from thy Lord: so be in no wise of those in doubt. (Yusuf Ali)

"And if thou (Muhammad) art in doubt concerning that which We reveal unto thee, then question those who read the Scripture that was before thee." (Pickthall)

قَبْلِكَ مِنَ ٱلْكِتَـٰبَ يَقْرَءُونَ إِلَيْكَ أَنزَلْنَآ مِّمَّآ شَكٍّ فِى كُنتَ فَإِن ٱلْمُمْتَرِينَ مِنَ تَكُونَنَّ فَلَا رَّبِّكَ مِنَ ٱلْحَقُّ جَآءَكَ لَقَدْ

Fa in kunta fee shakkin mimmaaa anzalnaaa ilaika fas'alil lazeena yaqra'oonal Kitaaba min qablik; laqad jaaa'akal haqqu mir Rabbika fa laa takoonanna minal mumtareen

SAHIH INTERNATIONAL:

So if you are in doubt, [O Muhammad], about that which We have revealed to you, then ask those who have been reading the Scripture before you. The truth has certainly come to you from your Lord, so never be among the doubters.

And in another Qur'anic verse Allah also gave Muhammad the same commandment to consult those who studied the Scriptures of the Bible:

Surah 21:7: "And We sent not before you (O Muhammad) but men to whom We inspired, so ask the people of the Reminder (Scriptures – the Taurat (Torah), the Injeel (Gospel)) if you do not know." (Hilali-Khan)

تَعْلَمُونَ لَا كُنتُمْ إِن ٱلذِّكْرِ أَهْلَ فَسْـَٔلُوٓا۟ إِلَيْهِمْ نُوحِىٓ رِجَالًا إِلَّا قَبْلَكَ أَرْسَلْنَا وَمَآ

Wa maaa arsalnaa qablaka illaa rijaalan nooheee ilaihim fas'aloo ahlaz zikri in kuntum laa ta'lamoon

At the time when these Qur'anic verses were revealed to Muhammad, all the Bibles in circulation throughout the world declared that Jesus died on the execution stake. The only Torah and Gospel that were available for Christians are the ones compiled in these Bibles. Therefore, when Allah commanded the Christians to observe the Torah and the Gospel, he was commanding them to observe the very Scriptures which prophesy and teach that Jesus was executed on the stake at the instigation of the Jews. And Allah also commanded Muhammad to consult the very people whose Scriptures confirms the death of Jesus. By affirming the Bible as the authoritative Word of God and yet at the same time denying the death of Jesus Christ, we find the Qur'an contradicting itself.

In fact, the Qur'an exposes the ignorance of Allah. He wrongly assumed that his denial of the death of Jesus did not conflict with his commandment that the Bible is the only reliable and authoritative guidance for Christians. The command for Christians to observe the Torah and the Gospel is still the standing order in the Qur'an today. These conflicting teachings prove that the author of the Qur'an is an impostor impersonating as the true God. This cast doubts on the inspiration of the Qur'an. The Qur'an is clearly in error since it affirms the authority of the Holy Bible while denying one of its essential teachings.

Internal contradictions

Even more troubling for Muslims is the fact that when the Qur'an denies the death of Jesus, it not only contradicts the Bible's clear testimony, but it also contradicts its very own teachings. This is not an uncommon occurrence in the Qur'an. We will now study the internal contradictions in the Qur'an. Reflect carefully on the evidences. The Qur'anic verse provided below records the statement of Jesus Christ:

Surah 19:33: Peace on me the day I was born, and the day I die, and the day I shall be raised alive! (Pickthall)

"There was peace on me the day I was born, and will be the day I die, and on the day I will be raised from the dead." (A. Ali)

حَيًّا أُبْعَثُ وَيَوْمَ أَمُوتُ وَيَوْمَ وُلِدتُّ يَوْمَ عَلَىَّ وَٱلسَّلَـٰمُ

Wassalaamu 'alaiya yawma wulidtu wa yawma amootu wa yawma ub'asu haiyaa

Muslim apologists find themselves in a dilemma when confronted with Qur'anic verses such as the ones cited above. Knowing that the above testimony of Jesus in Surah 19:33 clearly proves that he died *before* his ascension to heaven, Muslim apologists try to explain away the clear teaching of this Qur'anic verse. They respond by saying that the death of Jesus mentioned here will take place in the future. They assert that Jesus will die only after he comes back the second time and then be raised back to life. With no rhyme or reason, they desperately cling to this twisted explanation to evade an obvious contradiction in the Qur'an.

Well, what evidence do they provide to make such an outrageous claim? None! But this interpretation poses a serious problem for them. Why? Because the very same phrase used by Jesus is also expressed just a few verses earlier regarding John the Baptist. We can read an almost identical passage about John the Baptist in Surah 19:15. Note the similarity in the wordings:

Surah 19:15: And peace on him on the day he was born, and on the day he dies, and on the day he is raised to life. (Shakir)

حَيًّا يُبْعَثُ وَيَوْمَ يَمُوتُ وَيَوْمَ وُلِدَ يَوْمَ عَلَيْهِ وَسَلَـٰمٌ

Wa salaamun 'alaihi yawma wulida wa yawma yamootu wa yawma yub'asu haiyyaa (section 1)

According to Islamic belief, John the Baptist lived and died. And Muslims believe that he will be raised to life in Paradise on the Day of Resurrection. Muslims have no trouble whatsoever in recognizing the fact that this Qur'anic verse is not speaking about the death of John the Baptist in some distant future but his immediate death. Not only do they clearly understand but they also correctly apply the chronological sequence of the event mentioned here in the case of John. Yet, in the case of Jesus, we find Muslims having Jesus ascending to God *before* dying, destroying the very chronological sequence that Allah himself revealed in the Qur'an. They deliberately distort and destroy the chronological sequence of the event, even though the chronological sequence is identical in both cases. Since no Muslim shift the death of John to the future, no one should now shift the death of Jesus to the future.

Muslim apologists would rather make completely unsupportable arguments than admit that the death and resurrection of Jesus Christ is clearly taught in this Qur'anic verse. Of course, their refusal to come to terms with the truth is because they are aware that a correct interpretation of *Surah 19:33* will lead to a contradiction in the Qur'an. It will contradict *Surah 4:157* which denies the death of Jesus. Either Jesus died or he did not. It cannot be both. Since the Qur'an teaches both, Allah has left Muslims with little choice other than to deceive and manipulate a Qur'anic verse that really needs no explanation.

For the interpretation of the Muslims to be true, *Surah 19:33* should state: *"Peace on me the day I was born, and the day I shall be raised alive and the day I shall die."* Only when it is rendered in this manner, it will be in harmony with their absurd claim. Since *Surah 19:33* and *Surah 19:15* are identical in the description of the sequence of events, why don't Muslims also shift the death of John the Baptist to the future – after his resurrection – as they did in the case of Jesus? Why the discrepancy?

In fact, there is not a single passage in the entire Qur'an that shows that Jesus will return to die. Since the fulfillment of the parallel statement in the case of John the Baptist proves that he actually died before his resurrection, Jesus, too, must have died accordingly before his ascension. Muslims have a habit of shifting the goal posts to suit their agenda. The absolute supposition of *Surah 19:33* can be seen from the comment made by *Yusuf Ali*, the renowned translator of the Qur'an:

"..., Christ was not crucified (S. IV. 157). But those who believe that he never died should ponder over this verse." (Ali, "The Holy Qur'an," p.774, f. 2485.)

We will now expose the lies of these Muslim apologists even further. We will look at two separate Qur'anic verses to prove that Jesus actually died before his ascension to heaven. The first is Surah 3:55. This Qur'anic verse specifically points to the fact that Jesus died before his ascension to heaven. Allah said to Jesus:

Surah 3:55: Lo! God said: "O Jesus! Verily, I shall cause thee to die, and shall exalt thee unto Me, and cleanse thee of the presence of those who are bent on denying the truth; and I shall place those who follow thee far above those who are bent on denying the truth, unto the Day of Resurrection." (Asad)

God said, "O Jesus, I shall cause you to die and will raise you up to Me and shall clear you of the calumnies of the disbelievers, and shall place those who follow you above those who deny the truth, until the Day of Judgement." (W. Khan)

اتَّبَعُو الَّذِينَ وَجَاعِلُ كَفَرُواْ الَّذِينَ مِنَ وَمُطَهِّرُكَ إِلَيَّ وَرَافِعُكَ مُتَوَفِّيكَ إِنِّى يَـعِيسَىٰٓ اللَّهُ قَالَ إِذْ تَخْتَلِفُونَ فِيهِ كُنتُمْ فِيمَا بَيْنَكُمْ فَأَحْكُمُ مَرْجِعُكُمْ إِلَيَّ ثُمَّ ۖ الْقِيَـمَةِ يَوْمِ إِلَىٰ كَفَرُواْ الَّذِينَ فَوْقَ كَ

Iz qaalal laahu yaa 'Eesaaa innee mutawaffeeka wa raafi'uka ilaiya wa mutah hiruka minal lazeena kafaroo wa jaa'ilul lazeenattaba ooka fawqal lazeena kafarooo ilaa Yawmil Qiyaamati summa ilaiya marji'ukum fa ahkumu bainakum feemaa kuntum feehi takhtaliifoon

Surah 3:55 is part of a passage in the Qur'an that recounts the birth, death and ascension of Jesus. Two conditions are stipulated about Jesus in this Qur'anic verse: First, Allah will cause his death. Second, he will be raised to heaven. The second condition cannot take place till the first condition is met. In other words, before Jesus can be raised, he must first die. The sequence of the events is very clearly outlined with no ambiguity whatsoever. It plainly testifies that Allah will first cause Jesus to die *and* then raise him up to heaven. Therefore, whenever the Qur'an states the Jesus was raised to heaven, it has to be only after Allah caused him to die. The fact that Allah dictated the phrase, *"cause thee to die"* before the words *"exalt thee"* reveals the determined thoughts of Allah. What right has Muslims to change the order of the words of Allah in the Qur'an?

More remarkably, this Qur'anic verse shows that the *death* and *ascension* of Jesus occurred long before the *"Day of Judgement."* This is verified by the fact that after stating the *death* and *ascension* of Jesus, this Qur'anic verse states that the disciples of Jesus will be placed above the disbelievers until the *"Day of Judgement"* – clearly a future event that is yet to occur. This proves that the death of Jesus occurred long before the arrival of the *"Day of Judgement."* Since his *Second Coming* is closely related to the time of the arrival of the *"Day of Judgement,"* his death clearly took place long before his *Second Coming*. Therefore, the statement that Jesus will die only after his *Second Coming* is a deliberate lie concocted by Muslims to conceal an obvious error in the Qur'an.

According to the Qur'an, the *Second Coming* of Jesus serves as a sign of the nearness of the *"Day of Judgement."* The *"Day of Judgement"* is also referred to as the *"Last Hour"* in some translations of the Qur'an:

Surah 43:61: And surely when he, (Jesus), descends from heaven, he will be a sign of the nearness of the Last Hour. So do not doubt it at all. And keep following Me. This is the straight path. (Mohammad Tahir-ul-Qadri)

Now, let's look at the second Qur'anic verse which also strongly supports the fact that Jesus actually died before his ascension to heaven. This verse is important because it gives us a time-frame. In this verse, Jesus is conversing with Allah after his ascension to heaven. And this is what Jesus said to Allah:

Surah 5:117: Nothing did I tell them beyond what Thou didst bid me to say: 'Worship God, who is my Sustainer as well as your Sustainer.' And I bore witness to what they did as long as I dwelt in their midst; but since Thou hast caused me to die, Thou alone hast been their keeper: for Thou art witness unto everything. (Asad)

I was a witness to what they did as long as I remained among them, and when You did cause me to die, You were the watcher over them. You are the witness of all things. (W. Khan)

وَرَبَّكُمْ رَبِّى ٱللَّهَ ٱعْبُدُواْ أَنِ بِهِ أَمَرْتَنِى مَآ إِلَّا لَهُمْ قُلْتُ مَا عَلَيْهِمُ ٱلرَّقِيبَ أَنتَ كُنتَ تَوَفَّيْتَنِى فَلَمَّا ۚ فِيهِمْ دُمْتُ مَّا شَهِيدًا عَلَيْهِمْ وَكُنتُ ۚ شَهِيدٌ شَىْءٍ كُلِّ عَلَىٰ وَأَنتَ ۚ

Maa qultu lahum illaa maaa amartanee bihee ani'budul laaha Rabbeee wa Rabbakum; wa kuntu 'alaihim shaheedam maa dumtu feehim falammaa tawaffaitanee kunta Antar Raqeeba 'alaihim; wa Anta 'alaa kulli shai'in Shaheed

SAHIH INTERNATIONAL:

I said not to them except what You commanded me – to worship Allah, my Lord and your Lord. And I was a witness over them as long as I was among them; but when You took me up, You were the Observer over them, and You are, over all things, Witness.

Study the wordings of this Qur'anic passage carefully. This Qur'anic verse clearly shows that now in presence of Allah, after his ascension to heaven, Jesus spoke of his death as already having occurred. *"Thou hast caused me to die."* Thus, Allah caused him to die before his ascension to heaven. The claim that he will die only after his ascension and during his *Second Coming* is a deceitful attempt by Muslim apologists to cover an obvious contradiction in the Qur'an. Jesus clearly died before his ascension. The words of Jesus in the above Qur'anic verse clearly confirm the following sequence of events:

One: When Jesus was with his disciples on earth, he bore witness to them.

Two: But then Allah caused him to die.

Three: And now in heaven, Jesus says that Allah alone watches over them at present.

In the above Qur'anic verse, the term "die" is translated from the Arabic word, "mutawaffika." The term "mutawaffika" occurs over 25 times in the Qur'an, and in each case it refers to the death of someone. Especially enlightening is its usage in the following Qur'anic verse:

Surah 39:42: It is Allah that takes (mutawaffika) the souls of men at death; and those that die not He takes (mutawaffika) during their sleep: those on whom He has passed the decree of death. (Yusuf Ali)

مَنَامِهَا فِى تَمُتْ لَمْ وَٱلَّتِى مَوْتِهَا حِينَ ٱلْأَنفُسَ يَتَوَفَّى ٱللَّهُ
مُّسَمًّى أَجَلٍ إِلَىٰٓ ٱلْأُخْرَىٰٓ وَيُرْسِلُ ٱلْمَوْتَ عَلَيْهَا قَضَىٰ ٱلَّتِى فَيُمْسِكُ
يَتَفَكَّرُونَ لِّقَوْمٍ لَّءَايَٰتٍ ذَٰلِكَ فِى إِنَّ

Allaahu yatawaffal anfusa heena mawtihaa wallatee lam tamut fee manaamihaa fa yumsikul latee qadaa 'alaihal mawta wa yursilul ukhraaa ilaaa ajalim musammaa; inna fee zaalika la Aayaatil liqawmai yatafakkarroon

It is important to note that even if some Qur'an translators use the phrase, *"Thou didst take me up" (mutawaffika)* instead of *"Thou didst cause me to die" (mutawaffika)* in their translations, it means the same thing in the Arabic Qur'an. It means death.

All Messengers will die

We will now consider two Surahs that use the same pattern of words to state categorically that all messengers of God will certainly pass away in death:

Surah 5:75: The Messiah, son of Marium is but a messenger; messengers before him have indeed passed away; and his mother was a truthful woman; they both used to eat food. See how We make the communications clear to them, then behold, how they are turned away. (Shakir)

ٱلطَّعَامَ يَأْكُلَانِ كَانَا ۗ صِدِّيقَةٌ وَأُمُّهُ ٱلرُّسُلُ مِن خَلَتْ قَدْ رَسُولٌ إِلَّا مَرْيَمَ ٱبْنُ ٱلْمَسِيحُ مَّا
يُؤْفَكُونَ أَنَّىٰ ٱنظُرْ ثُمَّ ٱلْءَايَـٰتِ لَهُمُ نُبَيِّنُ كَيْفَ ٱنظُرْ ۗ

Mal Maseehub nu Maryama illaa Rasoolun qad khalat min qablihir Rusulu wa ummuhoo siddeeqatun kaanaa yaa kulaanit ta'aam; unzur kaifa nubaiyinu lahumul Aayaati summan zur annaa yu'fakoon

SAHIH INTERNATIONAL:

The Messiah, son of Mary, was not but a messenger; [other] messengers have passed on before him. And his mother was a supporter of truth. They both used to eat food. Look how We make clear to them the signs; then look how they are deluded.

Surah 3:144: And Muhammad is no more than a messenger; the messengers have already passed away before him; if then he dies or is killed will you turn back upon your heels? (Shakir)

أَعْقَـٰبِكُمْ عَلَىٰٓ ٱنقَلَبْتُمْ قُتِلَ أَوْ مَّاتَ أَفَإِيْن ۗ ٱلرُّسُلُ قَبْلِهِ مِن خَلَتْ قَدْ رَسُولٌ إِلَّا مُحَمَّدٌ وَمَا
ٱلشَّـٰكِرِينَ ٱللَّهُ وَسَيَجْزِى ۗ شَيْـًٔا ٱللَّهَ يَضُرَّ فَلَن عَقِبَيْهِ عَلَىٰ يَنقَلِبْ وَمَن ۗ

Wa maa Muhammadun illaa Rasoolun qad khalat min qablihir Rusul; afa'im maata aw qutilan qalabtum 'alaaa a'qaabikum; wa mai yanqalib 'alaa aqibaihi falai yadurral laaha shai'aa; wa sayajzil laahush shaakireen

The first Surah clearly states that all messengers "before" Jesus "have indeed passed away." A fact that no Muslims will deny. And the second Surah states that all messengers "before" Muhammad "have already passed away" in death. Islam teaches that no prophet arose between Jesus and Muhammad. Therefore, the immediate messenger who was sent forth "before" Muhammad was Jesus. As such, the second Surah specifically confirms that Jesus who came immediately before Muhammad must have also died – just as the rest of the messengers. If he did not die, then Muslims have to reject this Qur'anic verse as false.

In Arabic, the term for messengers used in the above two Surahs is "al-rasul" which literally means "the messengers." According to grammatical rules of classic Arabic, owing to the prefix "al" (the), the word messengers in the above two Qur'anic verses really means "all messengers." (Ref. Bahr al-Muhit, Volume 3, p. 68).

Additionally, if *Surah 3:144* intends to exclude Jesus as one of the messengers who passed away before Muhammad, then it would have read, "*All the Apostles before Muhammad died with the exception of Isa son of Maryam.*" But we find no such thing. Hence *Surah 3:144* proves that Jesus must have died as the Gospels clearly and honestly testify. Moreover, this disproves the Muslim claim that God would not allow his messenger to die violently at the hands of their enemies. The Qur'an itself teaches that evil men in the past have "*killed the prophets*" of God. We will just cite one example out of the many to prove our point:

Surah 2:91: When it is said to them, "Believe in what Allah Hath sent down," they say, "We believe in what was sent down to us:" yet they reject all besides, even if it be Truth confirming what is with them. Say: "Why then have ye slain the prophets of Allah in times gone by, if ye did indeed believe?" (*Yusuf Ali*)

أَلَّ وَهُوَ وَرَآءَهُ بِمَا وَيَكْفُرُونَ عَلَيْنَا أُنزِلَ بِمَا نُؤْمِنُ قَالُواْ ٱللَّهُ أَنزَلَ بِمَآ ءَامِنُواْ لَهُمْ قِيلَ وَإِذَا مُّؤْمِنِينَ كُنتُم إِن قَبْلُ مِن ٱللَّهِ أَنْبِيَآءَ تَقْتُلُونَ فَلِمَ قُلْ مَعَهُمْ لِّمَا مُصَدِّقًا حَقٌّ

Wa izaa qeela lahum aaminoo bimaaa anzalal laahu qaaloo nu'minu bimaaa unzila 'alainaa wa yakfuroona bimaa waraaa'ahoo wa huwal haqqu musaddiqal limaa ma'ahum; qul falima taqtuloona Ambiyaaa'al laahi min qablu in kuntum mu'mineen

The Muslim assertion that Jesus did not die prior to his ascension contradicts yet again the following Qur'anic verse. According to the Qur'an, every soul must experience death. We have provided three different translations:

Surah 21:35: Every soul must taste of death, and We try you with evil and with good, for ordeal. And unto Us ye will be returned. (*Pickthall*)

Every human being is bound to taste death; and We test you (all) through the bad and the good (things of life) by way of trial: and unto Us you all must return. (*Asad*)

Every Soul -no exception- shall taste death. (*Al-Muntakhab*)

And the following Qur'anic verse punctuates the fact that all messengers of Allah will die. It emphasizes that none of the messengers who came before Muhammad were "*exempt from death.*"

تُرْجَعُونَ وَإِلَيْنَا فِتْنَةً وَٱلْخَيْرِ بِٱلشَّرِّ وَنَبْلُوكُم ٱلْمَوْتِ ذَآئِقَةُ نَفْسٍ كُلُّ

Kullu nafsin zaaa'iqatul mawt; wa nablookum bi sharri walkhairi fitnatanw wa ilainaa turja'oon

SAHIH INTERNATIONAL:

Every soul will taste death. And We test you with evil and with good as trial; and to Us you will be returned.

Surah 21:7-8: Before thee, also, the messengers We sent were but men, to whom We granted inspiration: If ye realise this not, ask of those who possess the Message. Nor did We give them bodies that ate no food, nor were they exempt from death. (Yusuf Ali)

تَعْلَمُونَ لَا كُنتُمْ إِن ٱلذِّكْرِ أَهْلَ فَسْـَٔلُوٓا۟ ۖ إِلَيْهِمْ نُّوحِىٓ رِجَالًا إِلَّا قَبْلَكَ أَرْسَلْنَا وَمَآ

Wa maaa arsalnaa qablaka illaa rijaalan nooheee ilaihim fas'aloo ahlaz zikri in kuntum laa ta'lamoon

SAHIH INTERNATIONAL:

And We sent not before you, [O Muhammad], except men to whom We revealed [the message], so ask the people of the message if you do not know.

خَٰلِدِينَ كَانُوا۟ وَمَا ٱلطَّعَامَ يَأْكُلُونَ لَّا جَسَدًا جَعَلْنَٰهُمْ وَمَا

Wa maa ja'alnaahum jasadal laa ya'kuloonat ta'aama wa maa kaanoo khaalideen

SAHIH INTERNATIONAL:

And We did not make the prophets forms not eating food, nor were they immortal [on earth].

And the Qur'an makes it clear that this includes Jesus Christ since he is als o identified as one of the messengers:

Surah 5:75: The Messiah, the son of Mary, is only a Messenger: Messengers like him have passed away before him. (H. S. Aziz)

ٱلطَّعَامَ يَأْكُلَانِ كَانَا ۗ صِدِّيقَةٌ وَأُمُّهُ ٱلرُّسُلُ قَبْلِهِ مِن خَلَتْ قَدْ رَسُولٌ إِلَّا مَرْيَمَ ٱبْنُ ٱلْمَسِيحُ مَّا

يُؤْفَكُونَ أَنَّىٰ ٱنظُرْ ثُمَّ ٱلْءَايَٰتِ لَهُمُ نُبَيِّنُ كَيْفَ ٱنظُرْ ۗ

Mal Maseehub nu Maryama illaa Rasoolun qad khalat min qablihir Rusulu wa ummuhoo siddeeqatun kaanaa yaa kulaanit ta'aam; unzur kaifa nubaiyinu lahumul Aayaati summan zur annaa yu'fakoon

Of course, Christians believe that Jesus Christ is more than a Messenger. As we can see, the denial of the death of Jesus creates many theological problems for Muslims. The only way out of this difficulty is for Muslims to deny the Qur'an. Because of a single contradictory statement in *Surah 4:157*, Muslims have to now torture themselves to re-interpret the rest of the Qur'anic verses that clearly point to the death of Jesus Christ. Muslim are torn between accepting all the Qur'anic verses that speaks about the death of Jesus and the single account in *Surah 4:157* that denies his death.

As stated earlier, one of the excuses that Muslims use to deny the death of Jesus is by falsely reasoning that God would not allow his prophets or messengers to die in such a violent manner at the hands of their enemies. However, when interpreting Surah 3:144 and Surah 5:75, Muslim scholars in their Tafsirs (Commentaries) have understood that it includes death both naturally and by murder or execution:

Qanwa 'ala Baidawi, Volume 3, p.124:

"The Holy Prophet would leave the world as had done previous prophets, by natural death or murder."

It is vital to note that the Arabic word *"khala"* which is translated as *"passed away"* in Surah 3:144 and Surah 5:75, always refers to the death of the person when used in connection with that individual. *(Ref. Lisan al-'Arab and Aqrab al-Mawarad).*

Surah 3:144 further clarifies the meaning of this Arabic term *"khala"* by qualifying it with the words *"if he dies or is killed"* regarding the manner of Muhammad's death. Therefore, when the Qur'an speaks of the *"passing away"* of all previous prophets, it refers both to the *"dying a natural death"* and *"being killed."* As such, it is inexcusable for Muslims to deny the violent execution of Jesus at the hands of his enemies.

Prophetic evidence

Unlike the Qur'an which is confusing, the Gospel accounts of the Bible are quite consistent in the narratives regarding the death of Jesus. What Muslims failed to understand is that the death of Jesus was not something which caught him unaware destroying his plans. On the contrary, the very purpose for which he came into the world was to die a sacrificial death so as to open the way of salvation for mankind. The death of Jesus on the execution stake was not an afterthought. Neither was it an unforeseen tragedy. It was God's purpose right from the beginning. In harmony with his Father's will, it was the conscious choice of Jesus to lay down his life. Thus, the death of Jesus is a certainty in Christianity. Even before his death, Jesus declared:

Mark 10:45: For even the Son of man came, not to be ministered to, but to minister and to give his life as a ransom in exchange for many.

In fact, centuries before the arrival of Jesus, God "announced beforehand through the mouth all the prophets that his Christ would suffer." And Jesus fulfilled all these prophecies to the letter:

Acts 3:18: But in this way God has fulfilled the things he announced beforehand through the mouth of all the prophets that his Christ would suffer.

Given below are some examples of the astounding prophecies dealing with the Arrest, Trial and Death of Jesus Christ. They are all taken from written Biblical records of the Jewish prophets who were the descendants of Abraham, Isaac and Jacob. These prophetic accounts were written between 500 to 1000 years before the birth of Jesus.

Betrayed by a close companion
Prophecy: Psalms 41:9 — Fulfillment: Matthew 26:47-50; John 13:18
Betrayed for thirty pieces of silver
Prophecy: Zechariah 11:12 — Fulfillment: Matthew 26:14-15
Shepherd struck, flock scattered
Prophecy: Zechariah 13:7 — Fulfillment: Matthew 26:31, 56
Use of false witnesses
Prophecy: Psalms 27:12 — Fulfillment: Matthew 26:59-61
Tried and condemned
Prophecy: Isaiah 53:8 — Fulfillment: John 19:1-16
Silent before his accusers
Prophecy: Isaiah 53:7 — Fulfillment: Matthew 27:12-14
Struck and spat on him
Prophecy: Isaiah 50:6 — Fulfillment: Matthew 26:67
Pierced for our transgression
Prophecy: Isaiah 53:5 — Fulfillment: John 19:34
Pierced while on the stake
Prophecy: Zechariah 12:10 — Fulfillment: John 19:37
Reviled while impaled on the stake
Prophecy: Psalm 22:7-8 — Fulfillment: Matthew 27:39-43
Lots cast for his garments
Prophecy: Psalm 22:18 — Fulfillment: John 19:23-24

Poured out his life to the very death
Prophecy: Isaiah 53:12 — Fulfillment: Matthew 26:27-28; Luke 23:46
Counted among the sinners
Prophecy: Isaiah 53:12 — Fulfillment: Luke 23:32-33; Matthew 26:55-56
The Messiah will be cut off
Prophecy: Daniel 9:26 — Fulfillment: Matthew 26:2
No bones broken
Prophecy: Psalm 34:20 — Fulfillment: John 19: 32-36
Buried with the rich
Prophecy: Isaiah 53:9 — Fulfillment: Matthew 27:57-60
Will not be allowed to remain in death
Prophecy: Psalm 16:10 — Fulfillment: Acts 13:34-37
Exalted to the right hand of God
Prophecy: Psalm 110:1 — Fulfillment: Romans 8:34

The above prophecies and their fulfillments show the unity and cohesiveness between the Hebrew (Old Testament) and the Christian Greek Scriptures (New Testament). These prophecies were written over the centuries by the ancient prophets of God. And they point harmoniously to the circumstances leading to the death of Jesus Christ. The Book of Isaiah was written more than *700 years* before the birth of Jesus. Please read *Isaiah 53:1-12* and see the astounding prophecy which details the sacrificial death of Jesus in the outworking of God's divine purpose to redeem sinful mankind.

The fundamental Christian belief is that Jesus died and rose from the dead. In contrast, Muhammad claimed that he never died. Can we then put away all these evidences and place our trust in the judgment of one man who denies the death of Jesus when he lived some hundreds of miles away from the place of the event and some 600 years after the event, and who by his own admission is an illiterate? In contrast to the clear teachings of the Holy Bible, the Qur'an gives contradictory statements.

Islam's confusion

Muhammad's claim about the death of Jesus is confusing – even to Muslims. Islam does not give us a clear identity of the person who was nailed on the stake. Some Muslims believe it was Jesus who was nailed to the stake but he did not die. Others believe that he was not even placed on the stake but was taken up to heaven while somebody else was impaled in his place. And Muslims have differences of opinion about who this other somebody was.

Some believe it was Judas Iscariot while others say it was Simon of Cyrene. And still others believe it was one of the Roman soldiers. No Muslims seem to know conclusively. And all these different opinions have been suggested in different Muslim writings as a possible replacement of Jesus Christ. Some Muslims even believe Jesus was impaled on the stake. Yet he somehow revived in the tomb and died in India at the age of 120. Talk about clarity!

While secularist may not accept the Christian doctrine of salvation through the death of Jesus, they still recognize his death as an historical fact. Disagreeing with the doctrine would not change what actually happened in history. One can reject a doctrine but not history. Muslims confuse doctrine with history. Even if Muslims reject the Christian doctrine of salvation through the death of Jesus, they cannot reject the solid testimony of history.

Testimony of a Roma Historian

A number of secular writers who lived close to the time of Jesus made specific mention of him. Among them was the Roman historian and Senator, *Cornelius Tacitus.* He is considered as one of the most respected historians. He recorded the history of Rome under the emperors. Regarding a fire that devastated Rome in 64 C.E., Cornelius Tacitus relates that it was rumored that Emperor Nero was responsible for the disaster. Cornelius Tacitus wrote that Nero tried to place the blame on a group whom the populace called Christians. And Cornelius Tacitus added:

"Christus, from whom their name is derived, was executed at the hands of the procurator Pontius Pilate in the reign of Tiberius." — Annals (Book 15, Chapter 44)

Now compare how accurately the historical account of Cornelius Tacitus agrees with the earlier recorded account in the Holy Bible:

Mark 15:15: "At that Pilate, wishing to satisfy the crowd, released Barabbas to them, and, after having Jesus whipped, he handed him over to be executed."

Luke 23:24-25: "So Pilate gave sentence for their demand to be met: he released the man that had been thrown into prison for sedition and murder and whom they were demanding, but he surrendered Jesus to their will."

There are substantial historical evidences for the death of Jesus on the stake. The Old Testament prophets testified to the death of Jesus through numerous prophecies. Jesus himself testified to his death on multiple occasions. Eyewitnesses testified to the death of Jesus on the torture stake. Non-Christian historians also testified that Jesus died. Surprisingly the Qur'an also testifies to the fact that Jesus died.

The Problem with Surah 4:157

The Muslims denial of the execution and death of Jesus is based entirely on a single verse in the Qur'an. If it were not for *Surah 4:157*, Muslims would plainly understand *Surah 3:55* and *Surah 19:33* as referring to the death of Jesus. Let us look at *Surah 4:157* once again and analyze this Qur'anic verse further. We will now deal with other obvious errors in this Qur'anic verse:

Surah 4:157: And their saying: Surely we have killed the Messiah, Isa son of Marium, the messenger of Allah; and they did not kill him nor did they crucify him, but it appeared to them so (like Isa) and most surely those who differ therein are only in a doubt about it; they have no knowledge respecting it, but only follow a conjecture, and they killed him not for sure. (Shakir)

If you read the context of this account, you will understand that it the Jews who are saying: *"Surely we have killed the Messiah, Isa son of Marium, the messenger of Allah."* Think! Would the unbelieving Jews identify Jesus as the *"Messiah"* when they have rejected him as the Messiah in the first place? It must be remembered that the Jewish religious leaders even objected when Pilate wrote a title referring to Jesus as *"King of the Jews."* (John 19:19-22). As hysterical as they were in their rejection of Jesus, would it be logical for the Jews to address Jesus as the *"Messiah"*? Surely, had they recognized Jesus as the Messiah, do you think they would want to kill him? And equally ridiculous is statement in this Qur'anic verse where we find the Jews addressing Jesus as the *"messenger of Allah."*

Furthermore, the hostile Jews who rejected Jesus will never proclaim *"we have killed the Messiah"* as this Qur'anic verse claims. They will never say this even in sarcasm. This is because the Messiah is a reverential figure for whom the Jews are waiting for deliverance. Not even in mockery will the Jews say that they have killed the Messiah. And the Jews are still devotedly waiting for the Messiah to come.

Surah 4:157: And they did not kill him, nor did they crucify him; but another was made to resemble him to them. (Sahih International)

وَقَوْلِهِمْ إِنَّا قَتَلْنَا ٱلْمَسِيحَ عِيسَى ٱبْنَ مَرْيَمَ رَسُولَ ٱللَّهِ وَمَا قَتَلُوهُ وَمَا صَلَبُوهُ وَلَٰكِن شُبِّهَ لَهُمْ وَإِنَّ ٱلَّذِينَ ٱخْتَلَفُوا فِيهِ لَفِى شَكٍّ مِّنْهُ مَا لَهُم بِهِ مِنْ عِلْمٍ إِلَّا ٱتِّبَاعَ ٱلظَّنِّ وَمَا قَتَلُوهُ يَقِينًا

Wa qawlihim innaa qatal nal maseeha 'Eesab-na-Maryama Rasoolal laahi wa maa qataloohu wa maa salaboohu wa laakin shubbiha lahum; wa innal lazeenakh talafoo feehee lafee shakkim minh; maa lahum bihee min 'ilmin illat tibaa'az zann; wa maa qataloohu yaqeenaa

Because of this Qur'anic verse, Muslims believe that Allah took Jesus to heaven while someone else was nailed to the stake. Most Muslims believe that it was Judas Iscariot. Thus, according to the Qur'an, the person on the stake was made to *"resemble"* Jesus. This means Judas, died in the place of Christ. This is a massive theological problem because *Surah 4:157* presents Allah as a deceiver who misleads people into believing a lie for no valid reason at all. Allah deceived people into believing that Jesus had died on the stake when in fact he did not. If Allah was able to lift up Jesus instantly to safety, what is the advantage of this whole deception? Does not the deception of having someone replace Jesus actually conceal the powerful act of Allah's saving power? Thus, the entirety of Islam is but a mockery of the truth.

If Islam is correct, then Allah started this whole idea that Jesus died on the stake when he tricked his enemies into thinking that they had killed him. And the Disciples of Christ were also deceived into believing that he died. So who is responsible for the erroneous teaching of Christianity that Jesus died on the stake? And this now leads to even more theological problems for Islam.

CHAPTER XIV

THE QURAN VALIDATES THE DEATH OF JESUS

The Quran validates the death of Jesus.

The death and resurrection of Jesus Christ is central to the Christian faith. However, Muslims deny Jesus was put to death. They are taught to believe that Jesus did not die but was bodily raised to heaven. The Islamic view is that someone else was executed in the place of Jesus. Most Muslims believe that it was Judas Iscariot. According to Islam, Allah changed the appearance of Judas to resemble Jesus. Therefore, Allah allegedly deceived the Jews into believing they had killed Jesus when it was Judas. The Muslim denial of the death of Jesus is based solely on a single verse in the Qur'an:

Surah 4:157: They declared, We have put to death the Messiah, Jesus, son of Mary, the Messenger of Allah. They did not kill him, nor did they crucify him, but it only seemed to them as if it had been so. And those who differ in this matter are in doubt concerning it. They have no definite knowledge about it, but only follow mere conjecture. But they certainly did not kill him. (W. Khan)

لَهُ شُبِّهَ وَلَٰكِن صَلَبُوهُ وَمَا قَتَلُوهُ وَمَا ٱللَّهِ وَمَا رَسُولَ مَرْيَمَ ٱبْنَ عِيسَى ٱلْمَسِيحَ قَتَلْنَا إِنَّا وَقَوْلِهِمْ يَقِينًا قَتَلُوهُ وَمَا ۞ ٱلظَّنِّ ٱتِّبَاعَ إِلَّا عِلْمٍ مِن بِهِ لَهُم مَا ۞ مِّنْهُ شَكٍّ لَفِى فِيهِ ٱخْتَلَفُوا۟ ٱلَّذِينَ وَإِنَّ ۞ مْ

Wa qawlihim innaa qatal nal maseeha 'Eesab-na-Maryama Rasoolal laahi wa maa qataloohu wa maa salaboohu wa laakin shubbiha lahum; wa innal lazeenakh talafoo feehee lafee shakkim minh; maa lahum bihee min 'ilmin illat tibaa'az zann; wa maa qataloohu yaqeenaa

This deceptive miracle of Allah not only fooled the Jews but also the Disciples of Jesus into believing that Jesus was executed when he was not. Thus, Allah is clearly responsible for the existence of this false teaching in the Bible. Why did not Allah disclose the truth to the Disciples of Jesus? After all, did they not faithfully pledge their support to Allah?

Surah 61:14: O you who believe! Be helpers of Allah, as Jesus son of Mary said to his Disciples: "Who are my helpers of Allah?" The Disciples said, "We are helpers of Allah." (Hamid S. Aziz)

Allah waited 600 years to reveal that Jesus did not die. It was 600 years too late for billions of Christians who by then were thoroughly deceived by this deception of Allah. Moreover, if the sole intention of Allah is to save Jesus from his enemies, could he not just raise Jesus to heaven without all this deception? Would not this be a far better recourse since it would have saved countless Christians from becoming victims unjustly to this deception of Allah? What is the rationale behind this pointless deception of Allah? If Allah is truly Almighty, could he not save Jesus without victimizing the Disciples of Jesus? Is their salvation not precious to Allah? Allah deceived the Christians for no legitimate reason whatsoever. We have a couple of simple questions for Muslims: What do you call it when someone makes you believe something as true when it is not true? Does not this prove that Allah is a deceiver?

Of course, Christians do not believe in this false claim of Allah that Jesus did not die. However, this contrasting view of Islam is important since it now gives us an opportunity to determine which of these two religions is true. Is it Islam or Christianity? If it can be proven from both the Qur'an and the Bible that Jesus did die as Christians firmly believe, then this would mean that Islam is false. The Qur'an is clearly in error for the following reasons which we will now outline in this article.

The validity of the Bible

While contradicting the Bible on the essential teaching regarding the death of Jesus, the Qur'an at the same instant affirms the authority of the Bible as the Word of God. How is it possible for Allah to deny the death of Jesus in the Qur'an and at the same instant validate the authority of the Bible in the same Qur'an? If the Bible is wrong about the death of Jesus, then it means that it has become an unreliable guidance for Christians. And since the Christian doctrine of the sacrificial death of Jesus is based on the supposedly erroneous teachings of the Bible, is it not ironical for Allah to give Christians the following commandment in the Qur'an:

Surah 5:68: Say: "O followers of the Bible! You have no valid ground for your beliefs - unless you truly observe the Torah and the Gospel, and all that has been bestowed from on high upon you by your Sustainer!"(Asad)

قُلْ يَا أَهْلَ ٱلْكِتَابِ لَسْتُمْ عَلَىٰ شَىْءٍ حَتَّىٰ تُقِيمُواْ ٱلتَّوْرَاةَ وَٱلْإِنجِيلَ وَمَآ أُنزِلَ إِلَيْكُم مِّن رَّبِّكُمْ وَلَيَزِيدَنَّ كَثِيرًا مِّنْهُم مَّآ أُنزِلَ إِلَيْكَ مِن رَّبِّكَ طُغْيَٰنًا وَكُفْرًا فَلَا تَأْسَ عَلَى ٱلْقَوْمِ ٱلْكَٰفِرِينَ

Qul yaaa Ahlal Kitaabi lastum 'alaa shai'in hattaa tuqeemut Tawraata wal Injeela wa maaa unzila ilaikum mir Rabbikum; wa layazeedanna kaseeram minhum maa unzila ilaika mir Rabbika tugh yaananw wa kufran falaa taasa 'alal qawmil kaafireen

And Allah gave the following commandment to Muhammad:

Surah 10:94: But if you (Muhammad) are in doubt as to what We have revealed to you, ask those who read the Book before you. Verily the Truth from thy Lord hath come unto thee. So be not thou of the waverers. (Pickthall)

فَإِن كُنتَ فِى شَكٍّ مِّمَّآ أَنزَلْنَآ إِلَيْكَ فَسْـَٔلِ ٱلَّذِينَ يَقْرَءُونَ ٱلْكِتَٰبَ مِن قَبْلِكَ لَقَدْ جَآءَكَ ٱلْحَقُّ مِن رَّبِّكَ فَلَا تَكُونَنَّ مِنَ ٱلْمُمْتَرِينَ

Fa in kunta fee shakkin mimmaaa anzalnaaa ilaika fas'alil lazeena yaqra'oonal Kitaaba min qablik; laqad jaaa'akal haqqu mir Rabbika fa laa takoonanna minal mumtareen

Allah also reiterated a similar commandment in the following Qur'anic verse:

Surah 21:7: And We sent not before you (O Muhammad) but men to whom We inspired, so ask the people of the Reminder – (the Torah and the Gospel) – if you do not know. (Hilali-Khan)

تَعْلَمُونَ لَا كُنتُمْ إِن ٱلذِّكْرِ أَهْلَ فَسْـَٔلُوٓا۟ ۚ إِلَيْهِمْ نُّوحِىٓ رِجَالًا إِلَّا قَبْلَكَ أَرْسَلْنَا وَمَآ

Wa maaa arsalnaa qablaka illaa rijaalan nooheee ilaihim fas'aloo ahlaz zikri in kuntum laa ta'lamoon

"If you do not know this ask the followers of the earlier Revelation." (Muhammad Asad)

With reference to the term, "followers of the earlier Revelation," the exegesis of Muhammad Asad on Surah 21:7 states: Literally "Followers of the Bible."

Why is Allah commanding Christians to observe the very Torah which contains numerous prophesies concerning the death of Jesus? Why is Allah commanding the Christians to observe the very Gospel which teaches that Jesus was put to death? And why did Allah command Muhammad to consult the very people who believe in the death of Jesus? By denying the death of Jesus Christ and yet at the same instance affirming the Bible as the authoritative Word of God, Allah exposes his ignorance. He wrongly assumed that his denial of the death of Jesus did not conflict with his views that the Holy Bible is the preserved Word of God. This proves that the author of the Qur'an is untrustworthy. The Qur'an simply cannot be the inspired Word of the true God. The Qur'an is clearly in error since it affirms the preservation and authority of the Bible while denying its essential teachings.

Even more troubling for Muslims is the fact that the Qur'an not only contradicts the Bible but also its very own teachings when it denies that the death of Jesus. Such discrepancies are common in the Qur'an.

Contradictory teachings in the Quran

The following Qur'anic verse records Jesus as saying:

Surah 19:33: "Peace be upon me the day I was born, the day I die, and the day I will be raised back to life!" (The Clear Quran)

"There was peace on me the day I was born, and will be on the day I die, and on the day, I will be raised from the dead." (A. Ali)

Knowing that the testimony of Jesus in Surah 19:33 clearly proves that he will die before his ascension to heaven, Muslims deceptively distort the clear meaning of this Qur'anic verse. They try to explain away this Qur'anic verse by saying that the death of Jesus which is mentioned here is yet to come. And that he will die only after his second coming. They say this with no rhyme or reason except to evade an obvious contradiction in the Qur'an. Well, what evidence do they provide to make such an outrageous claim? None! Their interpretation is deceptive since the same formula of wordings are used just a few verses earlier to describe the death of John the Baptist. Note the similarity in the wordings:

Surah 19:15: And peace on him on the day he was born, and on the day he dies, and on the day he is raised to life. (Shakir)

In the case of John, Muslims are unanimous that he was killed and buried. They have no problem in understanding the sequence of the events: Birth – Death – Resurrection. No Muslim will shift the death of John to the future. Yet, in the case of Jesus, Muslims deceitfully postpone the death of Jesus until after his ascension to heaven. They deliberately distort the chronological sequence even though the chronological sequence is identical in both cases. Islam cannot survive without deception. Muslims are aware that coming to terms with the true meaning of this Qur'anic verse, would expose an irrefutable contradiction in the Qur'an. They know that an honest interpretation of Surah 19:33 will lead to a contradiction of Surah 4:157. Either Jesus died or he did not. Since the Qur'an teaches both, Muslims are left with no choice other than to deceive and manipulate a verse that really needs no explanation. However, we are glad that not all Muslim scholars are deceptive.

Dr. Mahmud Shaltut, the former Rector of Al-Azhar University, explains the meaning of Surah 19:33:

"Consequently, it is misleading to claim that the death of Jesus must occur after his triumphant return to Earth. It would be illogical. This verse deals with the relationship between Jesus and the people of his time and not with those of the time of his return."

The reality is that there is not a single passage in the entire Qur'an which testifies that Jesus will return to die. Since John died exactly in the order described in Surah 19:15, Jesus too must have died exactly in the order described in Surah 19:33. There is an interesting remark by the renowned Qur'an translator, Yusuf Ali, in his footnote to Surah 19:33:

" . . . Christ was not crucified (S. IV. 157). But those who believe that he never died should ponder over this verse." (Surah 19:33) (Ali, "The Holy Qur'an," p.774, f. 2485.)

We will now expose the lies of Muslims even further. We will look at two Qur'anic verses to prove beyond doubt that Jesus died before his ascension to heaven. The first is Surah 3:55 and the second is Surah 5:117. We will now consider Surah 3:55:

Surah 3:55: God said, "O Jesus, I shall cause you to die (mutawaffika) and will raise you up to Me and shall clear you (of the calumnies) of the disbelievers, and shall place those who follow you above those who deny the truth, until the Day of Judgment." (W. Khan)

The Arabic term "mutawaffika" (future tense) which is used in Surah 3:55 and the corresponding term "tawafaytani" (past tense) which is used in Surah 5:117 derive from the verb "tawaffa." Whenever this verb is used in association with Allah or the Angels as the ones executing this action, it always means "to cause one to die." In other words, whenever Allah or the Angels carry out "mutawaffika" (tawafaytani), it means death. And it is important to note that in both Surah 3:55 and Surah 5:117, it is Allah who executes this action. While translators like Yusuf Ali tries to obscure the true meaning, honest Muslim translators of the Qur'an know exactly what the term "mutawaffika" means. We will now provide ten additional translations of Surah 3:55 to validate our point. Only the relevant quote is cited below:

(1) Lo! God said: "O Jesus! Verily, I shall cause thee to die (mutawaffika) and shall exalt thee unto Me. (Asad)

(2) God said, "Jesus, I will cause you to die (mutawaffika) and raise you up to me. (Safi Kaskas)

(3) God said: "O Jesus, I will let you die (mutawaffika) and raise you to Me. (The Monotheist Group)

(4) Allah said: O 'Isa! Verily I shall make thee die (mutawaffika) and am lifting thee to myself. (Abdul Majid Daryabadi)

(6) Allah said: "O Iesa! Certainly, I am the Giver of death (mutawaffika) to you and the Raiser of you towards Me. (Dr. Kamal Omar)

(7) God said: Jesus, I make you die (mutawaffika) and bring you up to Me. (Ali Bakhtiari Nejad)

(8) Allah said: "O Jesus! I am indeed going to make you die (mutawaffika) and raise you up to Me. (Mohammad Shafi)

(9) Allah said: O Jesus, I will cause thee to die (mutawaffika) and exalt thee in My presence. (Maulana Muhammad Ali)

(10) God said: "You Jesus, I am making you die (mutawaffika) and raising you to Me. (Muhammad Ahmed/ Samira – Literal Translation)

We can quote many more translations but the above is sufficient to prove our point. As we can see, the term "mutawaffika" means "to cause one to die." And Surah 3:55 clearly states that Allah will cause Jesus to die before raising him to heaven. But what is equally vital to note is the fact that this Qur'anic verse also proves that the death and ascension of Jesus will occur before the "Day of Judgment." In other words, the death and ascension of Jesus will occur before his second coming. Surah 3:55 outlines the sequence of events. After mentioning the death and ascension of Jesus, Allah uses the conjunction "and" before describing the subsequent course of action that he will now execute. And that is to exalt the Disciples of Jesus until the "Day of Judgment." This clearly indicates a follow up course of action. Thus, not only does this Qur'anic verse prove the chronological order of the events but it also proves that the death and ascension of Jesus will precede the "Day of Judgment." This means that the claim by Muslims that Jesus will die only after his second coming is a preposterous lie.

It is also enlightening to note the usage of the term "mutawaffika" in Surah 39:42:

It is Allah that takes (mutawaffika) the souls of men at death; and those that die not He takes during their sleep, those on whom He has passed the decree of death. (Yusuf Ali)

Surah 39:42 proves a vital fact. It proves that even if translators of the Qur'an deceptively use phrases such as, "Allah takes" instead of translating mutawaffika accurately as "Allah causes to die" it still does not alter the fact that it means death in the Arabic language. Now, let's look at the second Qur'anic verse which strongly proves that Jesus actually died before his ascension to heaven. This verse is important because it gives us a time-frame. It recounts the conversation between Jesus and Allah after his ascension to heaven. Note carefully how Jesus recapitulates the chronology of events as they truly happened:

Surah 5:117: I was a witness to what they did as long as I remained among them, and when You did cause me to die (tawafaytani), You were the watcher over them. You are the witness of all things. (W. Khan)

I said nothing to them except that what You had commanded me, "Worship Allah, my Lord as well as your Lord." I was a witness over them only so long as I remained among them but ever since You caused me to die (tawafaytani), You Yourself have been the Watcher over them and You are the Witness to everything. (Amatul Rahman Omar)

Study the wordings of this Qur'anic verse carefully. Now in the presence of Allah, Jesus clearly spoke of his death as something that had already occurred prior to his ascension to heaven. Thus, Allah caused Jesus to die before raising him to heaven. Therefore, the claim that Jesus will die only after his second coming is a deceitful attempt by Muslims to cover up an obvious contradiction in the Qur'an. Jesus clearly died before his ascension. In summary, Surah 5:117 testifies to the following facts:

One: When Jesus was with his disciples on earth, he bore witness to them. Two: But then Allah caused him to die. Three: And now in the presence of Allah in heaven, Jesus states that since Allah caused him to die, Allah alone now watches over his disciples.

The following two Qur'anic verses state emphatically that all Messengers of God will die:

Surah 5:75: The Messiah, son of Mary, was only a Messenger, all the Messengers have like him passed away before him. (Amatul Rahman Omar)

And the same formula is applied with reference to Muhammad:

Surah 3:144: And Muhammad is but a Messenger. Surely, all Messengers have passed away before him. Would you recant if he dies or be killed. (Amatul Rahman Omar)

Surah 5:75 clearly states that all the "Messengers" who lived before the time of Jesus died. No Muslims will deny this. And Surah 3:144 likewise states that all the "Messengers" who lived before the time of Muhammad have passed away in death. Is Jesus not a Messenger of God who lived before the time of Muhammad? In fact, Islam teaches that no Messengers or Prophets were raised between the time of Jesus and Muhammad. Thus, the immediate Messenger who lived before Muhammad was Jesus. Therefore, according to Surah 3:144, since Jesus was a Messenger, he too must have died like the rest. If Jesus did not die before the time of Muhammad, then the statement of Allah in Surah 3:144 is a lie. This Qur'anic verse would still be false even if Jesus were to die after his second coming as Muslims claim. He has to die before the time of Muhammad for the Qur'an to be true.

One subtle excuse that Muslims use in denying the executional death of Jesus is by falsely claiming that God would never allow his prophets or messengers to die in such a violent manner at the hands of their enemies. However, in their Tafsirs (Commentary), Muslim scholars acknowledge that the passing away of the messengers or prophets of God would include both "natural death" and "murder." Even Muhammad is not exempted:

"The Holy Prophet would leave the world as had done previous prophets, by natural death or murder." (See Qanwa 'ala Baidawi, Volume 3, p.124)

The Arabic word "khala" in Surah 5:75 and Surah 3:144 which is translated as "passed away" always refers to the death of that individual with whom this word is associated with. (See Lisan al-'Arab and Aqrab al-Mawarad). It is also vital to note that Surah 3:144 clarifies the meaning of this Arabic term by qualifying it with the words "if he dies or is killed" with regards to

Muhammad. Therefore, the "passing away" of the prophets of God would include both "dying a natural death" and "being killed" by the enemy. Thus, it is inexcusable for Muslims to deny the execution of Jesus at the hands of his enemies.

If Jesus is an exception, then Surah 3:144 would state: "Surely, all Messengers with the exception of Jesus have passed away before him." But we find no such thing. Thus, this Qur'anic verse proves that Jesus died just as the Bible honestly testifies. Further disproving the Muslim claim that Allah will protect all his prophets from experiencing a violent death, the Qur'an itself teaches that evil men in the past have "killed the prophets" of God. We will cite just one example out of the many to prove our point:

Surah 2:91: When it is said to them, 'Believe in God's revelations,' they reply, 'We believe in what was revealed to us,' but they do not believe in what came afterwards, though it is the truth confirming what they already have. Say, 'Why did you kill God's prophets in the past if you were true believers?' (Abdel Haleem)

The Muslim claim that Jesus did not die contradicts yet again the following Qur'anic verses. These verses clearly state that all the messengers of God who lived before the time of Muhammad were human beings. And as such, none were exempt from death:

Surah 21:7-8: Before thee, also, the messengers We sent were but men, to whom We granted inspiration: If ye realize this not, ask of those who possess the Message. Nor did We give them bodies that ate no food, nor were they exempt from death. (Yusuf Ali)

The following Qur'anic verse reiterates that every human being, without exception, must taste death:

Surah 21:35: Every human being is bound to taste death; and We test you (all) through the bad and the good (things of life) by way of trial: and unto Us you all must return. (Asad)

Every Soul – no exception – shall taste death. (Al-Muntakhab)

It will be beneficial for Muslims to ponder on the full implication of this Qur'anic verse:

Surah 5:75: "The Messiah, the son of Mary, is only a Messenger: Messengers like him have passed away before him." (H. S. Aziz)

As we can see, the denial of the death of Jesus leads to many theological problems for Muslims. Because of the contradictory statement in Surah 4:157, Muslims have to torture themselves to re-interpret all the other Qur'anic verses that clearly testify to the death of Jesus. Muslims are torn between Allah's single testimony that Jesus did not die and all these other Qur'anic verses that testify he did. Unlike the Qur'an, which creates much confusion regarding the death of Jesus, the Bible is consistent in its teachings about the death and execution of Jesus. Numerous passages in the Hebrew Scriptures (Old Testament) prophesied about the death of Jesus Christ. We will cite just two examples:

One: Daniel 9:26 (Hebrew Scriptures): "And after the sixty-two weeks Messiah will be cut off, with nothing for himself."

Acts 3:18 (Christian Greek Scriptures): "But in this way God has fulfilled the things he announced beforehand through the mouth of all the prophets that his Christ would suffer."

Two: Isaiah 53:7 (Hebrew Scriptures): He was brought like a sheep to the slaughter, like an ewe that is silent before its shearers.

Acts 5:30 (Christian Greek Scriptures): The God of our forefathers raised up Jesus, whom you killed, hanging him on a stake.

If Muslims obeyed the commandment of Allah to learn from those who studied the Bible (Surah 10:94), they will understand not only the fact that Jesus died but also the reason why he had to die. When a disciple of Jesus tried to prevent him from facing his impending death, Jesus rebuked him saying:

Matthew 26:53-54: "Do you not think I cannot call on my Father, and he will at once put at my disposal more that twelve legions of angels? But how then would the Scriptures be fulfilled that say it must happen in this way?"

Is Allah qualified to correct Christianity?

Is Allah qualified to correct the inspired teachings of the Bible? We will prove why Allah is absolutely ineligible to do so.

We will consider evidence which is easily verifiable to expose the ignorance of Allah regarding the doctrines of Christianity. Provided below is just one out of the many errors we can find in the Qur'an. Allah wrongly presumed that just like the Muslims, Christians too have a Qiblah to direct their prayers to:

Surah 2:145: Even if you give every proof to the People of the Book, they will not accept your Qiblah, nor will you accept theirs. Neither of them (the Jews and Christians) are the followers of each other's Qiblah. If, after all the knowledge you have been given, you yield to their desires then surely you will be among the wrongdoers. (Farook Malik)

The Qiblah is the focal point to which every Muslim must face while praying. Muslims are commanded to face towards the direction of the Ka'ba during their daily prayers. After stating that the "people of the Book" (Jews and Christians) will not follow the Qiblah of the Muslims, Allah then added: "nor will they follow each other's Qiblah." In other words, the Jews will not pray facing the Qiblah of the Christians and vice versa. This is a gross error in the Qur'an. It is a well-known fact that Christians never had a Qiblah. They were never assigned a specific direction to face while praying. So, how can Allah then say that the Jews will not follow the Qiblah of the Christians? In the entire Bible there is not even a hint of a Qiblah for Christians. If there is truly a Qiblah for Christians as the Qur'an claims, then we would like to ask: What is the Qiblah of the Christians? And where are Christians supposed to face while praying?

The purpose of the above example is to demonstrate that if Allah is ignorant of even the basic observable facts about Christianity, can we then trust him to understand the deeper truths about Christianity? For that matter, can we trust him with anything? Men can err but not God. Therefore, when the Bible testifies that Jesus died on the stake, do not let Allah fool you into believing otherwise. He is ignorant!

Death is Jesus is an historical fact

The death of Jesus is an historical fact. It is firmly established as an historical event even by non-Christian sources. Scholars consider the Baptism of Jesus and his Death by Impalement to be two historically certainties about him. James Dunn who is a leading British New Testament scholar states:

These two facts in the life of Jesus command almost universal assent and rank so high on the 'almost impossible to doubt or deny' scale of historical facts that they are often the starting points for the study of the historical Jesus. ("Jesus Remembered" by James D. G. Dunn, page 339)

The Testimony of a Roman Historian

Cornelius Tacitus (b. 55 C.E.) is recognized as one of the greatest historians of his time. This Roman historian referred to both the execution of Christ by Pontius Pilate and the existence of Christians in Rome. These historical facts are recorded in his final works known as "Annals" (Book 15, Chapter 44).

Tacitus also recorded how Emperor Nero blamed the burning of Rome upon those "called Christians by the populace." He added: "Cristus, from whom the name had its origin, suffered the extreme penalty during the reign of Tiberius at the hands of one of our procurators, Pontius Pilatus." (The Complete Works of Tacitus, translated by A. Church and W. Brodribb, p. 380)

The "extreme penalty" that the Romans administer on a person is death by execution on a stake. Tacitus not only confirmed that Jesus was put to death but he also named "Pontius Pilatus" as the person responsible for his death. The "Annals" by Tacitus is recognized by historians as our best source of information concerning this period of time in history. Of course, Christians do not depend on secular history to verify the death of Jesus. They have the Holy Bible. Now compare how the historical account of Tacitus harmonizes with the accurate account recorded years in advance by the Gospel writers:

Mark 15:15: At that Pilate, wishing to satisfy the crowd, released Barabbas to them, and, after having Jesus whipped, he handed him over to be impaled.

Luke 23:24-25: So, Pilate made the decision that their demand be met. He released the man whom they were demanding, who had been thrown into prison for sedition and murder, but he surrendered Jesus to their will.

The teachings of Islam regarding the death of Jesus are confusing – even to Muslims. Most Muslims believe Jesus was never placed on the stake but was raised to heaven while somebody else was executed in his place. Muslims also differ as to who this substitute was. No one is certain whether it was Judas Iscariot, Simon of Cyrene or one of the Roman soldiers. Some other Muslims believe that Jesus was actually impaled but did not die on the stake. All these different opinions are recorded in the authoritative sources of Islam. Some Muslims even believe that Jesus somehow survived his execution and died in India at the age of 120. All this confusion is the result of Allah's incomplete and contradictory teachings in the Qur'an. Can you place your eternal salvation on a religion as unreliable and confusing as this?

It is also vital for Muslims to note that Muhammad came hundreds of years after the time of the death of Jesus. He lived hundreds of miles away from the place where this event happened. He had no knowledge of either Hebrew or Greek – the languages of the Holy Scriptures. He spoke a different language. And he did not produce a single shred of evidence to support his newfangled doctrine. So how can the lone testimony of Muhammad who admittedly is an illiterate outweigh the testimonies of hundreds of eyewitnesses who lived during the time of this event?

While secularist may not accept the Christian doctrine of salvation through the death of Jesus, they still recognize the death of Jesus as an historical fact. Muslims can reject the Christian doctrine of salvation through the death of Jesus, but they cannot deny history. Sadly, for Muslims, the Qur'an both affirms and denies the death of Jesus. Muslims, your eternal salvation depends on submitting to one of these two Books – the Qur'an or the Holy Bible. And your eternal salvation depends on submitting to one of these two religions – Islam or Christianity. One is true and one is false. Choose wisely!

CHAPTER XV

DID JESUS DIE AT THE CROSS?

Did Jesus die at the Cross?

It is a fact that the vast majority of Muslims believe in the substitution theory. Though modern thinkers like Dr. Ayoub and Dr. Hussein tell us that the theory of substitution makes mockery of divine justice, and belongs to the uncultured, the Muslim masses have been led to believe it and zealously defend it.

Not only do the masses believe in the substitution theory but they also believe that Jesus did not die.

However, modern thinkers insist that Jesus *did* die. Dr. Ayoub said that 'the verb, *tawaffa*, in general usage, means in its passive form, *tuwuffi*, to die.' [2] He then added, 'It was early reported on the authority of Ibn 'Abbas that the word *mutawaffika* means 'causing you to die', i.e. '*mumituka*.' Then in a footnote he said, 'Most commentators mention this as an alternative. Modern thinkers generally insist on it.' (For example, see 'abd al-Karim 'abd Allah al-Aniazi in his book, *Elaykum Ya 'Ulama' al-Gharb*, 1985, p. 27.)

It is amazing to know also that even Wahb spoke of the death of Jesus amongst the many versions of the stories he told. Suyuti relates that,

Ibn Garir and Ibn Abi Hatem on the authority of Wahb said, 'God caused Jesus Son of Mary to die three hours then lifted him up." Ibn 'Asaker said on the authority of Wahb that 'God caused Jesus son of Mary to die for three days then God resurrected and lifted him up.' And al-Hakem said on the authority of Wahb 'God caused Jesus son of Mary to die for seven hours then restored his life.' [emphasis added]

That was rejected by Tabari. It is fascinating to note that Wahb even said that Jesus died for three days and God resurrected him and lifted him up. Again Dr. Ayoub found no difficulty in stating that the Qur'an plainly asserts that Jesus did die:

The Qur'an ... does not deny the death of Christ. Rather it challenges human beings who in their folly have deluded themselves into believing that they would vanquish the divine Word, Jesus the messenger of God. The death of Christ is asserted several times and in various contexts, see for example, S.3:55; 5:117; 19:33.

According to Dr. Ayoub the Qur'an asserts the death of Christ several times and in various contexts. He does not appeal to any clever exegetical exercise, but to the clear passages of the Qur'an.

Some believe He was crucified

Not only do some Muslim thinkers assert Jesus did die, there are others who assert that Jesus died on the cross. The philosopher Abu Ya'qub Ishaq al-Sagastani said,

Without doubt murder and crucifixion were inflicted upon his body. The pronoun (hu) since it appeared at the end of the words 'murdered him' 'qataluhu', or crucified him is a pointing letter to the spirit (*huwiyya*) of Jesus. So, in this exists the evidence that he who suffered death and crucifixion was not the spirit (*huwiyya*) of Jesus. [empasis added]

The philosopher Sagastani sees that the Qur'an denies the crucifixion of the *spirit of Jesus* but undoubtedly affirms the physical crucifixion of the body of Jesus.

Mahmoud Mohammad Taha the leader of the Republican Brothers in Sudan, wrote in a booklet titled *al-Masih*:

The belief of the Muslims that Jesus did not die is based on Sura 4:157. But it is clear that that verse does not give that understanding ... specially if we take into consideration the other verse in which God said, 'Isa [Jesus] I am about to cause you to die and lift you up to me', and also the words, 'Peace be upon me, the day I was born, and the day I die, the day I am raised up alive'. Naturally the Qur'an does not contradict itself, for the expression *'mutawaffika'* means that he will die ... and also the expression 'the day I die' points in the same direction. So, the straight understanding becomes that the Christ was killed, then raised up. And that is what is pointed to by the words of God, 'and they slew him not of a certainty - no indeed', [10] which means that without any doubt they killed him, as they thought they did, but they slew him not of a certainty which is the same expression as 'they thought they did' ... this meaning appears in the Qur'an in other places such as the words of God, 'you did not slay them, but God did, and when thou throwest, it was not thyself that threw, but God threw'. And the meaning of that verse is that, when you killed them, it was not you who killed them, but it was God.

Thus, Mamoud Mohammad Taha, like the philosopher Sagastani understood from the same Qur'anic passages that Jesus was killed by the Jews without a doubt, then raised up by God. With Dr. Ayoub he found no difficulty in concluding that the Qur'an speaks plainly of the death of Jesus, otherwise the Qur'an would be contradicting itself. He then proceeded to prove that this mode of expressing the death of Christ is not unique but has a parallel in the Qur'an, indeed it is an affirmation in the form of negation.

Secular historians accept the crucifixion

What adds weight to the belief that the Christ was crucified is 'the fact that secular historians also accept the crucifixion as a fact. No serious modern historian doubts that Jesus was crucified.

Historians, regardless of their interpretation of the crucifixion, (that is, whether or not they attach any spiritual significance to it), have accepted the crucifixion as a historical fact. The experts, in sifting what belongs to history, compared with what belongs to myth or dogma, have cast their verdict in favor of the historicity of the crucifixion of Jesus. Not only historians, but other great minds like Tagore the brilliant Bengali poet and winner of the Nobel prize, accepted the crucifixion as a fact. Tagore wrote:

From His eternal seat Christ comes down to this earth, where, ages ago, in the bitter cup of death He poured His deathless life for those who came to the call and those who remained away.

He looks about Him, and sees the weapons of evil that wounded his own age.

The arrogant spikes and spears, the slim, sly knives, the scimitar in diplomatic sheath, crooked and cruel, are hissing and raining sparks as they are sharpened on monster wheels.

But the most fearful of them all, at the hands of the slaughterers, are those on which has been engraved His own name, that are fashioned from the texts of His own words fused in the fire of hatred and hammered by hypocritical greed.

He presses His hand upon His heart; He feels that the age-long moment of His death has not yet ended, that new nails, turned out countless in numbers by those who are learned in cunning craftsmanship, pierce Him in every joint.

They had hurt Him once, standing at the shadow of their temple; they are born anew in crowds.

From before their sacred altar, they shout to the soldiers, 'Strike'

And the Son of Man in agony cries, 'My God, My God why hast Thou forsaken Me?'

Tagore must have been aware of the view that the Christ was not crucified and someone else died on the cross, because he was living amongst millions of Muslims. But he chose to believe in the historicity of the crucifixion. He spoke of the crucifixion as an event that took place in time, 'where, ages ago, in the bitter cup of death He poured His deathless life'. Tagor, though a poet, was not talking about a myth. The tragedy of his own time, represented in the merciless murder of the innocent was of the same kind as that which killed the Christ. Listen to him say:

the age-long moment of His death has not yet ended, that new nails, turned out in countless numbers by those who are learned in cunning craftsmanship, pierce Him in every joint.

They had hurt Him once...

Tagore, did not question the historicity of the crucifixion, but accepted it, although he was aware of the views of his fellow countrymen who believed otherwise.

Ahmad Shawqi believed Jesus was crucified

The great Egyptian poet Ahmad Shawqi who is called by his people the prince of the poets accepted the historicity of the crucifixion.

In one of his poems, he wrote:

Jesus, your way was mercy, love, perfection and peace to the world.

You were not a shedder of blood, and the weak and the orphans to you were not insignificant.

You who are the bearer of the world's sufferings, yet sufferings were multiplied in your name.

You made the world into one brotherhood, but in your name, relationships are severed.

Shouts in the name of the cross are heard by those who are enemies of God and his Spirit.

They mixed your cross with knives, guns, and every tool of destruction and death.

Ahmad Shawqi, like Tagor, was aware of the beliefs of the majority of Muslims, yet he chose to believe in the suffering of Jesus on the cross.

Thirteen Hundred years of error

The Muslim masses, then, for almost thirteen hundred years have been believing not only a false report claiming that a substitute died for Jesus on the cross, and a teaching that is contrary to the Qur'an; namely that Jesus did not die, before his being lifted up. For modern thinkers tell us that the Qur'an plainly asserts the death of Jesus. For thirteen hundred years, not only has the average man in the street been mistaken in his belief on this issue, but many devout Muslims have blindly accepted it, and vigorously defended it as God's truth.

One might ask why millions upon millions of sincere Muslims have believed that which is error, for so long, while the Qur'an plainly asserts that Jesus did die.

If there was o substitute-what now?

It is important to note that in every Muslim story told about what happened to Jesus and his substitute, there is a *crucifixion.* This crucifixion of Jesus is denied, but nevertheless a crucifixion is mentioned in every single story. Dr. Ayoub said, "They [the commentators] accepted a crucifixion as an historical fact.... but denied it of Jesus." A crucifixion is accepted by the Jews, the Christians, and the Muslims. The dispute is over who was on that cross.

Now if there was no substitute on the cross, (the cross is the only undisputed historical fact), who then was on it? Someone was there, bleeding and dying.

Modern Muslim thinkers have discarded the substitution theory and insist that Jesus died. Most, however, prefer to leave the manner of his death alone. But if we bring together the historical fact of the cross, the impossibility of a substitute and the insistence of modern thinkers that Jesus did die, the answer is simple: It was Jesus who was on the cross. It *is* how he died.

Where are the Hawariyun (Disciples)?

Whatever theory we discuss we must ask ourselves the question: Where were the *Hawariyun?* That is, where were the disciples of Jesus in the plan and purpose of God? Men's theories can take them away from the scene of the cross, so that they could not be eye witnesses, and yet they had a critical place in the plan of God. The Qur'an says of them,

And when Jesus perceived their unbelief, he said, 'Who will be my helpers unto God?' The apostles said, 'We will be helpers of God' ... inscribe us therefore with those who bear witness.

The Qur'an called them 'helpers of God'; they were to make the Truth of God victorious and known. Where is their voice for God and His Truth concerning the crucifixion? If Jesus was not crucified, these 'helpers of God' would have spoken fiercely of what they believed to be the truth, and filled the whole world with it, and even died for it. Where then is the voice of God's helpers?

Mohammad Kamel Husein writes of them as 'the finest band of men that could be conceived, lacking neither in faith nor in resolve.' Did they just sit down to let the lies of the Jews spread like fire to be believed by the whole world? Could the disciples, whose rank had been elevated to those 'who bear witness' hide themselves in the shadows of forgetfulness, and silence? If so, they do not deserve to be called 'helpers of God' or 'witnesses', but disappointers of God and the Truth.

But that is not what they did, for they did speak fearlessly of the crucifixion and the resurrection; so much so that even those who are not followers of Jesus know the disciples' report, that Jesus died and rose again on the third day.

Did the clearest evidence end in confusion?

The theories we have studied are simply not consistent with the manner in which God was dealing with humanity in the life of Jesus. The Qur'an states that Jesus came with the clear evidence. This clarity was God's stamp throughout his life. Is it consistent with God's dealings, then, to cloud the last day of Jesus' time on earth with confusion? Or is it more consistent with God's ways, to say that this clarity was uninterrupted and that Jesus was crucified? The Jews did their worst and God did His best, raising Jesus up. In Q. 4:157 the Qur'an states:

And for their saying, 'We slew the Messiah, Isa [Jesus] son of Mary, the messenger of God' - yet they did not slay him, neither crucified him; only a likeness of that was shown to them. And those who are at variance concerning him are in doubt regarding him; they have no knowledge of him, except the following of surmise; and they slew him not of a certainty - no indeed; God raised him up to Him; God is All-mighty and Wise.

This verse is an emphatic denial of the Jews' boasting; it is an emphatic denial of their claim that theirs is the victory. That is what the Qur'an denies, not the actual death and the actual crucifixion of Jesus. The mode of expression in this verse is found in the Qur'an in different forms. When the Qur'an speaks of those who have eyes but do not see [20] it does not mean that they are blind, but that they do not perceive the truth. Similarly, when the

Qur'an speaks of those who do not hear, it is the perception of what they actually heard that they have denied. It is the same with the Jews, they killed the Christ, but their perception that they had finally destroyed him is denied. They thought that by their crucifying him, he would be finished, but he rose from the dead. The crucifixion was not the last word. The resurrection was. So, they thought they had killed him on the cross, but they had not, for he rose again.

There is a parallel between the death of Jesus and that of Mohammad's grandson, al-Husein. One writer, commenting on the tragic murder of al-Husein, said,

On the tenth of the month of Moharam in the year 61H, al-Husein was killed and all those who were with him of men, youth and children, except Imam Ali son of al-Husein. And people said that al-Husein wasted his life and the lives of those with him ... But time proved the opposite. For the pure blood of al-Husein did not dry up on the soil of Karbala'a until the throne of the Amawites was quaked and the seat of Yazid was shaken. They were days when the power of the Amawite crumbled in shame. And the wonderful victory was on the side of the reformation [of al-Husein]....

This is the same sentiment that answers the boasting of the Jews who said, 'We killed the Christ'. The people said that Al-Husein 'wasted his life... but time proved the opposite'; that is, he did not waste his life. But that is not to say he was not killed, for he was. And so, it was with Jesus. al-Husein was killed by those who were supposed to accept him and honor him, Jesus likewise.

The impact of Tabari and Wahb

If the Christ died on the cross why did the early commentators, and the many Muslim generations after them, believe (contrary to the plain teaching of the Qur'an, and to the understanding of modern Muslim thinkers) that Jesus did not die? Remember Dr. Mahmoud Ayoub's words: 'The substitutions theory will not do, regardless of its form or purpose. First, it makes a mockery of divine justice and the primordial covenant of God with humanity.'

Why have the commentators propounded many theories to avoid the historical facts and the teaching of other Muslim leaders that the Christ had been crucified?

The answer to that question can be traced back to two people, who in turn influenced subsequent commentators and hence the Muslim masses. These two are Tabari and Wahb Ibn Munabbeh.

Dr. Ayoub tells us: 'The traditions relating the story of Jesus are told on the authority of either Jewish converts like Wahb Ibn Munabbeh, or of unnamed Christian converts as in the traditions of Ibn Isaq.' In other words, the source of the stories about what is supposed to have happened could be traced back to some unknown Christian converts or a man called Wahb.

When Tabari was analyzing the different traditions, he preferred the two versions of Wahb's story. Tabari then influenced almost all the commentators after him.

On these two persons we shall now focus.
But first we must say a brief word about the phenomenon of recorded Islamic history.

The beginning of recording Islamic history

This phenomenon concerns fabricated historical reports that were mixed with early Islamic historical material. One scholar said about the transmission of early Islamic historical material in general:

The historical accounts of early Islam used to be transmitted orally .... then came a generation that committed this oral material to writing. And by the beginning of the third century (H) paper-making was introduced and this material began to take the form of written reports, with every report dealing with only one topic...

These first written reports formed the first nucleus for subsequent historians...

In spite of what has been said, i.e., that these reports were not well arranged and not carefully organized, and that most of them lack verification and accuracy and even include possible fabrication, they nevertheless provided historians like Tabari and Ya'qouby with a flood of historical material, though this flood was so overflowing that subsequent historians could not sift, and could not get rid of the contradictions, the exaggerations, and the forgery in it. They could not detect the work of the fabricators in it, for the fabricators - sad to say - have found such a wide entrance to these reports.

That is not to cast doubt on the historicity of basic Islamic events, but to warn readers of Islamic history that not everything is above board, that there are forgeries which have slipped in since the early period.

These forgeries are not single incidents here and there, but a great flood. The damage is irreversible for fabrication was mixed with fact to such an extent that later historians could not sift or eradicate the forgeries. Some scholars have collected up to 620 Hadith fabricators and liars [not 620 Hadiths, but Hadith transmitters] who were quoted by others as authorities in Hadith and history.

Some examples will be cited later. It is worth noting again, however, that Tabari was one of the commentators who drew on this vast volume of fabricated material.

Another kind of material that crept in, in many different forms was what scholars call 'al-Isra'iliyat': supposed stories some of which were in the form of historical material, others supposedly in the form of the revealed books of the Jews and the Christians. This material was transmitted through Christian and Jewish converts to Islam, like Wahb.

Dr. Qaradawi commented on the 'Isra'ilyiat' and Wahb Ibn Munabbeh in particular, as follows, (and I paraphrase):

What disfigured our literary heritage, especially the field of expounding the Qur'an *(Tafsir)*, were the 'Isra'iliyat' that crept into it, and disturbed its order. This started, regretfully, very early, that is, since the time of the companions and the followers [of the prophet]. It started with people like K'ab al-Ahbar and Wahb Ibn Munabbeh, and others who were converted to Islam from the People of the Book [i.e., Jews and Christians] - also through what reached the Muslims from Jewish and Christian books.

The infiltration of the 'Isra'iliyat' was small at the beginning, then it began to increase, unintentionally. This gave way to plotting, scheming and intentional conspiracy.

Because the Jews were defeated militarily by the Muslims and wanting to resist by using another weapon - an intellectual one - they slipped in the 'Isra'iliyat' and, within a short period, the books of Muslims were full of it.

Here again we notice the extent of the 'creeping in'. Dr. Qaradawi wrote that within a short time the books of the Muslims became full of it. The 'Isra'iliyat' particularly affected the science of Tafsir, that is, the expounding and explaining of the Qur'an.

The substitution theory belongs to the flood of forgery that later historians could not detect, and which Tabari used on the authority of Wahb, one of the instruments of transmitting the 'Isra'iliyat'. As we have seen, it is only recently that modern thinkers have discarded the theory.

More Wahb

Here are some extracts by Muhammad Abd El-Ghani Hasan, from his book Attarikh 'End al-Muslemeen, that give us a better picture of Wahb.

Wahb was from San'aa of Yemen; died 110 or 114 H. He was *Ikhbary* (a storyteller) and not a Hadith transmitter. But his main interest was what is called "Isra'iliyat" (that is, stories that were heard from the Jewish people) which were transmitted to him through men like K'aab al Ahbar (who died 32-34 H.) ... which Wahb inserted into Islamic stories.

The most important thing to note from the above is that Wahb was not a Hadith transmitter, that is, he was not counted or classed as an authority on the words or the Sunnah of the prophet. He was, rather, a storyteller, and his main interest was the 'Isra'iliyat'. The authority of a storyteller is far inferior to that of a Hadith transmitter, for the latter's final authority is the prophet, but the storyteller, specially of the Isra'iliyat, cannot claim that authority.

It is no wonder, then, that those storytellers (Ikhbariyeen) have no authority in any serious work, as one scholar commented: '...scrutineers of the truth place no weight on the reporting of those 'Ikhbariyeen' (storytellers). They do not rely on them and shame those who quote them in any serious scientific work.'

Muhammad Abd El-Ghani Hasan wrote:

We will not leave Wahb Ibn Munabeh without summarising the critics' opinion of him. They said that he did not seek accuracy in his reporting and he was not above making false claims. The historian al-Sakhawi, the author of, *'al-daw'a Allam'e* and *al-'Elan Be-Tawbikh Li-man Zama-Tarikh'*, considers the reporting of Wahb to be unworthy of serious historians ..

Other Muslims see 'Wahb Ibn Munabbeh as the First Zionist' and thus place him at the very top of the enemies of Islam.

So, Wahb, even as a storyteller, lacked integrity. For that reason, no serious historian relies on him. One can understand why modern thinkers shy away from the theory of substitution and treat it with contempt, for they see it as a mockery of God's justice, not only because it does not stand against the scrutiny of reason, but also because Wahb who was its perpetrator was a cheap storyteller.

There are guidelines for accepting or rejecting Hadith. The following is one of them:

The scholars and the critics of Hadith transmitters have agreed that whoever was proven to be a liar or a fabricator of Hadith is to be 'punished by rejecting even his truthfulness, ignoring his virtues, and his Hadith is not to be accepted after that.'

If only the commentators had applied this rule to Wahb, and rejected his report, a lot of confusion and error would have been avoided.

Here is another rule for determining the truth of any report:

Logic, accuracy and Islam are essential conditions for any transmitter. If these conditions are missing, or one of them, the transmitter's story must be rejected and his Hadith discarded.
As we have seen, Wahb's reporting lacked logic, and accuracy. There is even a question about his conversion to Islam. And some label him as the first Zionist. Wahb's reporting should have been rejected completely. But sadly, this was not so.

The influence of Tabari

Tabari's influence on subsequent commentators on this subject is unquestionable. Dr. Mahmoud Ayoub wrote:

The classical tradition is epitomized in the monumental commentary of Tabari (d. 310/923) which has influenced subsequent commentators down to the present. Other works of the classical period differ little from that of Tabari, which they take as their source and starting point.

Dr. Sobhy al-Saleh said, 'Almost all subsequent commentators after Tabari were entirely dependent on him.' Literally he said that they 'lived off him'.

Tabari is called *"Sheikh al-Mufasereen"*, that is, the chief and head of the commentators.

Dr. Yousif Qaradawi, in one of his many books, makes the following remark on this famous commentator as a historian:

The idea that dominated Tabari when he wrote his 'history' was to collect and record without sifting and examining either the authority or the reported events of his historical material.

So, whoever had something to report was quoted by Tabari, acknowledging the source of that report, even if the reporter was a weak one, or suspected one, or even a disregarded one ... some of those authorities, the researcher will find, were dropped completely, others differ in reliability, while others are reliable.

So out of Tabari's men:

Muhammad Ibn Ishaq, the author of 'The Life of the Prophet', was criticized bitterly by Imam Malek ...

Waqedi was accused of falsehood by some leading transmitters of Hadith ...

Hesham Ibn Muhammad al-Kalby and his father, were accused of being liars. And Saif Ibn 'Omar al-Tamimi was a fabricator of Hadith, and was accused of being an atheist ...

And there were many more, who are regarded as unworthy of mention by learned men of Hadith.

For that reason, scrutineers of the truth place no weight on the reporting of those 'Ikhbareyeen' (storytellers) - they do not rely on them and shame those who quote them in any serious scientific work.

No wonder then that Dr. Qaradawi acknowledges that 'Tabari treated historical issues in a careless and cheap manner.' He added

May Allah forgive Imam Tabari, for his carelessness has disfigured the history of the dawn of Islam, and harmed the first bearers of the message.

Modern thinkers like Dr. Ayoub would agree whole-heartedly with Dr. Qaradawi's last statement. Imam Tabari not only has disfigured the history of the dawn of Islam, but also made a mockery of the justice of God to this day, by propagating the reporting of the *Ikhbareyeen*, and Wahb in particular.

Even though, according to Dr. Qaradawi, "scrutineers of the truth place no weight on the reporting of the *Ikhbareyeen*, they do not rely on them and shame those who quote them in any serious scientific work", one *Ikhbary*, Wahb, has influenced the Islamic 'Ummah more than the most reliable Hadith transmitters on the issue of the crucifixion of Jesus.

Tabari as commentator

It is not only that Tabari as a historian 'treated historical issues in a careless and cheap manner', he also, as a commentator, made some serious errors.

Dr. Qaradawi wrote that 'in spite of his [Tabari's] high rank and the place of his commentary, he sometimes chose weak explanations - nay very weak explanations - such as [the explanation given of husbands disciplining of women in] "banish them to their couches, and beat them". Tabari said that this meant tie them by that which ties the camel, so the meaning becomes: 'Tie the women in order to force them to do that which they refused to do.'

Such a sentiment is abhorred by the cultured and the uncultured alike nowadays but that was Tabari's choice of meaning.

Also Dr. Qaradawi criticized Tabari's choice for the explanation of the verses, 'Whoso judges not according to what God has sent down; they are the unbelievers.' Tabari said 'those intended are the people of the Book (that is the Jews and the Christians)'. [43] Dr. Qaradawi, in disagreeing with Tabari's interpretation, said: 'What is under consideration here is the general wording, not the special causes.' He then added that the above verses were mentioned in front of Hazifah Ibn al-Yaman by a man who said that the people intended are the children of Israel. Hazifah then said: 'Yes, they are your brothers, the children of Israel, if to you belongs everything that is sweet and to them belongs everything that is bitter! Meaning, how can the children of Israel be described by blasphemy, injustice and iniquity if they do not judge according to what God has sent down upon them, and you are not so described if you do not judge according to what God has sent down upon you?'

Then Dr. Qaradawi concluded the chapter by saying: 'The goal is to avoid the weak interpretations and opinions, no matter what the authority of their source. For as 'Ali said, "Truth is not known by those who call themselves men of Truth, but know the Truth, then you shall know its men"'

The problem of fabrication

The advice of Dr. Qaradawi to avoid the weak interpretations (even if their authority is the chief of the commentators, Imam Tabari), is far too late. For unfortunately the rest of the commentators have been greatly influenced by Tabari. They almost lived off his original work.

Dr. Qaradawi was not the only one who admitted the existence of forgeries and criticized the lack of careful investigation by other writers in Islamic material. Appealing to Imam Tabari as a final authority, another author wrote:

The enemies of Islam who spread amongst its followers and pretended to be Muslims ... have managed to insert in the Hadith of the prophet and his biography, the biography of the companions, the history of Islam, and the Hadith that expounds the Qur'an, many [fabricated] things. For we will not find in the history of previous nations those who have invented for one of their prophets 150 imaginary companions. And, in spite of that, we find the great majority of Muslims have innocently accepted, as pure, what they inherited ... And when their research ends with an incident from the history of the companions by Tabari, or an incident of the biography of the prophet by Ibn Hisham, they then become confident, full of assurance and relaxed, and do not take the trouble to sift the errors from what has been written, but copy and follow the authors of those books like the blind who follows his guide. As we have seen in the book of 'Abd Allah Ibn Sab'a the extent of the fabrication in the historical work of Tabari, which is considered the most trusted historical source concerning the companions, disfigured and turned the historical facts upside down.

To invent and forge certain material is one thing, but to invent people who do not exist is completely another. These works of forgery did not turn only Islamic historical facts upside down, but also turned the historicity of the crucifixion upside down for generations of Muslims.

Fabrication and forgery did not only involve distant past histories of other nations, but also included a sacred branch of Islamic material known as *'asbab an-Nuzul* i.e.; the occasions of revelation which provide the historical context of the Qur'an. One scholar commented:

The writings of the older generations who wrote on the reasons of the inspiration [*'asbab al-nuzul*, i.e. the occasions in which a particular verse was revealed], were subjected to strong criticism, in spite of the fact that their authors were very pious, careful, scientific and faithful. Yet our criticism today will be stronger and more severe, and what we have against them will be more bitter and appalling ... The commentator Suyuti boldly criticized the shortcomings and weaknesses of these works. We had hoped the shortcomings were the only weaknesses in the old works, but they are also full of historical mistakes, illogical reasoning, incredible exaggerations and strange rarities!

'Al Wahidi, for example, when he read The Cow: 114, did not conclude that it was a general threat to those who trifled with places of worship and try to stop God's ordinances... but he fell into an ugly historical error. If that error was his personally, that would have been of no consequence. But to force error on the text of the Qur'an is a thing that is not permissible for him or for any other person.

It is amazing to see that al-Wahidi unashamedly mentions Qatadah who said that this verse is about Bakhtnassar the Babylonian and his friends who captured the Jews, and destroyed Bait al-Maqdes and were helped by the Nasara [the Christians]. He mentions that the Nasara were united with Bakhtnassar in the destruction of Bait al-Maqdes, despite the fact that this event took place 633 years before the birth of Christ.
He then added:

Al-Wahidi might be forgiven for this because he was not a historian ... " And even the ugly error made by al-Wahidi's ignorance of the historical events might be excused if we ascribe, he was referring to Adrinal the Roman, whom the Jews called Bakhtnassar the Second, who came 130 years after Christ. He had built a city on the ruins of Jerusalem, made Roman baths in it, built a temple for Zeus on the ruins of Solomon's temple, and prevented the Jews from entering the city.

If we have an excuse for al-Wahidi, what excuse can we find for Ibn Garir al-Tabari, the commentator and historian who not only mentioned Bakhtnassar's incident as al-Wahidi did, but he chooses it from a group of options declaring: 'The best explanation of them all concerning the Cow:114, "And who does greater evil than he who bars God's places of worship, so that His Name be not praised in them" is the Christians (Nasara). For they are the ones who sought to destroy Bait al-Maqdes, and helped Bakhtnassar in doing that, and prevented the believers of the children of Israel from praying in it after the return of Bakhtnassar to his own land.'

Then he added:

Why did Ibn Garir al-Tabari, the great historian and a trusted faithful one, prefer this opinion? Would it be scientifically honest to explain away his error by claiming that he meant Bakhtnassar the Second, thus defending him and being biased towards him? Or rather to acknowledge the historical error into which even the greatest scientists and the truest faithful fell? If we examine such historical errors that were forced on the reasons of inspiration (Asbab An-nuzul), and made the Qur'an say that which it did not say, it would take us a long time, and our wandering would be extensive.

Here is another example of one of Tabari's errors. This time it concerns a simple historical fact which can be seen by all. Piety and religious faithfulness are not a guarantee of freedom from error. Imam Tabari made mistakes that all can see. Would it be scientifically honest to explain away his errors, or to admit them? It is far better to side with the truth than to side with the greatest commentators. Just as Tabari chose from different options in the story concerning Bakhtnassar and was wrong, so he also chose from different options concerning the crucifixion of Jesus and was proven to be wrong again.

It is not only concerning the crucifixion (an event which occurred 900 years before the time of Tabari) that historical data was wrongly selected by Imam Tabari and others. His historical data concerning the reasons of inspiration was also incorrect, even though this was 300 (not 900) years before Tabari's time and transmitted by people who had its interest in heart. The listing of such historical errors would take us a long time, and our wandering too would be extensive.

Dr. Qaradawi quoted another Muslim scholar concerning the use of the 'Isra'iliyat':

Permission to talk about them [the 'Isra'iliyat'] is one thing, although we cannot prove or deny them, but to use them to explain the Qur'an, and to make it a quotation or a story in the meaning of the Qur'anic text, or to specify that which was not specified, or to detail that which is general is another thing. For accepting the 'Isra'iliyat' beside the word of Allah, gives the impression that that which we cannot prove or deny, stands to explain the word of Allah, ... God forbid. There is no stronger confirmation of their stories and sayings than to link them with the Book of Allah, and give them the place of clarifying and explaining the word of Allah. O Allah, forgive us.

The acceptance of the substitution theory is based on the specialty of Wahb, the 'Isra'iliyat'. It is the same 'Isra'iliyat that Imam Tabari used to explain the Qur'anic verses about the crucifixion of Jesus. After Tabari, most commentators have continued to do the same, to the present day.

Dr. Qaradawi requested forgiveness for Imam Tabari when he said: 'May Allah forgive Imam Tabari, for his carelessness has disfigured the history of the dawn of Islam, and harmed the first bearers of the message.' [49] He requested forgiveness from Allah on behalf of all who used the 'Isra'iliyat to expound the Qur'an, when he said 'O Allah forgive us.' But this plea for forgiveness should also include its use in relation to the crucifixion of Jesus. It is the only appropriate response if the record is to be set straight.

---

1. City of Wrong, Kenneth Cragg, London,1960, p. 222.
2. Ayoub, Mahmoud M., "Towards an Islamic Christology II", The

Muslim World, Vol. LXX, April 1980, No. 2, p. 107.

3. Ibid..

4. Suyuti, commenting on the Qur'an, 3:55.

5. Ayoub, Mahmoud M., Towards an Islamic Christology II, The Muslim World, Vol. LXX, April 1980, No. 2, p. 106.

6. Al-Sagastani, Abu Ya'qub Ishaq, Kitab Ithbat al-Nubuwat, Al-Matb'aa al-Kathulikiah, Beirut, Lebanon, 1966, p. 185.

7. The verse, "And for their saying, 'We slew the Messiah, Isa son of Mary, the messenger of God' - yet they did not slay him, neither crucified him; only a likeness of that was shown to them." (A.J. Arburry), or "They declared; 'We have put to death the Messiah Isa son of Mary, the apostle of Allah.' They did not kill him, nor did they crucify him, but they thought they did." (N.J. Dawood)

8. The Qur'an, 3:55, (N.J. Dawood)

9. The Qur'an, 19:33.

10. The Qur'an, 4:157,158.

11. The Qur'an, 4:157, (N.J. Dawood)

12. The Qur'an, 8:17.

13. Mamoud Mohammad Taha, al-Masih, first edition, 1981, al-'Ikhwan al-Gomhuriyun, 'Um Durman, Sudan, p.9,10.

14. Geoffery Parrinder, Jesus in the Qur'an, Sheldon P., London, 1976, p.116.

15. Tagore, Collected Poems and Plays of Rabindranath Tagore, the Macmillan Company, New York, 1937, pp. 453, 454.

16. Ahmad Shawqi, As-Shawqiyat, Poem al-Andalus al-Gadidah, Dar al-Kutub, al-'Elmeyah, Beirut Lebanon, p.179.

17. Ayoub, Mahmoud M., "Towards an Islamic Christology II", The Muslim World, Vol. LXX, April 1980, No. 2, p. 96.

18. The Qur'an, 3:52, 53.

19. 'Abd al-Tafahum, The Muslim World, commenting on City of Wrong, Vol. xlvi. No. 2, April 1956, p. 139.

20. The Qur'an, 7:179.

21. Mohammad Bahr al-'Uloum, al-Hasan wa al-Hosein Imaman in Qama wa in Qa'ada, Dar az-Zahra'a, Beirout Lebanon, 1983 second edition, p. 62.

22. Ayoub, Mahmoud M., "Towards an Islamic Christology II", The Muslim World, Vol. LXX, April 1980, No. 2, p. 104.

23. Ibid., p. 96.

24. Muhammad abd el-Ghani Hasan, at-Tarikh 'end al-Muslemeen, Ketabuka No. 32. Dar al-Ma'aref,1977, pp. 22, 23.

25. Mohammad Bahr al-'Uloum, al-Hasan wa al-Hosein Imaman in Qama wa in Qa'ada, Dar az-Zahra'a, Beirout Lebanon, 1983 second edition, p. 44.

26. Qaradawi, Dr. Yousif, Thaqafat al-Da'iah, Mu'asasat ar-Resalah, Beirut,1979, p. 41.

27. Muhammad Abd al-Ghani Hasan, at-Tarikh 'end al-Muslemeen, Ketaboka No. 32. Dar al-Ma'aref,1977, p. 12.

28. Qaradawi, Dr. Yousif, Thaqafat al-Da'iah, Mu'asasat al-Resalah, Beirut,1979, p. 109-110.

29. Muhammad Abd El-Ghani Hasan, at-Tarikh 'end al-Muslemeen, Ketaboka No. 32. Dar al-Ma'aref,1977, p. 13.

30. Mahmoud abu Rayah, abu Horayrah, third edition, Dar el-Ma'aref, Egypt, 1969, p. 93.

31. Sobhy as-Saleh, 'Uloum al-Hadith wa Mustalahatoh, Dar 'al-'Elm LelMalaayeen, Beirut Lebanon, Fifteenth Edition 1984, p. 69.

32. Ibid., p. 126.

33. Ayoub, Mahmoud M., "Towards an Islamic Christology II", The Muslim World, Vol. LXX, April 1980, No. 2, p. 92.

34. Sobhy as-Saleh, Mabaheth Fi 'Ulum Al-Qur'an, 1983, p. 290.

35. Qaradawi, Dr. Yousif, Thaqafat al-Da'iah, Mu'asasat al-Resalah, Beirut,1979, pp. 109-110.

36. Ibid., p. 111.

37. Ibid.

38. Ibid., pp. 109-110.

39. Ibid., p. 111.

40. The Qur'an, 4:34.

41. Qaradawi, Dr. Yousif, Thaqafat al-Da'iah, Mu'asasat al-Resalah, Beirut, 1979, p. 51.

42. The Qur'an, 5:45.

43. Qaradawi, Dr. Yousif, Thaqafat al-Da'iah, Mu'asasat al-Resalah, Beirut,1979, p. 51.

44. Ibid.

45. Ibid.

46. Megalat al-Hadi, fourth year second issue, an article by Mortada al-'askari, p. 70.

47. Sobhy as-Saleh, Mabaheth fi 'Ulum al-Qur'an, 1983, pp. 135-

139.
48. Qaradawi, Dr. Yousif, Thaqafat al-Da'iah, Mu'asasat al-Resalah, Beirut,1979, p. 43.
49. Ibid. p. 111.

CHAPTER XVI

WAS JESUS SUBSTITUTED AS CONSTRUED IN THE QURAN?

Was Jesus substituted as construed in the Qur'an?

It is a subject which has generated much heat and discussion, not only between Muslims and Christians, but also amongst Muslims themselves across the centuries.

The question is: 'Was Jesus lifted up, body and spirit to be with God, without experiencing death on the over or was he crucified, dead, then raised from the dead and lifted up?'

Here we deal with that old question, firstly by looking at the material presented by commentators of the Qur'an, tracing the thoughts of those of early times through to the present day; and secondly, by examining the contribution some modern thinkers have made on the subject.

Before we begin, however, we must remember that it is the Truth we seek to know, and not merely the traditions handed down by our forefathers. The truth is never afraid of testing, nor does it shy away from scrutiny. The Qur'an states:

God strikes both the true and the false. As for the scum, it vanishes as jetsam, and what profits men abides in the earth.

Dr. Qaradawi, commenting on this verse said,

The Qur'an likens the Truth with running water and a useful metal, and likens what is false with the scum or the foam of water which goes downstream ... and what remains is the Truth.

The truth, any truth, can stand the strikes of the hammers of investigation and criticism, but error and falsehood will burst and vanish at the slightest touch, as does foam. The Truth is not afraid of being handled, touched, examined from a closer vantage point, but error shrinks from any of these things. Error can only stand behind the label "Do Not Touch". Truth is so solid that it can bear to be struck by men, by demons, even by God Himself, as the above Qur'anic verse states.

The Quranic passages

The following are the passages in the Qur'an which deal with our subject. Two translations will be cited, N.J. Dawood of the Penguin Classics, and A.J. Arburry of the World's Classics.

1. 'Peace be upon me, the day I was born, and the day I die, the day I am raised up alive' (A.J. Arburry). Dawood's translation is substantially the same.

2. 'He said: "Isa (Jesus), I am about to cause you to die and lift you up to me. I shall take you away from the unbelievers and exalt your followers above them till the Day of the Resurrection."' (N.J. Dawood) 'When God said, "Isa, I will take thee to me, and will raise thee to me, and I will purify thee of those who believe not. I will set thy followers above the unbelievers till the resurrection day."' (A.J. Arburry)

3. 'They declared: "We have put to death the Messiah Isa son of Mary, the apostle of Allah." They did not kill him, nor did they crucify him, but they thought they did. Those that disagreed about him were in doubt concerning his death, for what they knew about it was sheer conjecture, they were not sure that they had slain him. Allah lifted him up to His presence; He is mighty and wise.' (N.J. Dawood)

'And for their saying, "We slew the Messiah, Isa son of Mary, the messenger of God"- yet they did not slay him, neither crucified him; only a likeness of that was shown to them. And those who are at variance concerning him are in doubt regarding him; they have no knowledge of him, except the following of surmise; and they slew him not of a certainty - no indeed; God raised him up to Him; God is All-mighty and Wise.' (A.J. Arburry)

4. 'And when God said, 'O Isa son of Mary, didst thou say unto men "take me and my mother as gods, apart from God?". He said "To Thee be Glory! It is not mine to say what I have no right to ...I was a witness over them, while I remained among them, but when thou didst take me to Thyself, Thou wast Thyself the watcher over them, Thou Thyself art witness of everything."' (A.J. Arburry). Dawood's translation is substantially the same.

A survey of the interpretations of the Quranic passages

Following the development of the interpretation of the above passages, beginning with the earliest reports (as far as possible) to the latest theories, we will rely on Tabari's commentary, as it is the earliest commentary available dealing with the subject at some length, and it is also the one which influenced subsequent commentators, right up to the present day.

Tabari records two kinds of reports about what is believed to have happened to Jesus. We will cite the samples that typify each kind, then survey Tabari's analysis of them. Later on, we will survey the subsequent interpretations of the Qur'anic passages by other commentators.

TABARI'S REPORTS

The first kind of report

Tabari gives the following report which seems to be the earliest report on the belief that someone else was substituted for Jesus and so was killed instead of Jesus.

According to one group of traditions, as a result of Jesus' request for a substitute to be killed in his place, *only one person* had the likeness of Jesus cast upon him. Tabari records six traditions with this particular feature, of which this is a representative example:

The Jews surrounded Jesus, and nineteen of his disciples in a house. Jesus then said to his disciples, 'Who will take my likeness and get killed, and Paradise will be his?' One of the disciples accepted, and Jesus was lifted up. When the disciples came out the

Jews saw that they were nineteen in number. The disciples told the Jews that Jesus was lifted up to heaven. The Jews counted them and found that one of their number was missing, yet they saw that one who accepted the likeness of Jesus amongst them, so they were in doubt concerning him. They then killed that man, thinking him to be Jesus, and crucified him.

In another tradition *all* the disciples were turned to the likeness of Jesus. There is only one report with this particular feature.

Tabari relates; on the authority of a Jewish convert called Wahb, the following story:

Jesus and seventeen of his disciples went into a house. There, they were surrounded [by the Jews who were seeking Jesus]. So, when they entered, God cast the likeness of Jesus on the whole group. The Jews exclaimed, 'You have cast a spell on us! Either bring forth Jesus or we shall kill you all' Jesus then said to the disciples: 'Who amongst you will buy today Paradise in exchange of his life?'. One of the disciples said: 'I will' So he went out saying: I am Jesus. Being changed into the likeness of Jesus, they then took him and killed him, believing him to be Jesus. Hence, 'It was made only to appear so to them'. And the Christians also believed the same. And God lifted Jesus up that day.

The second kind of report

Here is the only sample of the second kind of Tabari's reports. This version differs in many ways from the others, the essential difference being that in this one, Jesus does not ask for a volunteer to take his place and so die instead of him, but God cast the likeness of Jesus on some unspecified person. This report is also related on the authority of the same man called Wahb.

When God informed Jesus that he would soon leave this world, He was troubled by death, and grieved. He therefore called the disciples together for a meal saying, 'Come all of you tonight for I have a favor to ask of you.' When they all had come, He served them Himself, and when they had finished eating, He washed their hands and helped them to perform their ablutions with His own hands, and wiped their hands on His garments. The disciples considered this as an act below the master's dignity and expressed their disapproval. But Jesus said, 'Anyone who disagrees with Me in what I do tonight is not of me, nor I of him.' Thus, they accepted. When He had finished, he said, 'As for what I have done for you tonight, serving you at table and washing your hands with My own hands, let that be an example for you. You consider Me the best of you, so let no one among you consider himself better than the others, and let each one of you offer his life for the others as I have laid down (or sacrificed) my life for you. As for the favor I ask of you, it is that you pray to God fervently that He may prolong My life.'

But when the disciples stood up to pray, they were overcome by sleep, so they were unable to pray. He began to rouse them, but they were too sleepy ... Then Jesus said, 'The shepherd will be taken away and the sheep will be scattered'. He continued, 'In truth, I say to you, one of you will deny Me three times before the cock crows. And another will sell Me for a few pieces of silver and consume My price'.

After this they left Him and went out, each going his own way. The Jews then came seeking Him, and they seized Sham'un, saying, 'He is one of his companions', but he denied, saying, 'I am not his companion'. Others also seized him and he likewise denied. Then he heard the crowing of a cock, and he wept bitterly.

The next morning, one of His disciples went to the Jews and said, 'What will you give me if I lead you to the Christ?' They gave him thirty pieces of silver, which he took and led them to Him. Before that, however, they became under an illusion [or an apparition appeared to them or they imagined it]. Thus, they took Him after ascertaining that it was, He, and tied Him with a rope. They dragged Him, saying, 'You raised the dead and cast out Satan, and healed those who were demon possessed, can you not save yourself from this rope?' They also spat on Him and placed thorns upon His head. Then they brought Him to the wood on which they wanted to crucify Him. God, however, took Him up to Himself and they crucified the man who seemed to them to be Jesus.

Then Jesus remained seven days. Then His mother and the woman whom Jesus cured from madness came to weep in the place where the crucified one was. Jesus came to them and said, 'For whom do you weep?' They answered, 'For you' He said, 'God had taken Me up to Himself and no harm befell Me. For this is a thing which only appeared to them. Go now and tell the disciples to meet Me at such and such a place' So eleven disciples went and met Him, but the one who sold Him and led the Jews to Him was missing. Jesus asked His companions about Him and they said, 'He regretted what he did, so he hanged and killed himself.' Jesus said, 'Had he repented, God surely would have pardoned him.'

Tabari's analysis of the first kin fog report

Let us consider Tabari's analysis of the first kind of report, that is, where Jesus asked for someone to have his likeness cast upon him.

Tabari found a problem with all versions of these reports because they included this request, since it would have made the disciples fully aware of what actually happened. And that, according to Tabari's understanding of the Qur'anic verse (Q. 4:157,158), would make the followers of Jesus certain of what actually happened, not uncertain and confused, following conjecture, as the Qur'anic verse states. The request of Jesus for a volunteer (according to Tabari's understanding of that verse) contradicts the Qur'an.

Tabari believed that neither the disciples nor the Jews knew what actually happened. The disciples of Jesus sincerely believed that Jesus was crucified, and so were not lying. They simply reported what they saw with their eyes, but their eyes deceived them. What they saw was not in reality Jesus dying on the cross. From that time on all the followers of Jesus did not know what actually happened to him, until the time of the Qur'an, when the true story was revealed.

Here, the problem is stated in Tabari's words:

The disciples would have been eye witnesses of the lifting up of Jesus, and eye witnesses of the transforming of the disciple who consented to have the likeness of Jesus cast upon him. So, the disciples would not be confused or in doubt as to what actually happened. Though their enemies the Jews would have been confused as they thought that the one, they killed was Jesus.... For how can the disciples be confused when they heard the words of Jesus: 'Who among you would consent to have my likeness *(shabahi)* cast upon him, be killed, and be my companion in Paradise?'... and also heard the answer of his disciple: 'I would', and witnessed the transforming of that disciple into the likeness of Jesus?

In the second version, where all the disciples had the likeness of Jesus cast upon them, there is an atmosphere of confusion. In this case, everywhere the disciples looked they saw the likeness of Jesus. But the problem of Jesus' request for a volunteer to take his place still remains. Although all had the likeness of Jesus, yet they knew the one who volunteered was the one then killed. This version also would leave only the Jews confused about the true identity of the crucified one, and not the disciples of Jesus. Again, that is contrary to the belief that both the Jews and the disciples did not know what actually happened. For both the Jews and the followers of Jesus say that Jesus was crucified.

It is not only that the above versions pose this problem but it could be argued they also make one of the disciples to be a liar, with the consent of Jesus, for he claimed to be Jesus when he was not.

These stories then have problems. Tabari, however, prefers the two reports given on the authority of Wahb. He prefers the report in which all the disciples were changed to look like Jesus, but with the provision that Jesus' request for a substitute be omitted altogether from the report.

The alternative acceptable report also given on the authority of Wahb, has Jesus betrayed by one of his disciples. In this report, Jesus does not ask for a substitute to take his place:

The disciples of Jesus deserted him before the Jews came to arrest him. Jesus then remained alone, but his likeness was cast on one of his disciples who had been with him in the house and subsequently left him. In this way he was changed. This man was killed and the disciples and the Jews thought that the one who was killed was Jesus, since they saw his likeness on him. The truth was hidden from them ... the disciples then cannot be considered as liars because they simply told what they saw as it appeared to them.

Tabari's finding then is this: Jesus did not ask for a volunteer, but somehow the likeness of Jesus was cast on someone who then died on the cross instead of Jesus.

Tabari's theory challenged

Tabari's theory has been challenged, for without Jesus' request for a volunteer to die on the cross instead of him, God is presented as an unjust God who made an innocent man to suffer for another against his will. Here is what Dr. Mahmoud Ayoub had to say concerning this problem:

Important to most of the substitutions interpretations is the idea that whoever bore the likeness of Jesus, and consequently his suffering and death, did so voluntarily. It must have been felt by Hadith transmitters and commentators that for God to cause an innocent man to die unjustly to save another would be divine wrongdoing *(zulm)*, which cannot be predicated of God. Thus, the theory which eventually gained most popularity was that one of the disciples voluntarily accepted death as a ransom for his master.

So, we are back to square one, with a theory retaining the inherent problem of Jesus' request for a volunteer, that was rejected by Tabari. If that substitute voluntarily accepted death in place of Jesus, then we have the inescapable objection which was rightfully and logically raised by Tabari. How can the disciples be confused, having heard the request of Jesus and the answer of his disciple, and having witnessed the transforming of that disciple into the likeness of Jesus? [18] This being contrary to the Qur'an 4:158.

If, however, we accept Tabari's theory, that would make God to be unjust; for He cast the likeness of Jesus on someone against his will, causing one that was innocent to be killed. This substitution theory, contradicts the Qur'an as well as the character of God!

The punishment substitution

After Tabari the substitution theory was not totally rejected, but took a new form. In this new form, God is completely clear of the charge of injustice.

Some versions of this theory go like this:

When God changed those who insulted Jesus and his mother into animals, [as a result of Jesus' request to God], Judas the leader of the Jews heard about it, and was afraid that he might be transformed to an animal too. So, he gathered the Jews together and agreed to kill Jesus. Gabriel made Jesus enter the top part of a house with a sky light in the ceiling. Then Gabriel lifted him up. Judas the leader of the Jews sent one of his friends, whose name was Titanus, into the house to kill him, but he could not see him, so he delayed. The people outside thought he was fighting with him in the upper part of the house. There God cast the likeness of Jesus on that man, and when he came out to his friends, they killed him and crucified him. Some say that God cast the likeness of Jesus only on the man's face and not on his body. The people said, 'The face is Jesus' face but the body is Titanus' body" Others said, 'If this is Titanus, then where is Jesus, and if this is Jesus, where is Titanus?'

In this version Jesus did not ask for a volunteer, and the one who was killed and crucified was not an innocent man, so he deserved to be killed. In this report neither the Jews nor the disciples knew what actually happened. Indeed, they were confused, for the face was that of Jesus but the body was that of Titanus. Here Tabari's lost link is found, and his objection is answered. Also, God is not portrayed as unjust.

This report was related on the authority of Ibn 'Abbas, who was one of the very early companions of the Prophet (he was four years old when the Prophet died). So that tradition must have been known to Tabari. One wonders why, then, Tabari did not use this report. It would have been a perfect one for his understanding of Q. 4:157,158. Indeed, this report does not appear at all in Tabari's collection of the reports he mentions in his commentary!

The problem of the substitution theory

The theory of substitution in whatever form it took was not safe from the scrutiny of those who wrestled with this issue. A commentator who carefully analyzed and discussed the substitution theory and its implications at great length was Fakhr ad-Din al-Razi (d. 606/1209).

Razi, after surveying all the forms of the substitution theory, said, 'These forms (of the substitution theory) are contradictory and conflicting and God knows the truth of the matter.' But this contradictory nature did not cause Razi to reject the substitution theory totally, for he understood the Qur'anic verse, 'They did not kill him, nor did they crucify him, but they thought they did' to mean that God did cast the likeness of Jesus upon someone, who was killed instead of Jesus. Razi, however, admits there are six problems with the theory of substitution.

1. Razi asked the question, 'If it can be claimed that the likeness of one man could be cast on another, this would open the gate of sophistry. For if we see Zayd, maybe he is not Zayd, but it is the likeness of Zayd that was cast on another. Then no marriage or ownership rights could be ascertained. Further, this would lead to doubt concerning historically transmitted reports. This historical transmission provides a sure source of knowledge... If, however, we allow the possibility of the occurrence of such confusion of identity, this would lead to doubt concerning the historically transmitted reports and in turn this would finally lead people to doubt all sacred laws... 'In sum, the opening of such a gate of sophistry necessitates doubting the truthfulness of historical reports, and this in turn leads to doubt in fundamentals, and that leads to doubting the prophethood of all prophets. This is a path leading to doubt in fundamentals, and must therefore be rejected.'

2. Since 'the Most High God commanded Gabriel to accompany Jesus in most circumstances (for that is what the commentators said of His words 'I confirmed you with the Holy Spirit'), and since the tip of one of the wings of Gabriel is sufficient to destroy the whole world, how then is it that Gabriel was unable to protect him from the Jews? Besides he [Jesus] himself was able to raise the dead and heal the blind and the leper. How is it that he could not destroy those Jews who intended to harm him...?'

3. If 'God, the Most High, was able to save him from his enemies by lifting him up to Himself, what was the advantage of casting the likeness of Jesus on another, except the charge that the innocent substitute died to no real gain for himself?'

4. 'If the likeness of Jesus was cast on someone else and Jesus was lifted up to heaven, leaving people to believe that the crucified was Jesus when he was not; that amounts to forcing ignorance and deception on people. And that is not worthy of God's wisdom.'

5. 'The Christians in masses, east and west, in spite of their strong love for Jesus, and their exaggeration concerning him, reported that they saw him dying on the cross. If we deny their

report, that would be doubting the historically transmitted reports, and such doubt necessitates doubt in the prophethood of Mohammad, and the prophethood of Jesus, even their existence, and the existence of all the prophets.'

6. 'It is historically transmitted that the crucified remained alive for quite a while on the cross, if he was not Jesus, he must have expressed his own agony, and said 'I am not Jesus but I am someone else'. He also must have tried very hard to convince people of his case. But since nothing like that was reported, it follows then that the claim of a substitute is not true.'

The important point drawn from Razi's writings is this: Once we doubt that Zayd is Zayd, but suspect that Zayd might be someone else, what guarantee is there that Jesus was Jesus or Mohammad was Mohammad? And what guarantee is there now that what they said is truly what they said? If divine knowledge or anything is to be reliable, such confusion cannot be admitted, for then how can we be certain of anything at all?

Razi's possible scenario

Razi offers the opinion of some who said:

When Christ was taken up, the Jews took a man whom they killed, claiming that he was Jesus, for Jesus was a man little given to social intercourse, and thus known only to a few chosen companions. The Christian agreement in the transmission of the crucifixion goes back to a few people whose agreement on a false report is not improbable."

Dr. Ayoub gives a more detailed account of the above story: 'The Jews sought to kill Jesus, but God took him up to Himself. They therefore took another whom they crucified on a high and isolated hill, allowing no one to come near him until his features had changed beyond recognition. They were thus able to conceal the fact of Jesus' Ascension, *which they witnessed*, and to spread false reports of his death and crucifixion.' (Emphasis added)

The main idea behind the above story is to remove the problem that God is the author of this deception and the cause of this confusion of identity, because 'for God to allow such confusion of identity for whatever reason would be too irrational and therefore inadmissible.'

In this solution, it is not God who is the author of this confusion of identity, but the Jews. God is not portrayed here as a deceiver but as helpless against the scheming of the Jews. For the Jews win and God loses control. His purpose has been defeated. For the Jews have managed to conceal the fact of Jesus' Ascension, which is a mighty work of God. The Jews managed to make it void as if God did not do it. In the above solution while God's justice and rationality are met, as far as those who hold this view are concerned, God's purpose in the Ascension of Jesus, is thwarted and the Jews are seen as outsmarting God. This theory makes a mockery of God's sovereignty and greatness. The earliest form of substitution was based on divine deception, but this one is based on human deception which turns the power of God to naught.

Furthermore, according to the above story, if the Jews were eye witnesses of the Ascension, were the disciples also eye witnesses? Would God reveal the Ascension to the unbelieving Jews and hide it from the faithful band of the followers of Jesus, and leave them in darkness, ignorance and grief? And if they were eye witnesses, then the disciples could have told everyone that the crucified one was not Jesus but that it was a lie, and that Jesus was lifted up to be with God.

If this theory were true then the Jews have also succeeded in misleading the followers of Jesus, and thus thwarted God's purpose. These disciples believed in him and the Qur'an called them *'Shuhoud'*, that is 'eye witnesses' when it said of them: 'Count us amongst the witnesses'

Razi himself, commenting on the description of the disciples as witnesses said, 'The request of the disciples to be counted amongst the witnesses was answered, and God made them prophets and apostles.'

Could those disciples whom God made prophets and apostles be so cut off from God that they knew neither what actually happened to Jesus, nor that the Jews were only lying concerning the crucified one?

Razi also said that 'since the disciples were described as witnesses, their testimony was associated with God's mention, and this is a high degree and a great rank.' If those whose mention is placed alongside God's witness were deceived by the Jews, that would make a mockery of the testimony of God to the disciples of Jesus. Besides God could have easily revealed to those disciples of

Jesus that he was not crucified, and that the Jews were only telling a lie. Such a theory would run contrary to the purpose of God in establishing His truth, and contrary to the nature of God, who miraculously lifted Jesus up but could do nothing for his followers. If the substitution theory makes a mockery of divine justice this theory would make mockery of God's covenant with the faithful band that followed Jesus.

The influence of the Gospel of Barnabas

The 'Gospel of Barnabas' did not appear until the sixteenth century. With the appearing of this 'gospel' we see the return of one of the old forms of the substitution theory. This gospel tells us:

Judas Iscariot led the Jews and Roman soldiers to arrest Jesus at night in a house. When God saw the danger approaching his servant, He ordered Gabriel and Mikhaiel and Rafaiel and Oryiel, His ambassadors, to take Jesus from the world. So, they took Him out of the southern window of the house and carried Him up to heaven. All the disciples were asleep, and the wonderful God acted wonderfully, insomuch that Judas was so changed in speech and in face that the disciples believed him to be Jesus. And Judas, having awakened the disciples, was seeking where the master was. The disciples marveled, and answered: 'Thou, Lord, art our master'. He smiling said: 'Now are ye foolish, that know not me to be Judas Iscariot.' ... The soldiers came and arrested Judas, then he was taken and crucified. He lost his mind so that his incoherent protests were considered as those of a madman. Jesus, on the other hand, appeared after three days to his mother and the rest of the disciples to comfort and reassure them that he did not die, he even requested from the four angels to testify that he did not die. Then before their eyes the four angels carried him up into heaven.

After so many modifications to the substitution theory, Dr. Ayoub had this to say about the Gospel of Barnabas:

This is most probably a late work, written under Islamic influence and agreeing with Islam on many crucial points.

In other words, it is most probably a forged work, written under Islamic influence. Because of that influence the author took an obvious Islamic position on many crucial points in the debate between Christians and Muslims. This gospel also contradicts the

Qur'an in that it calls Mohammad the 'Christ'. Nowhere in the Qur'an do we find that Mohammad is called the Christ, rather it is Jesus Son of Mary who is called the Christ.

The Gospel of Barnabas, then, teaches a version of the old substitution theory, with Judas as the one who was crucified. But the earliest reports tell us that Judas committed suicide, so the Gospel of Barnabas contradicts the earliest reports collected by Tabari.

Thus, we have come back full circle back to the earliest interpretation of the words *'shubbiha lahum'* as meaning 'another took his likeness and was substituted for him'. Once more we are back to square one!

The rejection of the substitution theory

Traditional commentators like Sayed Qutb clung to the Gospel of Barnabas as their evidence for the substitution theory, while modern thinkers shy away from it.

So, the latest interpretations of the Qur'anic verses on the subject fall into two groups. One group insists on the substitution theory, like that of Sayed Qotb, while others, mainly modern thinkers, refuse the substitution theory totally.

Modern thinkers are aware of the embarrassment caused by this confusion. Here is what Dr. Kamel Hussein had to say:

The idea of a substitute for Christ is a very crude way of explaining the Qur'anic text. They had to explain a lot to the masses. *No cultured Muslim believes in this nowadays.* The text is taken to mean that the Jews thought they killed Christ but God raised Him in a way we can leave unexplained among the several mysteries which we have taken for granted on faith alone. [emphasis added]

Dr. Hussein rejects the substitution theory. It so lacked simplicity and the ring of truth that it had to be modified repeatedly to cover all the holes. It is a crude way of explaining the Qur'anic text; the idea of a substitute is not well thought out. Even after almost one thousand years of modifications, thinkers still discard it as a backward thing that belongs to the uncultured, and hopefully to the past. It is an insult to the intelligence of the thinking man.

Dr. Mahmoud Ayoub also said:

The substitution theory will not do, regardless of its form or purpose... it makes a mockery of divine justice and the primordial covenant of God with humanity.

The theory of substitution in any form is rooted in and based on *divine deception*, whether the deception of Jesus' disciples or the deception of the Jews. If it involves the deception of the disciples, then it turns the Merciful God into a monster (God forbid), for how can God deceive the disciples of Jesus, the faithful band that believed His messenger, and after them the followers of Jesus generation after generation? And if it involves the deception of the Jews, that also does not fit the character of God; nor does it confound the arrogance of the Jews, for they still believe that they killed Jesus, and boast about it. What the Jews needed, was to be shown without a shadow of a doubt that they had no power over Jesus.

And if some say that the Jews did see Jesus ascending to heaven, but the disciples did not (hence the report of the Christians that Jesus was crucified) then this amounts to saying that God allowed the infidel Jews to see the Ascension, but the faithful followers were denied this sight and were left in darkness and despair. If this was so, what sort of message would those Hawariyun (the disciples of Jesus) have had for the world, if all they had to say was that Jesus was only crucified and did not ascend? If they claimed he ascended, yet did not see him ascending they would have been the greatest liars in the history of mankind.

How could the prophet to whom God gave the clearest evidence, confuse his disciples and his followers?

The Gospel of Barnabas tells us that although Jesus appeared to the disciples after his Ascension, they all dispersed into the different parts of the world, and kept silent about the true story, which they knew very well. Only the supposed Barnabas had the courage to write the true story and the world had to wait for sixteen centuries after the event to know what actually happened. Is this the way God reveals His truth?

The historically transmitted reports by the followers of Jesus are well known all over the world, as Razi observed: 'The Christians in their masses, east and west, in spite of their strong love for Jesus, and their exaggeration concerning him, reported that they saw him dying on the cross.'

This must have been what the disciples of Jesus taught as they spread east and west.

The substitution theory insults and mocks both man and God, and therefore must be rejected.

---

1. The Qur'an, 13:17.

2. Dr. Qaradawi, al-Iyman wal-Hayat, seventh ed., Cairo, Maktabat Wahbah, 1980 , P. 5.

3. The Qur'an, 19: 33.

4. The Qur'an, 3: 55.

5. The Qur'an, 3: 55.

6. The Qur'an, 4:157,158.

7. The Qur'an, 4:157,158.

8. The Qur'an, 5:116-120.

9. Ayoub, Mahmoud M., "Towards an Islamic Christology II", The Muslim World, Vol. LXX, April 1980, No. 2, p. 92.

10. Tabari, commenting on Q. 4:157, ref. No. 10783.

11. Ibid., ref. No. 10779.

12. Ibid., ref. No. 10780.

13. Ibid., 4:157.

14. Tabari, comments after ref. No. 10789.

15. Tabari, commenting on the Qur'an, 4:157.

16. Ibid.

17. Ayoub, Mahmoud M., "Towards an Islamic Christology II", The Muslim World, Vol. LXX, April 1980, No. 2, P 97.

18. Tabari, comments after ref. No. 10789.

19. Magma'u al-Bayan, Abu 'Ali al-Fadl Ibn al-Hasan al-Tubrusi, commenting on Q. 4:157.

20. Razi, at-Tafsir al-Kabir, Commenting on Q. 4:157.

21. The Qur'an, 4:157,158.

22. Razi, at-Tafsir al-Kabir, Commenting on Q. 3: 55.

23. Ibid., Commenting on Q. 4:157.

24. Ibid., Commenting on Q. 3:55.

25. Ibid., Commenting on Q. 3:55.

26. Ibid., Commenting on Q. 4:157.

27. Ayoub, Mahmoud M., "Towards an Islamic Christology

II", The Muslim World, Vol. LXX, April 1980, No. 2, P. 102.
28. Ibid., P. 102.
29. The Qur'an 3:53.
30. Razi, at-Tafsir al-Kabir, Commenting on Q. 3: 53.
31. Ibid.
32. The Gospel of Barnabas, translated from Italian MS by Lonsdale and Laura Ragg, sections 214-221.
33. Ayoub, Mahmoud M., "Towards an Islamic Christology II", The Muslim World, Vol. LXX, April 1980, No. 2, P. 113.
34. Sayed Qutb, Fi Zelal al- Qur'an, commenting on Q. 4:157.
35. City of Wrong, Kenneth Cragg, London, 1960, P. 222.
36. Ayoub, Mahmoud M., "Towards an Islamic Christology II", The Muslim World, Vol. LXX, April 1980, No. 2, P. 104.

CHAPTER
XVII

IS JESUS LIKE ADAM

Is Jesus like Adam?

The Quran claims that Jesus' similitude, or likeness, before God is like that of Adam whom he created from dust by his creative command:

Truly, the likeness of Jesus, in God's sight, is as Adam's likeness; He created him of dust, then said He unto him, 'Be,' and he was. S. 3:59

Muslims see this as a rather impressive refutation of the Christian arguments for the uniqueness of the Lord Jesus. However, on closer inspection this a rather poor response to the Christian claims for the eternal majesty of God's Son.

In the first place, the Quran is not clear on how Allah created Adam. The above reference claims that Allah spoke and created him from dust. Yet other references assert that Allah actually fashioned Adam from clay with his own hands and breathed his spirit into him:

When thy Lord said to the angels, *'See, I am creating a mortal of a clay. When I have shaped him, and breathed My spirit in him,* fall you down, bowing before him!' Then the angels bowed themselves all together, save Iblis; he waxed proud, and was one of the unbelievers. Said He, 'Iblis, what prevented thee to bow thyself before *that I created with <u>My own hands</u>?* Hast thou waxed proud, or art thou of the lofty ones?' S. 38:71-75

Q. 3:59 is actually formulated in a rather strange and confusing manner, even without comparing it with other passages. Note that it says that Allah created him of dust and THEN spoke the word "Be!" to him.   Does this mean that Adam didn't have a being, didn't exist until Allah said "Be!"? He obviously did, since Allah already created him from dust.   Then why would Allah even need to say "Be!" after he had already created him? Does the "Be!" refer to Allah giving life to Adam's lifeless body? If so, why did he breathe his spirit into Adam?

Wasn't it for the purpose of animating his body? Then why would he need to say "Be!"?

In light of the foregoing what are we supposed to believe about the creation of the first man? Did Allah create him with his own hands from clay, from stinking mud as another verse says, and then breathe the spirit of life into his body? Or did Allah merely speak life into him after fashioning him out of dust?

Secondly and more importantly, the Quran itself is a witness against its own assertion of Adam being similar to Jesus. The Quran ascribes to Jesus certain roles and characteristics which not only demonstrate his vast superiority to Adam, but which also elevate him higher than any other prophet or messenger.

Here are a host of qualities and functions that both the Quran and Islamic literature assign to Jesus which place him far above and beyond Adam.

1. Jesus was born of a virgin, Adam was not.

The Quran emphatically affirms Jesus' virgin birth:

'Lord,' said Mary, 'how shall I have a son seeing no mortal has touched me?' 'Even so,' God said, God creates what He will. When He decrees a thing, He does but say to it "Be," and it is. S. 3:47

And mention in the Book Mary when she withdrew from her people to an eastern place, and she took a veil apart from them; then We sent unto her Our Spirit that presented himself to her a man without fault. She said, 'I take refuge in the All-merciful from thee! If thou fearest God ... He said, 'I am but a messenger come from thy Lord, to give thee a boy most pure.   She said, 'How shall I have a son whom no mortal has touched, neither have I been unchaste?' He said, 'Even so thy Lord has said: "Easy is that for Me; and that We may appoint him a sign unto men and a mercy from Us; it is a thing decreed."' S. 19:16-21

A good question to ask at this point is why was a virgin birth necessary seeing that God's law of reproduction had already been set in motion? Adam's creation was due primarily to the circumstances in which he was created, i.e., seeing that he was the first man there could have been no possible way for him to have been born from human parents. Yet the situation with Christ was different and a virgin birth wasn't required, unless there was something special and unique about Jesus.

Islam does not give a good or valid reason for the virgin birth, apart from the assertion that Allah wanted to show that he could create anyway he sees fit. But this still wouldn't explain why Allah chose to demonstrate his creative ability by causing Jesus to be conceived from a virgin, as opposed to someone else, whether Abraham, Moses, Muhammad etc.

The Holy Bible gives us the reason why Jesus was born of a virgin:

"And Mary said to the angel, 'How shall this be, since I have no husband?' And the angel said to her, 'The Holy Spirit will come upon you, and the power of the Most High will overshadow you; Therefore, the child to be born will be called holy, the Son of God.'" Luke 1:34-35

God decreed the virgin birth since the Lord Jesus is his unique and beloved Son. God ordained Christ's entrance into human existence by means of a virgin since this is what befitted the eternal glory and dignity of his immortal Son.

Thus, Adam's creation is *unlike* Jesus' birth from a virgin. The creation of the former was determined by his circumstances whereas the virginal conception and birth of the latter was due to his unique relationship with God as his beloved Son.

2. Jesus was sinless, Adam was not.

The Quran, in several places, mentions Adam's sin in eating of the forbidden tree:

"O Adam! dwell thou and thy wife in the Garden, and enjoy (its good things) as ye wish: but approach not this tree, or ye run into harm and transgression." Then began Satan to whisper suggestions to them, bringing openly before their minds all their shame that was hidden from them (before): he said: "Your Lord only forbade you this tree, lest ye should become angels or such beings as live forever." And he swore to them both, that he was their sincere adviser. *So, by deceit he brought about their fall: when they tasted of the tree, their shame became manifest to them*, and they began to sew together the leaves of the garden over their bodies. And their Lord called unto them: "Did I not forbid you that tree, and tell you that Satan was an avowed enemy unto you?" They said: "Our Lord! *We have wronged our own souls*: If thou forgive us not and bestow not upon us Thy Mercy, we shall certainly be lost." (God) said: "*Get ye down. With enmity between yourselves*. On earth will be your dwelling-place and your means of livelihood, - for a time." He said: "Therein shall ye live, and therein shall ye die; but from it shall ye be taken out (at last)." O ye Children of Adam! We have bestowed raiment upon you to cover your shame, as well as to be an adornment to you. But the raiment of righteousness, - that is the best. Such are among the Signs of God, that they may receive admonition! O ye Children of Adam! Let not Satan seduce you, *in the same manner as He got your parents out of the Garden, stripping them of their raiment, to expose their shame*: for he and his tribe watch you from a position where ye cannot see them: We made the evil one's friends (only) to those without faith. S. 7:19-27

And:

We had already, beforehand, taken the covenant of Adam, but he forgot: *and We found on his part no firm resolve*. When We said to the angels, "Prostrate yourselves to Adam", they prostrated themselves, but not Iblis: he refused. Then We said: "O Adam! verily, this is an enemy to thee and thy wife: so, let him not get you both out of the Garden, so that thou art landed in misery. There is therein (enough provision) for thee not to go hungry nor to go naked, nor to suffer from thirst, nor from the sun's heat." But Satan whispered evil to him: he said, "O Adam! shall I lead thee to the Tree of Eternity and to a kingdom that never decays?" In the result, they both ate of the tree, and so their nakedness appeared to them: they began to sew together, for their covering, leaves from the Garden: *thus did Adam disobey his Lord, and allow himself to be seduced.* But his Lord chose him (for His Grace): He turned to him, and gave him Guidance. He said: "*Get ye down, both of you, - all together, from the Garden, with enmity one to another*: but if, as is sure, there comes to you Guidance from Me, whosoever follows My Guidance, will not lose his way, nor fall into misery." S. 20:115-123

Contrast this with what the Quran says about the sinlessness of both Jesus and his blessed mother:

When the wife of Imran said, 'Lord, I have vowed to Thee, in dedication, what is within my womb. Receive Thou this from me; Thou hearest, and knowest.' And when she gave birth to her, she said, 'Lord, I have given birth to her, a female.' (And God knew very well what she had given birth to; the male is not as the female.) 'And I have named her Mary, and commend her to Thee with her seed, to protect them from the accursed Satan.' S. 3:35-36

Muhammad purportedly interpreted the preceding passage as implying that only Mary and her glorious Son were protected from Satan when they were born:

Narrated Said bin Al-Musaiyab:

Abu Huraira said, "I heard Allah's Apostle saying, 'There is none born among the off-spring of Adam, but Satan touches it. A child therefore, cries loudly at the time of birth because of the touch of Satan, EXCEPT MARY AND HER CHILD." Then Abu Huraira recited: "And I seek refuge with You for her and for her offspring from the outcast Satan" (3.36) *(Sahih Al-Bukhari, Volume 4, Book 55, Number 641; see also Volume 4, Book 54, Number 506)*

And here is what the Quran says God's Spirit told Mary about the birth of her glorious Son:

... He said, 'I am but a messenger come from thy Lord, to give thee a boy *most pure (ghulaman zakiyyan)*. S. 19:19

This next report brings out the contrast between Jesus' absolute purity with Adam's sinfulness much more clearly:

Narrated Anas:

The Prophet said, "On the Day of Resurrection the Believers will assemble and say, 'Let us ask somebody to intercede for us with our Lord.' So, they will go to Adam and say, 'You are the father of all the people, and Allah created you with His Own Hands, and ordered the angels to prostrate to you, and taught you the names of all things; so please intercede for us with your Lord, so that He may relieve us from this place of ours.' Adam will say, 'I am not fit for this (i.e., intercession for you).' Then Adam will remember his sin and feel ashamed thereof. He will say, 'Go to Noah, for he was the first Apostle Allah sent to the inhabitants of the earth.' They will go to him and Noah will say, 'I am not fit for this undertaking.' He will remember his appeal to his Lord to do what he had no knowledge of, then he will feel ashamed thereof and will say, 'Go to the Khalil--r-Rahman (i.e., Abraham).' They will go to him and he will say, 'I am not fit for this undertaking. Go to Moses, the slave to whom Allah spoke (directly) and gave him the Torah.' So, they will go to him and he will say, 'I am not fit for this undertaking.' and he will mention (his) killing a person who was not a killer, and so he will feel ashamed thereof before his Lord, and he will say, 'Go to Jesus, Allah's Slave, His Apostle and Allah's Word and a Spirit coming from Him.' Jesus will say, 'I am not fit for this undertaking, go to Muhammad the Slave of Allah whose past and future sins were forgiven by Allah.'... (*Sahih al-Bukhari*, Volume 6, Book 60, <u>Number 3</u>)

Let the reader note that Jesus is the only prophet in this list who doesn't mention any personal sins. Even Muhammad was a sinner, unlike the Lord Jesus, according to this so-called sound hadith!

In fact, the famous Muslim historian and commentator al-Tabari cited a Muslim scholar named Qatadah who said that:

"Jesus and his mother did not commit any of the sins which the rest of the children of Adam commit." (Mahmoud M. Ayoub, *The Quran and Its Interpreters: The House of Imran* [State University of New York Press (SUNY), Albany 1992], Volume II, p. 94)

Thus, if anyone would be worthy of interceding it wouldn't be Muhammad, but the sinless Savior, the Lord Jesus.

3. Jesus is a Spirit proceeding from God and his very own Word, whereas Adam was given life by God's Spirit and was created by God's command.

When the angels said, 'Mary, God gives thee good tidings of a Word from Him whose name is Messiah, Jesus, son of Mary; high honored shall he be in this world and the next, near stationed to God. S. 3:45

People of the Book, go not beyond the bounds in your religion, and say not as to God but the truth. The Messiah, Jesus Son of Mary, was only the Messenger of God, and His Word that He committed to Mary, and a Spirit from Him. So, believe in God and His Messengers, and say no, 'Three.' Refrain; better is it for you. God is only One God. Glory be to Him -- That He should have a son! To Him belongs all that is in the heavens and in the earth; God suffices for a guardian. S. 4:171

Q. 4:171 presupposes that Jesus existed before he was born from the virgin. After all, for the Quran to identify Jesus as God's Word which he *committed* or gave to Mary indicates that he was with God even before he was given to his mother. Furthermore, both Christians and Muslims agree that God's Word is uncreated since he has never lacked his communicative ability. Thus, for Jesus to be God's Word implies that he is uncreated, that he is eternal. Notice the logic behind this:

A. God's Word is eternal.

B. Jesus is God's Word.

C. Therefore, Jesus is eternal.

The expression, "a Spirit from Him", provides further substantiation for this understanding. This phrase is used only one other time in the Quran:

Thou shalt not find any people who believe in God and the Last Day who are loving to anyone who opposes. God and His Messenger, not though they were their fathers, or their sons, or their brothers, or their clan. Those -- He has written faith upon their hearts, and He has confirmed them with a Spirit from Himself; and He shall admit them into gardens underneath which rivers flow, therein to dwell forever, God being well-pleased with them, and they well-pleased with Him. Those are God's party; why, surely God's party -- they are the prosperous. S. 58:22

Here, the Spirit from God is present with all true believers in order to strengthen them in faith. This presupposes that this Spirit is both omnipresent and omnipotent, qualities which belong only to God. This, perhaps, accounts for why the late Muslim commentator, Abdullah Yusuf Ali, viewed this Spirit as being Divine:

"... Cf. ii 87 and 253, where it is said that God strengthened the Prophet Jesus with the holy spirit. Here we learn that all good and righteous men are strengthened by God with the holy spirit. If anything, the phrase used here is stronger, 'a spirit from Himself'. Whenever anyone offers his heart in faith and purity to God, God accepts it, engraves that faith on the seeker's heart, and further fortifies him with the Divine Spirit, which we can no more define adequately than we can define in human language the nature of God." (Ali, *The Meaning of the Holy Quran*, p. 1518, fn. 5365; bold emphasis ours)

Since the Quran uses the same expression to describe Jesus as a Spirit from God this therefore means that Christ is one who "we can no more define adequately than we can define in human language the nature of God." The Quran, at this point, is confirming the Deity and prehuman existence of the Lord Jesus.

4. Jesus is the Messiah, a King, whereas Adam was not. The Quran knows of only one Messiah, namely Jesus:
(And remember) when the angels said: O Mary! Lo! Allah giveth thee glad tidings of a word from him, <u>whose name is the Messiah, Jesus, son of Mary</u>... S. 3:45 Pickthall

According to the Holy Bible, the Messiah is God's appointed King who rules over the nations:

"Jesus said to them, 'I tell you the truth, at the renewal of all things, *when the Son of Man sits on his glorious throne*, you who have followed me will also sit on twelve thrones, judging the twelve tribes of Israel.'" Matthew 19:28

"And I confer on you a kingdom, just as my Father conferred one on me, so that you may eat and drink at my table *in my kingdom* and sit on thrones, judging the twelve tribes of Israel." Luke 22:29-30

"Then the whole assembly rose and led him off to Pilate. And they began to accuse him, saying, 'We have found this man subverting our nation. He opposes payment of taxes to Caesar *and claims to be Christ, a king.*' So, Pilate asked Jesus, 'Are you the king of the Jews?' 'Yes, it is as you say,' Jesus replied." Luke 23:2-3

"Pilate then went back inside the palace, summoned Jesus and asked him, 'Are you the king of the Jews?' 'Is that your own idea,' Jesus asked, 'or did others talk to you about me?' 'Am I a Jew?' Pilate replied. 'It was your people and your chief priests who handed you over to me. What is it you have done?' Jesus said, '*My kingdom is not of this world.* If it were, my servants would fight to prevent my arrest by the Jews. But now my kingdom is from another place.' 'You are a king, then!' said Pilate. Jesus answered, '*You are right in saying I am a king.* In fact, for this reason I was born, and for this I came into the world, to testify to the truth. Everyone on the side of truth listens to me.'" John 18:33-37

"From then on, Pilate tried to set Jesus free, but the Jews kept shouting, 'If you let this man go, you are no friend of Caesar. *Anyone who claims to be a king opposes Caesar.*' When Pilate heard this, he brought Jesus out and sat down on the judge's seat at a place known as the Stone Pavement (which in Aramaic is Gabbatha). It was the day of Preparation of Passover Week, about the sixth hour. 'Here is your king,' Pilate said to the Jews. But they shouted, 'Take him away! Take him away! Crucify him!' 'Shall I crucify your king?" Pilate asked. 'We have no king but Caesar,' the chief priests answered... Pilate had a notice prepared and fastened to the cross. It read: JESUS OF NAZARETH, THE KING OF THE JEWS. Many of the Jews read this sign, for the place where Jesus was crucified was near the city, and the sign was written in Aramaic, Latin and Greek. The chief priests of the Jews protested to Pilate, 'Do not write "The King of the Jews," *but that this man claimed to be king of the Jews.*' Pilate answered, 'What I have written, I have written.'" John 19:12-15, 19-22

The following Islamic commentary agrees that this is what the term means:

((And remember) when the angels) i.e., Gabriel (said: O Mary! Allah giveth you glad tidings of a Word from Him) of a son who shall come into being by means of a Word from Allah, (whose name is the Messiah) because he travels from one country to another; it is also said: the Messiah means the king, (Jesus, Son of Mary, illustrious in the world) he has standing and position amidst people in the life of this world (and the Hereafter) he has standing and position with Allah, (and one of those brought near) unto Allah in the Garden of Eden. (*Tanwîr al-Miqbâs min Tafsîr Ibn 'Abbâs*; source Al Tafsir)

5. Jesus is highly honored in the next world, something which the Quran never explicitly says of anyone else.

... illustrious in the world and the Hereafter, and one of those brought near (unto Allah) ... S. 3:45 Pickthall

According to the expositors, God will highly honor Jesus in the next life by making him an intercessor:

Mention, when the angels, namely, Gabriel, said, 'O Mary, God gives you good tidings of a Word from Him, that is, a boy, whose name is the Messiah, Jesus, son of Mary, He addresses her attributing him to her in order to point out that she will give birth to him without a father, for, the custom is to attribute the child to its father, honored shall he be in this world, through prophethood, and the Hereafter, through [his] intercession and the high stations [*al-darajat al-'ula*, cf. Q. 20:75], and of those brought close, to God. (*Tafsir al-Jalalayn*; source; underline emphasis ours)

This leads us to our next point.

6. Jesus ascended alive into God's very own presence; Adam died.

When God said, 'Jesus, I will take thee to Me and will raise thee to Me and I will purify thee of those who believe not. I will set thy followers above the unbelievers till the Resurrection Day. Then unto Me shall you return, and I will decide between you, as to what you were at variance on. S. 3:55

God raised him up to Him; God is All-mighty, All-wise. S. 4:158

Jesus' high honor is seen in the fact that he has ascended into the very presence of God himself. The Quran never says this of any other person, that there is someone else along with Jesus whom God has taken to be with himself.

When we tie this in with the fact that Jesus is the Messiah then this means that Jesus is currently a King who is ruling in God's own presence! This, perhaps, explains why Jesus returns as a judge, which is the focus of our next point.

7. Jesus will return as a just judge and kill the antichrist, whereas Adam will remain dead till the day of resurrection.

According to some expositors the following verse:

And (Jesus) shall be a Sign (for the coming of) the Hour (of Judgment): therefore, have no doubt about the (Hour), but follow ye Me: this is a Straight Way. S. 43:61 Y. Ali

Refers to Jesus' Second Advent:

And indeed he, that is, Jesus, is a portent of the Hour - [the arrival of] it is known by the sending down of him - so do not doubt it (*tamtarunna*: the indicative *nun* has been omitted for apocopation together with the *waw* of the [third] person [plural] on account of two unvowelled consonants coming together) but, say to them: 'Follow me, in the affirmation of [God's] Oneness. This, to which I command you, is a straight path'. (*Tafsir al-Jalalayn*; <u>source</u>)

(And lo! Verily) in the coming of Jesus the son of Mary (there is knowledge of the Hour) there is an indication of the coming of the Hour; it is also said that this means: his coming is a sign of the advent of the Hour. (So, doubt ye not concerning it) so have no doubt in the coming of the Hour, (but follow Me) by professing Allah's divine Oneness. (This) profession of divine Oneness (is the right path) an established religion with which Allah is pleased: i.e., the religion of Islam. (*Tanwîr al-Miqbâs min Tafsîr Ibn 'Abbâs*; <u>source</u>)

The hadith literature expressly states that Jesus is returning to judge the earth:

Narrated Abu Huraira:

Allah's Apostle said, "By Him in Whose Hands my soul is, surely (Jesus,) the son of Mary will soon descend amongst you and will judge mankind justly (as a Just Ruler); he will break the Cross and kill the pigs and there will be no Jizya (i.e., taxation taken from non-Muslims). Money will be in abundance so that nobody will accept it, and a single prostration to Allah (in prayer) will be better than the whole world and whatever is in it." Abu Huraira added "If you wish, you can recite (this verse of the Holy Book): -- 'And there is none of the people of the Scriptures (Jews and Christians) But must believe in him (i.e., Jesus as an Apostle of Allah and a human being) Before his death. And on the Day of Judgment, He will be a witness Against them." (4.159) (See Fateh Al Bari, Page 302 Vol 7) (*Sahih Al-Bukhari*, Volume 4, Book 55, Number 657)

'Abdullah b. 'Amr reported that a person came to him and said: What is this hadith that you narrate that the Last Hour would come at such and such time? Thereupon he said: Hallowed be Allah, there is no god but Allah (or the words to the same effect). I have decided that I would not narrate anything to anyone now. I had only said that you would see after some time an important event that the (sacred) House (Ka'ba) would be burnt and it would happen and definitely happen. He then reported that Allah's Messenger (may peace be upon him) said: The Dajjal would appear in my Ummah and he would stay (in the world) for forty-I cannot say whether he meant forty days, forty months or forty years. And Allah would then send Jesus' son of Mary who would resemble 'Urwa b Mas'ud. He (Jesus Christ) would chase him and kill him ... (*Sahih Muslim*, Book 041, Number 7023)

Hence, Jesus the Messianic King returns to the earth from heaven in order to rule and judge the nations.

8. Jesus performed miracles, Adam did not.

And He will teach him the Book, the Wisdom, the Torah, the Gospel, to be a Messenger to the Children of Israel saying, "I have come to you with a sign from your Lord. *I will create for you out of clay as the likeness of a bird*; then I will breathe into it, and it will be a bird, by the leave of God. I will also heal the blind and the leper, and bring to life the dead, by the leave of God. I will inform you too of what things you eat, and what you treasure up in your houses. Surely in that is a sign for you, if you are believers. S. 3:48-49

When God said, 'Jesus Son of Mary, remember My blessing upon thee and upon thy mother, when I confirmed thee with the Holy Spirit, to speak to men in the cradle, and of age; and when I taught thee the Book, the Wisdom, the Torah, the Gospel; *and when thou createst out of clay, by My leave, as the likeness of a bird, and thou breathest into it, and it is a bird, by My leave*; and thou healest the blind and the leper by My leave, and thou bringest the dead forth by My leave; and when restrained from thee the Children of Israel when thou camest unto them with the clear signs, and the unbelievers among them said, "This is nothing but sorcery manifest." S. 5:110

It is rather intriguing that the Quran not only acknowledges Jesus' ability to perform supernatural signs and wonders such as raising the dead, it even admits that Jesus had the power to create and give life in the same way that Allah does! Compare, for instance, Jesus' ability to create a bird from clay and infuse life into it by his breath with the way Allah created Adam:

Behold! thy Lord said to the angels: "*I am about to create man, from sounding clay* from mud moulded into shape; When I have fashioned him (in due proportion) *and breathed into him of My spirit,* fall ye down in obeisance unto him." S. 15:28-29

Hence, the Quran has both Allah and Jesus fashioning creatures from clay and animating their bodies by their breath!

With all of these vast and profound differences one is left wondering in what way Adam is supposed to be similar to Jesus. The Quran intimates that it is in their creation, i.e., that Allah created Adam in a miraculous manner much like he created Jesus. But, as we saw earlier, this is not a valid argument and does absolutely nothing to refute the Christian position regarding Jesus' unique relationship with God. Besides, the Quran itself implies that Jesus, unlike Adam, had a prehuman existence, having existed before his virgin birth as God's Word and as his Spirit which proceeded from him.

This leads us to the final point we want to touch on. The Quran says that Allah commanded the angels to worship Adam on the grounds that he created him with his own hands:

And when we said to the angels, "Bow down and worship Adam," then worshipped they all, save Iblis. He refused and swelled with pride, and became one of the unbelievers. S. 2:34

[Remember] when we said unto the angel's worship Adam: And they worshipped, except Iblis, who was one of the jinn, and departed from the command of his Lord. Will you therefore take him and his offspring for patrons besides me, notwithstanding they are your enemies? Miserable shall such an exchange be to the ungodly! S. 18:50; cf. 38: 71-75

For the moment we will set aside the problem with worshiping a creature like Adam, which would be idolatry, since we want to focus on something else. Seeing that the Quran itself agrees that Jesus is more exalted and far greater than Adam one would expect that Christ, more so than the first man, is deserving of the worship of the angels. This is precisely what the NT teaches, namely, that the entire angelic assembly is worshiping the risen Christ:

"And again, when God brings his firstborn into the world, he says, 'Let all God's angels worship him.'" Hebrews 1:6

"And they sang a new song: 'You are worthy to take the scroll and to open its seals, because you were slain, and with your blood you purchased men for God from every tribe and language and people and nation. You have made them to be a kingdom and priests to serve our God, and they will reign on the earth.' Then I looked and heard the voice of many angels, numbering thousands upon thousands, and ten thousand times ten thousand. They encircled the throne and the living creatures and the elders. In a loud voice they sang: 'Worthy is the Lamb, who was slain, to receive power and wealth and wisdom and strength and honor and glory and praise!' Then I heard every creature in heaven and on earth and under the earth and on the sea, and all that is in them, singing: 'To him who sits on the throne and to the Lamb be praise and honor and glory and power, for ever and ever!' The four living creatures said, 'Amen,' and the elders fell down and worshiped." Revelation 5:9-14

Interestingly, there are certain Muslim sources which claim that John the Baptist prostrated before Christ Jesus while both of them were still in their mothers' wombs! Noted Muslim exegete Al-Qurtubi mentions Elizabeth's visitation (called Mary's sister) shortly after both women had conceived their sons:

"The sister visited Mary and said, 'O Mary, do you perceive that I am with child?' Mary answered, 'Do you see that I am also with child?' Her sister went on, *'I feel the child in my womb bowing down to the child in your womb.'*"

Al-Qurtubi further says that:

"It is reported that she felt the fetus in her womb bow down with its head turned toward Mary's womb." (Mahmoud M. Ayoub, *The Qur'an and Its Interpreters, Volume II, The House of 'Imran* [State University of New York Press, Albany 1992], p. 108; bold and italic emphasis ours)

Al-Tabari, the renowned exegete, writes:

"She [Mary] came to her sister who was then pregnant and to whom the birth of the Baptist had been announced. When the two met, the Baptist's mother felt that her child was bowing within her in recognition of Jesus ..." (History of Al-Tabari: The Ancient Kingdoms,

translated by Moshe Perlmann [State University of New York Press, Albany, 1987], Volume IV, p. 114; bold emphasis ours)
And:

"... Her sister, the wife of Zechariah, came to visit her at night. When Mary opened the door for her, the sister clung to her. The wife of Zechariah said, 'Oh Mary, do you know I am with child?' Mary replied, 'Do you know, that I too am with child?' Zechariah's wife then said, 'I felt that the child in me was bowing to the child in you,' as it is written, 'confirming the Word of God.'" (Ibid., p. 119; bold emphasis ours)

These scholars were simply repeating what is found in the Gospel:

"When Elizabeth heard Mary's greeting, the baby leaped in her womb, and Elizabeth was filled with the Holy Spirit. In a loud voice she exclaimed: 'Blessed are you among women, and blessed is the child you will bear! But why am I so favored, that the mother OF MY LORD should come to me? As soon as the sound of your greeting reached my ears, the baby in my womb leaped for joy.'" Luke 1:41-44

John the Baptist was caused by God to leap in his mother's womb in honor of Christ being the Sovereign Lord. Notice that Elizabeth called the recently conceived baby in Mary's womb her Lord which foreshadows what the angels would later announce at Christ's birth:

"Today in the town of David *a Savior* has been born to you; he is Christ *the Lord.*" Luke 2:11

The evidence we have presented here conclusively shows that the Quran itself admits and agrees that Jesus is vastly superior to Adam, and is therefore more deserving of honor and glory than the first man.

Our interpretation is not merely an imposed Christian understanding upon the Islamic data, since there are Muslims who also see it this way. For example, the following Muslim writer candidly admits that, according to the Quran, Jesus is the greatest of all prophets. After citing Q. 2:253, 3:42-46, and 3:59, the author says:

Moslem religious leaders try to isolate Muhammad from all other prophets by saying, "God kept the best for last." Again, this directly contradicts the Koran's teachings. The Koran says that some prophets have been given more than others - that some even talk to God. The example it gives is that of Jesus Christ, not Muhammad...

These passages clearly show that God considered Jesus to be His best prophet, not Muhammad. After all, Jesus revealed himself to be a prophet from childhood, while Muhammad was not inspired until he was forty years old. The Koran relates a number of miracles from Jesus' childhood, but says nothing of this phase of Muhammad's life. The name "Christ" is also used. Unlike Jesus, Muhammad was not a special messenger of God, but a mere helper, who brought justice to the world, and glorified the name of Jesus by setting the record straight about his deeds on earth. His mission was also to eliminate the corruption of the message of those prophets who had gone before him. On the other hand, of Jesus it is said that he was created in a similar way to Adam...

Bear in mind that when God announced His creation of Adam to the angels, He commanded them to bow to him. (Dr. Nader Pourhassan, *The Corruption of Moslem Minds* [Barbed Wire Publishing, Las Cruces, New Mexico 2002], pp. 34-35)

Christian readers especially will be interested to learn that the Koran teaches that Jesus was God's best prophet, and that Christians will be placed above non-believers until the Day of Judgment... (Ibid., p. 61)

Moslem religious leaders claim that Muhammad was the greatest prophet ever sent. If this was true, then God would have stated so in the Koran. Instead, when God talks of a prophet being greater than others, the name He mentions is that of Jesus. (Ibid., p. 101)

CHAPTER
XVIII

WHY ISLAM IS FALSE REGARDING
THE DEATH OF JESUS?

Why Islam is false regarding the death of Jesus?

The death and execution of Jesus is not only taught in the Bible but it is also recognized as an historical fact by prominent historians and scholars – both ancient and modern. However, Muslims deny the death of Jesus.   Their denial of the death of Jesus is based solely on one single verse in the Qur'an:

Surah 4:157: And for their saying, "Indeed, we have killed the Messiah, Jesus, the son of Mary, the messenger of Allah." And they did not kill him, nor did they crucify him; but another was made to resemble him to them. And indeed, those who differ over it are in doubt about it. They have no knowledge of it except the following of assumption. And they did not kill him, for certain. (Sahih International)

لَهُ ۚ شُبِّهَ وَلَكِن صَلَبُوهُ وَمَا قَتَلُوهُ وَمَا ٱللَّهِ رَسُولَ مَرْيَمَ ٱبْنَ عِيسَى ٱلْمَسِيحَ قَتَلْنَا إِنَّا وَقَوْلِهِمْ يَقِينًا قَتَلُوهُ وَمَا ۚ ٱلظَّنِّ ٱتِّبَاعَ إِلَّا عِلْمٍ مِنْ بِهِ مَا ۚ لَهُم مِّنْهُ شَكٍّ لَفِى فِيهِ ٱخْتَلَفُوا ٱلَّذِينَ وَإِنَّ ۚ مْ

Wa qawlihim innaa qatal nal maseeha 'Eesab-na-Maryama Rasoolal laahi wa maa qataloohu wa maa salaboohu wa laakin shubbiha lahum; wa innal lazeenakh talafoo feehee lafee shakkim minh; maa lahum bihee min 'ilmin illat tibaa'az zann; wa maa qataloohu yaqeenaa

Surah 4:157 states that Jesus was neither killed nor executed on the stake. According to this Qur'anic verse, Allah made it appear to the onlookers as if Jesus died on the stake when he did not. To put it bluntly, Allah deceived everyone who witnessed the execution of Jesus – including the Disciples of Jesus – into believing that he died. Allah waited for some 600 years before revealing in the Qur'an that Jesus did not actually die. Meanwhile, billions were deceived into believing the lie. In the preceding article, we addressed this issue quite extensively.

This article which you are now reading is designed as an *Appendix* to the preceding article. We will now refute this denial of the death of Jesus from a different perspective. Let's begin.

The *Law Covenant* which God established with the ancient nation of Israel went into effect during the time of Moses. The *Law Covenant* set apart ancient Israel as God's chosen nation. Jehovah became their Judge and Lawgiver. And Moses was chosen as the mediator. The *Torah* clearly states that the *Law Covenant* was validated through the shed blood of animals. After sprinkling *the blood of the sacrificed animals* on the people, Moses declared: *"This is the blood of the Covenant that Jehovah has made with you."* Thus, God instituted the *Law Covenant* with ancient Israel:

Exodus 24:6-8: Then Moses took half of the blood and put it in bowls and half of the blood he sprinkled on the altar. Then he took the book of the Covenant and read it aloud to the people. And they said: "All that Jehovah has spoken we are willing to do, and we will be obedient." So, Moses took the blood and sprinkled it on the people and said: "This is the blood of the Covenant that Jehovah has made with you in harmony with all these words."

The Qur'an also acknowledges this divine requirement of animal sacrifices under the *Law Covenant* which God mediated through Moses:

Surah 2:67: Moses said to his people, "God commands you to sacrifice a heifer." (Rashad Khalifa)

أ أَنْ بِٱللَّهِ أَعُوذُ قَالَ هُزُوًا أَتَتَّخِذُنَا قَالُوا بَقَرَةً تَذْبَحُوا أَن يَأْمُرُكُمْ ٱللَّهَ إِنَّ لِقَوْمِهِ مُوسَىٰ قَالَ وَإِذْ ٱلْجَٰهِلِينَ مِنَ كُونَ

Wa iz qaala Moosaa liqawmiheee innal laaha yaamurukum an tazbahoo baqaratan qaalooo atattakhizunna huzuwan qaala a'oozu billaahi an akoona minal jaahileen

Before we proceed any further, it is vital to understand the purpose of the *Law Covenant*. The following verses clearly define the divine purpose of the *Law Covenant:*

Hebrews 10:1-4: The Law is a shadow of the good things to come, but not the very reality of the things. Therefore, the sacrifices which are offered year after year can never make those offering them perfect. Otherwise, these sacrifices would have been stopped since those once cleansed would not have the burden of sins anymore. On the contrary, these sacrifices are a reminder of sins year after year, for it is not possible for the blood of bulls and of goats to take sins away.

The Bible reveals that the "Law is a shadow of the good things to come." Therefore, it is only a shadow and not the actual substance or the reality of the things it foreshadows. Thus, the requirement of animal sacrifices under the Law Covenant foreshadows something greater to come. Confirming this, the above verses testify that "it is not possible for the blood of bulls and of goats to take sins away." Therefore, the animal sacrifices are only a shadow of a greater Sacrifice to come. We do not have to guess to whom the reality of this shadow belongs to. The Bible provides the answer:

Colossians 2:17: Those things are a shadow of the things to come, but the reality belongs to the Christ.

This is why God foretold in advance that the Law Covenant will eventually be replaced with a New Covenant when Jesus Christ to whom the "reality belongs" arrives. This truth was revealed in the Hebrew Scriptures (Old Testament) centuries before the arrival of Jesus. Through the prophet Jeremiah, God foretold:

Jeremiah 31:31-33: "Look! The days are coming," declares Jehovah, "when I will make with the house of Israel and with the house of Judah a New Covenant. It will not be like the Covenant that I made with their forefathers on the day when I led them out of Egypt, which they broke even though I was their true master."

"After those days I will make a New Covenant with the house of Israel," declares Jehovah. "I will put my law within them, and in their heart, I will write it. And I will become their God, and they will become my people."

When the time came, God established the New Covenant not with fleshly Israel but with spiritual Israel. In other words, with the anointed members of the Christian congregation. Jesus Christ confirmed this truth when spoke to his faithful apostles on the final night before his death:

Luke 22:20: "This cup means the new covenant by virtue of my blood, which is to be poured out in your behalf."

Just as the blood of the animals validated the Law Covenant between God and ancient Israel, the blood of Jesus validated the New Covenant. This was fulfilled when Jesus poured out his blood in sacrificial death on the execution stake. Just as Moses was the mediator of the Law Covenant, Jesus became the mediator of the New Covenant. The Christian Greek Scriptures (New Testament) clearly document both the establishment and the details of the New Covenant:

Hebrews 9:12-17: He (Jesus) entered into the holy place, not with the blood of goats and of young bulls, but with his own blood, once for all time, and obtained an everlasting deliverance for us. For if the blood of goats and of bulls and the ashes of a heifer sprinkled on those who have been defiled sanctifies for the cleansing of the flesh, how much more will the blood of the Christ, who through an everlasting spirit offered himself without blemish to God, cleanse our consciences from dead works so that we may render sacred service to the living God?

That is why he is a mediator of a new covenant, in order that because a death has occurred for their release by ransom from the transgressions under the former covenant, those who have been called may receive the promise of the everlasting inheritance. For where there is a covenant, the death of the human covenanter needs to be established, because a covenant is valid at death.

Hebrews 12:24: "And Jesus the mediator of a new covenant . . ."

Of course, all these Scriptural truths would be far too deep for Muslims to fathom. However, what is essentially for Muslims to understand for now is that in agreement with the Bible's testimony that God established a *Covenant* with the *Christians*, the Qur'an too acknowledges this fact. It confirms that God did make a *Covenant* with the *Christians:*

Surah 5:14: "Likewise, We also made a covenant with those who call themselves Christians . . ." (Farook Malik)

ٱلْعَدَاوَ بَيْنَهُمْ فَأَغْرَيْنَا بِهِ ذُكِّرُواْ مِّمَّا حَظًّا فَنَسُواْ مِيثَـٰقَهُمْ أَخَذْنَا نَصَـٰرَىٰٓ إِنَّا قَالُوٓاْ ٱلَّذِينَ وَمِنَ
يَصْنَعُونَ كَانُواْ بِمَا ٱللَّهُ يُنَبِّئُهُمُ وَسَوْفَ ۚ ٱلْقِيَـٰمَةِ يَوْمِ إِلَىٰ وَٱلْبَغْضَاءَ ةَ

Wa minal lazeena qaalooo innaa nasaaraaa akhaznaa meesaaqahum fanasoo hazzam mimmaa zukkiroo bihee fa aghrainaa bainahumul 'adaawata walbaghdaaa'a ilaa yawmil Qiyaamah; wa sawfa yunabbi'uhumul laahu bimaa kaanoo yasna'oon

SAHIH INTERNATIONAL:

And from those who say, "We are Christians" We took their covenant; but they forgot a portion of that of which they were reminded. So We caused among them animosity and hatred until the Day of Resurrection. And Allah is going to inform them about what they used to do.

Apart from admitting that God made a *Covenant* with the *Christians,* the Qur'an provides no other details. That is why the Bible is an indispensable source of information since it alone contains all the facts that are essential for our discussion on this subject. The information that we provided above can only be found in the Bible. Only when we consider all the conditions that are involved in the establishment and validation of the *Covenant* that God made with the *Christians,* we will be able to see an irrefutable contradiction in the Qur'an.

For God to establish a *Covenant* with the *Christians,* a sacrifice would be absolutely necessary to validate that *Covenant.* Jesus became that *Sacrifice* when he was executed on the stake. And history verifies this. Therefore, when *Surah 5:14* confirms the fact that God made a *Covenant* with the *Christians,* it actually validates the Christian position regarding the sacrificial death of Jesus. Thus, this Qur'anic verse actually proves that the denial of the death of Jesus in the Qur'an is a lie. In fact, *Surah 4:157* which denies the death of Jesus contradicts many other verses in the Qur'an which clearly confirm that Jesus died. Please read the previous article.

The *Christian Covenant* came into force through the *shed blood* of Jesus. It is crucial for Muslims to understand why this *Covenant* is important not only for Christians but also for Muslims. The eternal salvation of all Muslims depends not only in understanding God's purpose for establishing this *Covenant* but more importantly in accepting this divine arrangement of God:

'*Romans 3:23-25: For all have sinned and fall short of the glory of God, and it is as a free gift that they are being declared righteous by his undeserved kindness through the release by the ransom paid by Christ Jesus. God presented him as an offering for propitiation through faith in his blood.*

It is vital for Muslims to note that there is perfect harmony between the Jewish and the Christian Scriptures. There is perfect harmony between the Law Covenant and the New Covenant. One foreshadows the other. The Qur'an does not fit into this equation. The Qur'an is clearly in error for denying the death of Jesus Christ. *Hebrews 13:20: Now may the God of peace, who brought up from the dead the great shepherd of the sheep, our Lord Jesus, with the blood of an everlasting Covenant.*

We have compelling evidences to put our full trust in this *Covenant* which Jehovah God has arranged to save mankind from sin and death.

CHAPTER XIX

MUSLIMS SHOULD REJECT ISLAM
FOR CHRISTIANITY

After reading about Jesus in the Quran, here are the reasons why you should reject Islam for Christianity.

For your information, today a growing number of Muslims are leaving Islam. While some are turning to atheism, many are embracing Christianity. As a result, Muslim leaders in Islamic countries have organized anti-Christian seminars to discredit Christianity. What many ordinary Muslims fail to realize is the amount of lies that is deliberately passed off as facts at these seminars by the scholars of Islam. This willful deceit is carried out in a desperate effort to tarnish the image of Christianity. For the benefit of sincere Muslims, we will begin this article by first looking into an example of the deception of these self-appointed champions of Islam. After which, we will discuss the 10 REASONS WHY MUSLIMS SHOULD BECOME CHRISTIANS. Let's begin.

Some pseudo-Islamic scholars claim that the Christians are betraying God by consuming pork which is forbidden in the *Torah (Old Testament).* By using this argument to their advantage, they subtly claim for the legitimacy of Islam since it likewise prohibits the eating of pork. Is it really true that everything that is forbidden for the Jews under the Mosaic Law applies also to the Christians? We will use a verse from the Qur'an to answer this question. Addressing the early Christians, Jesus revealed a vital truth in the following Qur'anic verse:

Surah 3:50: I have come to you, to attest the Law which was before me. And to make lawful to you part of what was before forbidden to you; I have come to you with a Sign from your Lord. So fear God, and obey me." (Yusuf Ali)

عَلَيْكُمْ حُرِّمَ ٱلَّذِى بَعْضَ وَلِأُحِلَّ ٱلتَّوْرَٰةِ مِنَ يَدَىَّ بَيْنَ لِّمَا وَمُصَدِّقًا
وَأَطِيعُونِ ٱللَّهَ فَٱتَّقُوا۟ رَّبِّكُمْ مِّن بِـَٔايَةٍ وَجِئْتُكُم

Wa musaddiqal limaa baina yadaiya minat Tawraati wa liuhilla lakum ba'dal lazee hurrima 'alaikum; wa ji'tukum bi Aayatim mir Rabbikum fattaqul laaha wa atee'oon

SAHIH INTERNATIONAL:

And [I have come] confirming what was before me of the Torah and to make lawful for you some of what was forbidden to you. And I have come to you with a sign from your Lord, so fear Allah and obey me.

According to the above Qur'anic verse, Jesus clearly stated that he will make *"lawful"* for the Christians what was *"forbidden"* for them before under the Mosaic Law. This makes perfect sense since the Bible which precedes the Qur'an by centuries also teaches that with the coming of Jesus, Christians are no longer under the Law Covenant but under the Law of the Christ. As such, it was no longer mandatory for the Christians to observe the Mosaic Law. And this included the dietary restrictions of the Mosaic Law. The amendments initiated by Jesus for the Christians will certainly be reflected in their abstaining from observing the regulations that were specifically sanctioned for the Jews. And this is also true of Christians today. Hence, if these pseudo-Islamic scholars were to insist that the Christians also observe the Mosaic Law in the same way as the Jews do, then the above Qur'anic verse becomes false instantly since it clearly presupposes a change in the regulations for the Christians with the coming of Jesus.

These pseudo-Islamic scholars clearly fail to understand that the words of Jesus in *Surah 3:50* will inevitably result in changes for the Christians. In fact, this Qur'anic verse is saying the very opposite of what these pseudo-Islamic scholars are erroneously accusing the Christians of committing. Contrary to their claims, Christians would be acting in disobedience not for failing to observe the restrictions but for persisting to observe the restrictions that were removed and made *"lawful"* by Jesus. Therefore, to insist that Christians must observe the restrictions will amount to a denial of the teachings of Jesus Christ in Surah 3:50.

Furthermore, since the early Christians were commanded to preach the message of the Gospel to the far ends of the earth, many left the Jewish nation to distant lands. (*Matthew 28:19-20, Acts 1:8*) As such, the lifting of the dietary restrictions of the Jews wisely eliminated any unnecessary burden for the Christians who were now living among the Gentiles.

We will now expose the hypocrisy of these pseudo-Islamic scholars. What these pseudo-Islamic scholars do not reveal to the Muslims is that it is the Qur'an that violates many of the teachings which God gave to the Jews. And they also do not disclose to the Muslims that it is Islam which does not follow the dietary laws that were given to the Jews under the Mosaic Law. In fact, Islam is guilty of the very accusation that these pseudo-Islamic scholars deceitfully raise against the Christians. Consider for example the divine approval of camel flesh for consumption in Islam. Did you know that camel flesh is strictly forbidden under the Law given to Moses in the Torah?

Deuteronomy 14:6-7: You may eat any animal that has a split hoof divided into two and that chews the cud. But you must not eat the camel, the hare, and the rock badger, because they chew the cud but do not have split hooves. They are unclean for you.

And even the Qur'an acknowledges that God's law in the Torah prohibited the Jews from consuming camel flesh:

Surah 6:146: And to those imbued with Jewish doctrines and principles We forbade every animal with undivided hoof – camels, rabbits, hares – and of the oxen and the sheep We forbade them only their fat except the fat covering their backs and their entrails and the fat attached to the bones. (Al-Muntakhab)

ظُفُرٍ ذِى كُلَّ حَرَّمْنَا هَادُواْ ٱلَّذِينَ وَعَلَى

ٱخْ مَا أَوِ ٱلْحَوَايَآ أَوْ ظُهُورُهُمَا إِلَّا شُحُومَهُمَا عَلَيْهِمْ حَرَّمْنَا وَٱلْغَنَمِ ٱلْبَقَرِ وَمِنَ

لَصَٰدِقُونَ وَإِنَّا بِبَغْيِهِمْ جَزَيْنَٰهُم ذَٰلِكَ بِعَظْمٍ تَلَطَ

Wa 'alal lazeena haadoo harramnaa kulla zee zufurinw wa minal baqari walghanami harramnaa 'alaihim shuhoo mahumaaa illaa maa hamalat zuhooruhumaaa awil hawaayaaa aw makhtalata bi'azm; zaalika jazainaahum bibaghyihim wa innaa la saadiqoon

Yet, in contradiction with itself, the Qur'an authorizes the Muslims to consume camel flesh which according to the divine Law of God in the Torah is considered unclean for food:

Surah 22:36: And the camels and cows did We make lawful for you to use in the event of your oblation of thanks giving and in your offering. They serve as a store from which you obtain advantages in plenty. Therefore, pronounce Allah's Name on them as they are lined up, slaughtered and laid on their sides. You may eat therefrom and feed him who is content and satisfied in mind despite poverty. (Al-Muntakhab)

صَوَآفَّ عَلَيْهَا ٱللَّهِ ٱسْمَ فَٱذْكُرُواْ خَيْرٌ فِيهَا لَكُمُ ٱللَّهِ شَعَٰٓئِرِ مِّن لَكُم جَعَلْنَٰهَا وَٱلْبُدْنَ

وَٱلْمُعْتَرَّ ٱلْقَانِعَ وَأَطْعِمُواْ مِنْهَا فَكُلُواْ جُنُوبُهَا وَجَبَتْ فَإِذَا

تَشْكُرُونَ لَعَلَّكُمْ لَكُمْ سَخَّرْنَٰهَا كَذَٰلِكَ

Walbudna ja'alnaahaa lakum min sha'aaa'iril laahi lakum feehaa khairun fazkurusmal laahi 'alaihaa sawaaff; fa izaa wajabat junoobuhaa fakuloo minhaa wa at'imul qaani'a walmu'tarr; kazaalika sakhkharnaahaa lakum la'allakum tashkuroon

What explanation will these pseudo-Islamic scholars now conjure up to reconcile this contradiction in Islam? According to the Qur'an, Allah clearly made it unlawful for the Jews to consume camel flesh as food. How can Allah then permit the Muslims to consume camel flesh? Is Allah suffering from schizophrenia? We can cite many more examples but this is sufficient to expose the deceit of these pseudo-Islamic scholars. What Muslims need to understand is that these pseudo-Islamic scholars are not deceiving the Christians but their own fellow Muslims with their lies.

There are numerous valid reasons why Muslims should leave Islam and become Christians. Either Christianity is true or Islam is. Both cannot be equally true. Muslims need to make a choice. However, their decision should not be based on emotion or sentiment but on evidences. Ironically, evidences from both the Qur'an and the Sources of Islam themselves incriminate Islam. In this article we will provide 10 REASONS WHY MUSLIMS SHOULD BECOME CHRISTIANS if they truly value their eternal salvation. We encourage Muslims to read this article carefully. Our objective for writing this article is not to challenge or condemn the Muslims but to show them the true path of salvation. We sincerely care for the spiritual welfare of our Muslim friends. We believe that Muslims are the primary victims of Islam.

CHAPTER XX

ONE: THE DISQUALIFICATION OF ISLAM

One: The disqualification of Islam.

Muslims, please read *Surah 3:81* very carefully. And please read it with understanding. This single Qur'anic verse disqualifies Allah as the true God, disqualifies Muhammad as a true prophet, and disqualifies the Qur'an as the inspired Word of God. We sincerely invite you to respond to the incriminating evidences of this Qur'anic verse against the legitimacy of Islam. If you are unable to do so, then it is time to leave Islam. If you find this allegation unbelievable, we encourage you to examine the facts presented here. We will start with the reading of *Surah 3:81:*

And remember when Allah took the Covenant of the Prophets, saying: "Take whatever I gave you from the Book and Hikmah (understanding of the Laws of Allah), and afterwards there will come to you a Messenger (Muhammad SAW) confirming what is with you; you must, then, believe in him and help him." Allah said: "Do you agree to it and will you take up My Covenant which I conclude with you?" They said: "We agree." He said: "Then bear witness; and I am with you among the witnesses for this." (Hilali-Khan)

لَ مَعَكُمْ لِمَا مُصَدِّقٌ جَاءَكُمْ رَسُولٌ ثُمَّ وَحِكْمَةٍ كِتَـٰبٍ مِّن ءَاتَيْتُكُم لَمَآ ٱلنَّبِيِّـۧنَ مِيثَـٰقَ ٱللَّهُ أَخَذَ وَإِذْ
أَقْرَرْنَا قَالُوٓا۟ ۚ إِصْرِى ذَٰلِكُمْ عَلَىٰ وَأَخَذْتُمْ ءَأَقْرَرْتُمْ قَالَ ۚ وَلَتَنصُرُنَّهُۥ بِهِۦ تُؤْمِنُنَّ
ٱلشَّـٰهِدِينَ مِّن مَعَكُم وَأَنَا۠ فَٱشْهَدُوا۟ قَالَ ۚ

Wa iz akhazal laahu meesaaqan Nabiyyeena lamaaa
aataitukum min Kitaabinw wa Hikmatin summa jaaa'akum
Rasoolum musaddiqul limaa ma'akum latu'minunna bihee wa
latansurunnah; qaala a'aqrartum wa akhaztum alaa zaalikum
isree qaalooo aqrarnaa; qaala fashhadoo wa ana ma'akum minash
shaahideen.

SAHIH INTERNATIONAL:

And [recall, O People of the Scripture], when Allah took the
covenant of the prophets, [saying], "Whatever I give you of the
Scripture and wisdom and then there comes to you a messenger
confirming what is with you, you [must] believe in him and
support him." [Allah] said, "Have you acknowledged and taken
upon that My commitment?" They said, "We have acknowledged
it." He said, "Then bear witness, and I am with you among the
witnesses."

A careful examination of *Surah 3:81* reveals the following
facts:

*(1) Allah made a Covenant with the Prophets who lived before the time
of Muhammad.*

*(2) These Prophets were called upon by Allah to pledge their support to a
forthcoming Messenger who will to appear to them later.*

*(3) The Prophets agreed and Allah secured their pledge to help the
forthcoming Messenger by establishing a Covenant with them.*

*(4) This upcoming Messenger will confirm the previous Scripture of
Allah which is in the possession of the Prophets. Since the Prophets will
be present at the time when this Messenger arrives, they will personally
witness his confirmation of their sacred Book.*

*(5) Allah concludes the Covenant and bears witness with the Prophets to
ensure the fulfillment of his Covenant.*

As acknowledged by all Muslim scholars and clearly
testified in Hilali-Khan's translation of the Qur'an, the Messenger
in this Qur'anic verse refers to none other than Muhammad. This
raises some very vital questions. Who were the Prophets who
lived during the time of Muhammad's appearance as the
Messenger of Allah? Who were the Prophets on hand to assist

him? And who were the Prophets at hand to witness his confirmation of the previous Scripture? None!

Not a single *Prophet* lived during the time of Muhammad. And this is especially true regarding the *Prophets* with whom Allah concluded the Covenant. Yet, the Qur'an testifies that there would be *Prophets* present during the time of this *Messenger*. In fact, Allah swore these *Prophets* into his service to assist this forthcoming *Messenger*. And Allah himself bore witness with the *Prophets* that he will be with them to ensure the accomplishment of this Covenant. But there were no *Prophets* present during the time of Muhammad. This leaves us with two options.

One: Allah was mistaken in his claim that there would be other *Prophets* during the appearance of this *Messenger*.

Two: The *Messenger* mentioned in Surah 3:81 is referring to someone other than Muhammad. Either option spells disaster for Islam.

What is even more damaging for Islam is the fact that Muhammad excluded himself as the *Messenger* of Surah 3:81. Why do we say that? This is because Muhammad clearly ruled out the prospect for the co-existence of any other *Prophets* during his career as the *Messenger* of Allah. In other words, no other *Prophets* are supposed to exist anywhere on planet earth as a contemporary of Muhammad. Muhammad openly testified to this conclusion when he precisely informed his early Companions of this outcome in the following Hadith.

Sahih Muslim, Book 30, Number 5835:

Abu Huraira reported Allah's Messenger (may peace be upon him) as saying: I am most akin to Jesus Christ among the whole of mankind, and all the Prophets are of different mothers but belong to one religion and no Prophet was raised between me and Jesus.

Muhammad testified that no Prophets were raised between the time of Jesus and him. In other words, the only Prophet raised by Allah after the time of Jesus was Muhammad. And Islamic history is on the side of Muhammad. Historically, no other Prophets existed during his time as a Messenger of Allah. Yet, Allah testified in Surah 3:81 that there would be Prophets to help this new Messenger in his mission. Muhammad was more accurate than Allah and the Qur'an.

Since all Islamic scholars without exception recognize Muhammad as the Messenger of Surah 3:81, they must now explain why there were no Prophets at the time of Muhammad. Muslims cannot name a single Prophet who was a contemporary of Muhammad. The instant they come up with a name, Muhammad becomes a liar since he clearly testified that there would be no other Prophets after Jesus beside him. Thus, if the Qur'an is right about the presence of other Prophets at the time of this Messenger, then Muhammad cannot be the Messenger of Surah 3:81. Therefore, for the Qur'an to be true, Muhammad has to be disqualified. And for Muhammad to be true, the Qur'an has to be disqualified. Muslims have to now decide between a false prophet and a false book.

Surah 3:81 poses a real dilemma for Muslims. If the *Qur'an* is the inspired Word of God, then the prophetic proclamation of *Allah* stating that there would be *Prophets* to assist Muhammad should have taken place exactly as foretold by *Allah* in the *Qur'an.* But it did not. This is a double blow for Islam since both Allah and the Qur'an are completely mistaken. The only way out of this dilemma for Muslims is to deny Muhammad as the *Messenger* of Surah 3:81. However, this is even more damaging since Muslims will have to now reject Muhammad as their *Messenger.* Without Muhammad there will be no Islam. Furthermore, since the Qur'an declares that Muhammad is the final *Messenger* of Allah in Surah 33:40, then surely no other *Messenger* can be expected to appear at a later time to fulfill the *Covenant* in Surah 3:81.

Can Allah who commits multiple errors in a single Qur'anic verse qualify as the true God? His Covenant with the *Prophets* turns out to be false. His prophetic decision about the unification between the *Prophets* and the *Messenger* did not materialize as he foretold. There was not a single *Prophet* present at the time of Muhammad to validate his claim in Surah 3:81. This confirms that Allah is a fraud and the Qur'an is a lie.

If Muslims insist that Muhammad is indeed the *Messenger* of Surah 3:81, then the Qur'an is absolutely wrong in saying that there would be *Prophets* at hand to assist him in his mission. Thus, the Qur'an contains a serious error in it and it is as false as the unfulfilled Covenant of Allah. Either Allah was deliberately deceiving the Muslims with a false revelation in the Qur'an or he is downright ignorant and does not know the future. Either way, this disqualifies Allah as the true God. Since Islam disqualifies itself, and since the Qur'an destroys itself, it will be prudent for Muslims to leave Islam and turn to Christianity.

About 700 years before the arrival of Jesus, the prophet Isaiah was inspired by Jehovah to prophesy regarding the role of Jesus Christ as the Messiah:

Isaiah 61:1-2: The Spirit of the Sovereign Lord Jehovah is upon me, because Jehovah has anointed me to bring good news to the suffering and afflicted. He has sent me to comfort the brokenhearted, to announce liberty to captives, and to open the eyes of the blind. To proclaim the year of Jehovah's goodwill. And the day of vengeance of our God and to comfort all who mourn.

All four Gospel accounts of the Bible clearly testify to the precise fulfillment of the above prophecy of Jehovah. This prophecy was fulfilled word for word by Jesus when he accomplished his ministry here on earth. Do Muslims need proof to confirm the fulfillment of this outstanding prophecy of Jehovah? Read the following Qur'anic verses:

Surah 5:110: God said: "O Jesus son of Mary, recall My blessings upon you and your mother that I supported you with the Holy Spirit..., and you heal the blind and the leaper by My leave; and you brought out the dead by My leave. (The Monotheist Group)

إِذْ قَالَ ٱللَّهُ يَٰعِيسَى ٱبْنَ مَرْيَمَ ٱذْكُرْ نِعْمَتِى عَلَيْكَ وَعَلَىٰ وَٰلِدَتِكَ إِذْ أَيَّدتُّكَ بِرُوحِ ٱلْقُدُسِ تُكَلِّمُ ٱلنَّ

وَكَهْلًا ٱلْمَهْدِ فِى اسَ وَإِذْ عَلَّمْتُكَ ٱلْكِتَٰبَ وَٱلْحِكْمَةَ وَٱلتَّوْرَٰئَةَ وَٱلْإِنجِيلَ

بِإِذْنِى طَيْرًا فَتَكُونُ فِيهَا فَتَنفُخُ بِإِذْنِى ٱلطَّيْرِ كَهَيْئَةِ ٱلطِّينِ مِنَ تَخْلُقُ وَإِذْ

بِإِذْنِى ٱلْمَوْتَىٰ تُخْرِجُ وَإِذْ بِإِذْنِى وَٱلْأَبْرَصَ ٱلْأَكْمَهَ وَتُبْرِئُ

إِ هَٰذَآ إِنْ مِنْهُمْ كَفَرُواْ ٱلَّذِينَ فَقَالَ بِٱلْبَيِّنَٰتِ جِئْتَهُم إِذْ عَنكَ إِسْرَٰءِيلَ بَنِى كَفَفْتُ وَإِذْ

مُبِينٌ سِحْرٌ لَّا

Iz qaalal laahu yaa 'Eesab-na-Maryamaz kur ni'matee 'alaika wa 'alaa waalidatika; iz aiyattuka bi Roohil Qudusi tukallimun naasa fil mahdi wa kahlanw wa iz 'allamtukal kitaaba wal Hikmata wa Tawraata wal Injeela wa iz Takhluqu minat teeni kahai 'atit tairi bi iznee fatanfukhu feeha fatakoonu tairam bi iznee wa tubri'ul akmaha wal abrasa bi iznee wa iz tukhrijul mawtaa bi iznee wa iz kafaftu Baneee Israaa'eela 'anka iz ji'tahum bil baiyinaati fa qaalal lazeena kafaroo minhum in haazaaa illaa sihrum Mubeen

Surah 2:87: We gave Jesus, son of Mary, profound miracles and supported him with the Holy Spirit. (Khalifa)

وَأَيَّدْنَـٰهُ ٱلْبَيِّنَـٰتِ مَرْيَمَ ٱبْنَ عِيسَى وَءَاتَيْنَا بِٱلرُّسُلِ مِنْ وَقَفَّيْنَا ٱلْكِتَـٰبَ مُوسَى ءَاتَيْنَا وَلَقَدْ تَ وَفَرِيقًا كَذَّبْتُمْ فَفَرِيقًا ٱسْتَكْبَرْتُمْ أَنفُسُكُمُ تَهْوَىٰ لَا بِمَا رَسُولٌ جَآءَكُمْ أَفَكُلَّمَا ٱلْقُدُسِّ بِرُوحِ تَقْتُلُونَ

Wa laqad aatainaa Moosal Kitaaba wa qaffainaa mim ba'dihee bir Rusuli wa aatainaa 'Eesab-na-Maryamal baiyinaati wa ayyadnaahu bi Roohil Qudus; afakullamaa jaaa'akum Rasoolum bimaa laa tahwaaa anfusukumus takbartum fafareeqan kazzabtum wa fareeqan taqtuloon

Surah 3:49: As a messenger to the Children of Israel: "I come to you with a Sign from your Lord..., I restore vision to the blind, heal the leprous, and I revive the dead by God's leave. I can tell you what you eat, and what you store in your homes. This should be a proof for you, if you are believers." (Khalifa)

رَّبِّكُمْ مِّن بِـَٔايَةٍ جِئْتُكُم قَدْ أَنِّى إِسْرَٰٓءِيلَ بَنِىٓ إِلَىٰ وَرَسُولًا
ٱللَّهِ بِإِذْنِ طَيْرًا فِيهِ فَأَنفُخُ ٱلطَّيْرِ كَهَيْئَةِ ٱلطِّينِ مِّنَ لَكُم أَخْلُقُ أَنِّىٓ
ٱللَّهِ بِإِذْنِ ٱلْمَوْتَىٰ وَأُحْىِ وَٱلْأَبْرَصَ ٱلْأَكْمَهَ وَأُبْرِئُ
بُيُوتِكُمْ فِى تَدَّخِرُونَ وَمَا تَأْكُلُونَ بِمَا وَأُنَبِّئُكُم
مُّؤْمِنِينَ كُنتُم إِن لَّكُمْ لَـَٔايَةً ذَٰلِكَ فِى إِنَّ

Wa Rasoolan ilaa Baneee Israaa'eela annee qad ji'tukum bi Aayatim mir Rabbikum annee akhluqu lakum minatteeni kahai 'atittairi fa anfukhu feehi fayakoonu tairam bi iznil laahi wa ubri'ul akmaha wal abrasa wa uhyil mawtaa bi iznil laahi wa unabbi'ukum bimaa taakuloona wa maa taddakhiroona fee buyootikum; inna fee zaalika la Aayatal lakum in kuntum mu'mineen

The Qur'an did not exist when the prophecy regarding Jesus was recorded in the *Book of Isaiah*. Neither did the Qur'an exist when this prophecy was fulfilled by Jesus' centuries later. Thus, the source behind the inspiration and the eventual fulfillment of this prophecy cannot be Allah but Jehovah–the author of the Holy Bible. Yet, what is important for Muslims to recognize is the fact that the Qur'an acknowledges the fulfillment of this divine prophecy which God inspired centuries earlier in the Holy Bible. Of course, the Qur'an's purpose for doing so is merely to take advantage of the authentic accounts of the Bible to validate itself. We sincere hope that you as a Muslim will come to you sense and leave Islam. And we hope you will turn to Jehovah, the living God whose prophecies never fail.

CHAPTER XXI

TWO: THE FAILURE OF ALLAH'S PROPHECY IN THE QURAN

Two: The failure of Allah's prophecy in the Quran

Muslims, if you really believe that you are worshipping the true God, it would benefit you greatly to examine and evaluate the following prophecy of Allah in the Qur'an:

Surah 8:65: O Prophet! Rouse the Believers to the fight. If there are twenty amongst you, patient and persevering, they <u>will vanquish</u> two hundred: if a hundred, they <u>will vanquish</u> a thousand of the Unbelievers. (Yusuf Ali)

ٱلْقِتَالِ عَلَى ٱلْمُؤْمِنِينَ حَرِّضِ ٱلنَّبِىُّ يَـٰٓأَيُّهَا
مِّائَتَيْنِ يَغْلِبُوا۟ صَـٰبِرُونَ عِشْرُونَ مِّنكُمْ يَكُن إِن
يَفْقَهُونَ لَّا قَوْمٌ بِأَنَّهُمْ كَفَرُوا۟ ٱلَّذِينَ مِّنَ أَلْفًا يَغْلِبُوٓا۟ مِّائَةٌ مِّنكُم يَكُن وَإِن

Yaaa aiyuhan Nabiyyu harridil mu'mineena 'alal qitaal; iny-yakum minkum 'ishroona saabiroona yaghliboo mi'atayn; wa iny-yakum minkum min'atuny yaghlibooo alfam minal lazeena kafaroo bi anahum qawmul laa yafqahoon

Allah prophesied in no uncertain terms that from now on–from the time this prophecy was revealed in the Qur'an–a single Muslim warrior who ventures into battle *"will vanquish"* enemies ten times more numerous. A ratio of 1:10. Allah guarantees this stunning victory at every confrontation encountered between the Muslims and their enemies. This means the Muslim victory is an inevitable conclusion. Thus, the victory is assured even before the Muslims actually engage their enemies in battle. Hence, the success of the battle rests not in the hands of the Muslim warriors but in the mighty power of Allah the Almighty. It is the predetermined will of Allah that his Muslim warriors will vanquish all their enemies–every one of them. Allah was so sure of the outcome that he even sealed the prophecy by permanently inscribing it in the Qur'an. Can anyone or anything change the determined will of Allah?

However, just *one verse* later, Allah *abrogated* his own infallible prophecy. He *abolished* the prophecy wherein he foretold the exact ratio of the number of enemies that the Muslim warriors would be able to overcome in battle. Allah guaranteed this much but, in the end, he failed to ensure its success. Therefore, Allah had to dishonorably abrogate and replace his failed prophecy with yet another prophecy. The substituted prophecy of Allah now states:

Surah 8:66: For the present, Allah hath lightened your task, for He knoweth that there is a weak spot in you: But even so, if there are a hundred of you, patient and persevering, they will vanquish two hundred, and if a thousand, they will vanquish two thousand, with the leave of Allah: for Allah is with those who patiently persevere. (Yusuf Ali)

Well, why did Allah invalidate his own divine prophecy and change the ratio from 1:10 to 1:2? It was because the Muslim warriors did not trust Allah with their lives. When Muhammad related Allah's prophetic message to them, they became fearful. Even though the *prophecy* which guarantees that they *"will vanquish"* enemies more numerous than them is inscribed in the Qur'an, the Muslim warriors knew better. Just as much as they did not trust Allah, neither did they trust the Qur'an. And they complained bitterly at the impossible odds they would have to now encounter when engaging their enemies in battles. There are numerous authentic Islamic sources confirming this as the only reason for the abrogation of Allah's prophecy. Provided below is just one out of the many Hadiths to substantiate this fact.

Sahih Bukhari, Volume 6, Book 60, Number 176:

Narrated Ibn Abbas: When the Verse: – 'If there are twenty steadfast amongst you (Muslims), they will overcome two-hundred (non-Muslims).' was revealed, it became hard on the Muslims when it became compulsory that one Muslim ought not to flee (in war) before ten (non-Muslims). So (Allah) lightened the order by revealing:
'But now Allah has lightened your task for He knows that there is weakness in you. So, if there are of you one-hundred steadfast, they will overcome two-hundred (non-Muslims).' (Surah 8:66) So when Allah reduced the number of enemies which Muslims should withstand, their patience and perseverance against the enemy decreased as much as their task was lightened for them.

As we can see, Surah 8:66 was revealed only after the Muslim warriors became fearful and complained bitterly to Muhammad. Thus, lack of faith led to the invalidation of the eternal Word of Allah. Allah was forced to change his divine prophecy because of the failings of humans to follow his divine direction. And as a result, Allah changed the prophetic ratio from 1:10 to 1:2 in the mother of all books–the Holy Qur'an. This proves that either Allah has no knowledge of the future or he just does not have the power to see through to the fulfillment of his prophecies. We would like to ask the Muslims the following questions:

- How can the failings of humans to follow a divine direction result in the failure of Allah's prophecy?
- Can mere humans effect the invalidation of a divine prophecy?
- Why did not Allah know that his warriors would not be able to cope with his demand to defeat enemies ten times their number?
- Is it not because Allah did not know the weakness of the Muslims?
- Why did not Allah know their weakness just one verse away?
- Why did Allah choose to lower the prophesied ratio from 1:10 to 1:2 instead of raising the power, strength

and courage of his warriors to measure up to task as he had predicted in his prophecy?

- Can Muslims trust Allah with their eternal salvation when he could neither foresee nor prevent the failure of his divine prophecy?

Concerning Jehovah God, the Holy Bible states:

Isaiah 46:10: The One telling from the beginning the finale, and from long ago the things that have not been done.

And every single prophecy of Jehovah is certain to be fulfilled without fail:

Isaiah 55:11: So, my word that goes out of my mouth will be. It will not return to me without results. It will certainly accomplish whatever is my delight. And it will certainly succeed in what I send it to do.

There are hundreds of inspired prophecies in the Bible. And they cover a wide range of subjects. However, Jesus is the focal point on which all prophecies concentrate, and they shed light on his central role in the outworking of God's divine purpose. Many of these prophecies center on the birth, life and the death of Jesus Christ. We will consider just one example to prove the reliability of Jehovah's prophecies. More than *700 years* before the birth of Jesus took place, Jehovah prophesied the *virgin-birth* of Jesus in the *Book of Isaiah:*

Isaiah 7:14: "Therefore the Lord himself will give you a sign: behold, a virgin shall conceive, and bear a son."

Exactly as foretold, Jesus was conceived without a human father. And the Bible records the fulfillment of this absolutely unique prophecy:

Luke 1:30-35: And the angel said to her: "Do not be afraid, Mary, for you have found favor with God. Behold! You will conceive in your womb and bear a son, and you are to call his name Jesus. This one will be great and will be called Son of the Most High; and the Lord God will give him the throne of David his father, and he will rule as king over the house of Jacob forever, and there will be no end of his kingdom." But Mary said to the angel: "How is this to be, since I am a virgin?" In answer the angel said to her: "Holy Spirit will come upon you and power of the Most High will overshadow you. Therefore the child to be born will be called holy — the Son of God."

Matthew 1:22-23: All this actually came about for that to be fulfilled which was spoken by the Lord God through his prophet, saying: "Look! The virgin will become pregnant and will give birth to a son."

Do Muslims need a confirmation that the prophecy of Jehovah in Isaiah came to its fulfillment exactly as the Gospel accounts of Luke and Matthew testify? The Qur'an itself confirms the fulfillment of this divine prophecy of Jehovah in the following verses:

Surah 3:45-47: Behold! The angels said: "O Mary! God giveth thee glad tidings of a Word from Him: his name will be Christ Jesus, the son of Mary, held in honour in this world and the Hereafter and of (the company of) those nearest to God...She said: "O my Lord! How shall I have a son when no man hath touched me?" He said: "Even so: God createth what He willeth: When He hath decreed a plan, He but saith to it, 'Be,' and it is!" (Yusuf Ali)

وَجِيهًا مَرْيَمَ ٱبْنُ عِيسَى ٱلْمَسِيحُ ٱسْمُهُ مِّنْهُ بِكَلِمَةٍ يُبَشِّرُكِ ٱللَّهَ إِنَّ يَٰمَرْيَمُ ٱلْمَلَٰٓئِكَةُ قَالَتِ إِذْ ٱلْمُقَرَّبِينَ وَمِنَ وَٱلْٓءَاخِرَةِ ٱلدُّنْيَا فِى

Iz qaalatil malaaa'ikatu yaa Maryamu innal laaha yubashshiruki bi Kalimatim minhus muhul Maseehu 'Eesab nu Maryama wajeehan fid dunyaa wal Aakhirati wa minal muqarrabeen

SAHIH INTERNATIONAL:

[And mention] when the angels said, "O Mary, indeed Allah gives you good tidings of a word from Him, whose name will be the Messiah, Jesus, the son of Mary - distinguished in this world and the Hereafter and among those brought near [to Allah].

ٱلصَّٰلِحِينَ وَمِنَ وَكَهْلًا ٱلْمَهْدِ فِى ٱلنَّاسَ وَيُكَلِّمُ

Wa yukallimun naasa filmahdi wa kahlanw wa minassaaliheen

SAHIH INTERNATIONAL:

He will speak to the people in the cradle and in maturity and will be of the righteous."

بَشَرٌ يَمْسَسْنِى وَلَمْ وَلَدٌ لِى يَكُونُ أَنَّىٰ رَبِّ قَالَتْ   يَشَآءُ مَا يَخْلُقُ ٱللَّهُ كَذَٰلِكِ قَالَ

فَيَكُونُ كُن لَهُ يَقُولُ فَإِنَّمَا أَمْرًا قَضَىٰٓ إِذَا

Qaalat Rabbi annaa yakoonu lee waladunw wa lam yamsasnee basharun qaala kazaalikil laahu yakhluqu maa yashaaa'; izaa qadaaa amran fa innamaa yaqoolu lahoo kun fayakoon

SAHIH INTERNATIONAL:

She said, "My Lord, how will I have a child when no man has touched me?" [The angel] said, "Such is Allah; He creates what He wills. When He decrees a matter, He only says to it, 'Be,' and it is.

Another passage in the Qur'an also recognizes the fulfillment of the prophecy of Jehovah regarding the unique conception of Jesus Christ:

Surah 19:17-21: She placed a screen (to screen herself) from them; then We sent her our angel, and he appeared before her as a man in all respects. She said: "I seek refuge from thee to (God) Most Gracious: (come not near) if thou dost fear God." He said: "Nay, I am only an apostle from thy Lord, (to announce) to thee the gift of a holy son." She said: "How shall I have a son, seeing that no man has touched me, and I am not unchaste?" He said: "So it will be: Thy Lord saith, 'that is easy for Me: and (We wish) to appoint him as a Sign unto men and a Mercy from Us': It is a matter so decreed." (Yusuf Ali)

سَوِيًّا بَشَرًا لَهَا فَتَمَثَّلَ رُوحَنَا إِلَيْهَا فَأَرْسَلْنَآ حِجَابًا مِن دُونِهِمْ فَٱتَّخَذَتْ

19:17

Fattakhazat min doonihim hijaaban fa arsalnaaa ilaihaa roohanaa fatamassala lahaa basharan sawiyyaa

SAHIH INTERNATIONAL:

And she took, in seclusion from them, a screen. Then We sent to her Our Angel, and he represented himself to her as a well-proportioned man.

تَقِيًّا كُنتَ إِن مِنكَ بِٱلرَّحْمَـٰنِ أَعُوذُ إِنِّىٓ قَالَتْ

19:18

Qaalat inneee a'oozu bir Rahmaani minka in kunta taqiyyaa

SAHIH INTERNATIONAL:

She said, "Indeed, I seek refuge in the Most Merciful from you, [so leave me], if you should be fearing of Allah."

زَكِيًّا غُلَـٰمًا لَكِ لِأَهَبَ رَبِّكِ رَسُولُ أَنَا إِنَّمَآ قَالَ

19:19

Qaala innamaa ana rasoolu Rabbiki li ahaba laki ghulaaman zakiyyaa

SAHIH INTERNATIONAL:

He said, "I am only the messenger of your Lord to give you [news of] a pure boy."

بَغِيًّا أَكُ وَلَمْ بَشَرٌ يَمْسَسْنِى وَلَمْ غُلَمٌ لِى يَكُونُ أَنَّىٰ قَالَتْ
19:20

Qaalat anna yakoonu lee ghulaamunw wa lam yamsasnee bashrunw wa lam aku baghiyyaa

SAHIH INTERNATIONAL:

She said, "How can I have a boy while no man has touched me and I have not been unchaste?"

مَّقْضِيًّا أَمْرًا وَكَانَ مِّنَّا وَرَحْمَةً لِّلنَّاسِ ءَايَةً وَلِنَجْعَلَهُ هَيِّنٌ عَلَىَّ هُوَ رَبُّكِ قَالَ كَذَٰلِكِ قَالَ
19:21

Qaala kazaaliki qaala Rabbuki huwa 'alaiya haiyimunw wa linaj 'alahooo Aayatal linnaasi wa rahmatam minnaa; wa kaana amram maqdiyyaa

SAHIH INTERNATIONAL:

He said, "Thus [it will be]; your Lord says, 'It is easy for Me, and We will make him a sign to the people and a mercy from Us. And it is a matter [already] decreed.' "

Since the Qur'an did not exist before the time of Jesus, it would be simply impossible for the Qur'an to contain a single prophecy regarding him. And since the Qur'an did not exist during the time of Jesus presence, it simply could not be on hand to record the unfolding of the prophecies surrounding his virgin-birth. Therefore, when the Qur'an acknowledges the virgin-birth of Jesus, it is testifying to something beyond itself. It is testifying to the absolute reliability of the prophecies of Jehovah and their unfailing fulfillment. The Qur'an also recognizes the fact that the miraculous conception was *"decreed"* by God. Since it was not Allah but Jehovah who prophesized the virgin-birth of Jesus centuries in advance in the Holy Bible, it must surely be Jehovah who decreed this unique conception of Jesus Christ. In contrast to the reliability of the prophecies of Jehovah, Surah 8:65-66 is an indisputable proof that even the very short-termed prophecies of Allah failed in their fulfillment. This should give Muslims another compelling reason to leave Islam and become Christians.

CHAPTER XXII

THREE: ALLAH CONSPIRES WITH THE DEMONS

Three: Allah conspires with the Demons

Muslims, we sincerely hope that the following Qur'anic verse will alert you to come to your senses and leave the cult of Islam. Surah 6:112 clearly admits that Allah has "appointed devils of men and Jinns (demons)" to serve as enemies to mislead the Prophets of God:

Surah 6:112: "So have We appointed for every Prophet an enemy - devils of men and Jinns; who inspire each other with seductive, deceptive speech which leads astray, but had your Lord willed they would not have done so." (H. S. Aziz)

أَلْقَوْ زُخْرُفَ بَعْضٍ إِلَىٰ بَعْضُهُمْ يُوحِى وَٱلْجِنِّ ٱلْإِنسِ شَيَٰطِينَ عَدُوًّا لِكُلِّ نَبِىٍّ جَعَلْنَا وَكَذَٰلِكَ
يَفْتَرُونَ وَمَا فَذَرْهُمْ ۚ فَعَلُوهُ مَا رَبُّكَ شَآءَ وَلَوْ ۚ غُرُورًا ال

Wa kazaalika ja'alnaa likulli nabiyyin 'aduwwan Shayaateenal insi waljinni yoohee ba'duhum ilaa ba'din zukhrufal qawli ghurooraa; wa law shaaa'a Rabbuka maa fa'aloohu fazarhum wa maa yaftaroon

SAHIH INTERNATIONAL:

And thus We have made for every prophet an enemy - devils from mankind and jinn, inspiring to one another decorative speech in delusion. But if your Lord had willed, they would not have done it, so leave them and that which they invent.

The above Qur'anic verse clearly confirms the following facts. One: Allah took it upon himself to personally appoint *"devils of men and Jinns"* to oppose the Prophets of God–every single one of them. Two: Allah is in union with the Jinns who are actually demonic spirit creatures. This shady character of Allah should alert sincere Muslims. The objective of these enemies–both humans and demons–is to use *"seductive, deceptive speech which leads astray"* to mislead the Prophets of God. Additionally, this Qur'anic verse also reveals that these appointed enemies of the Prophets *"would not have done so"* had it not been the intention of Allah. In other words, it is the determined will of Allah to use these *"devils of men and Jinns"* to resist the Prophets of God. Would the true God act in such an evil manner towards his Prophets?

In complete contrast to Allah, the Bible reveals how Jehovah God cares for his Prophets. And it reveals how he protects them from being deceived by their adversaries:

Psalms 105:14-15: "And God did not allow any human to defraud them, But on their account he reproved kings, Saying: 'Do not you men touch my anointed ones, And to my Prophets do nothing bad.'"

Can you not see the immense difference between Allah and Jehovah? One ensnares the Prophets of God by appointing evil enemies to deceive them, while the other protects them from the deception of the evil enemies. Who do you think acts like the true Creator? Is it Jehovah or Allah? In fact, not only Jehovah protects his Prophets but he also invites all true worshippers to come under his protection:

James 4:7: Therefore, subject yourselves to God; but oppose the Devil, and he will flee from you.

Think! If Allah personally appoints *"devils of men and Jinns"* to serve as enemies to the very appointed Prophets of God, where do ordinary Muslims stand? And even more damaging is the fact that instead of protecting the Prophets of God, Allah protects the evil demons:

Surah 21:81-82: "(It was Our power that made) the violent (unruly) wind flow (tamely) for Solomon, to his order, to the land which We had blessed: for We do know all things. And of the evil ones, were some who dived for him, and did other work besides; and it was We Who guarded them." (Yusuf Ali)

Surah 21:82: And from the devils who dive for him, and they make/do a work/deed other than that, and We were for them protecting/observing. (Literal Translation by Samira)

رَبِّعِ بِكُلِّ وَكُنَّا فِيهَأ بُرَكَنَا تِي ٱلْأَرْضِ إِلَى بِأَمْرِةٍ تَجْرِي عَاصِفَةً ٱلرِّيحَ وَلِسُلَيْمَٰنَ لِمِينَ

21:81

Wa li Sulaimaanar reeha 'aasifatan tajree bi amriheee ilal ardil latee baaraknaa feehaa; wa kunnaa bikulli shai'in 'aalimeen

SAHIH INTERNATIONAL:

And to Solomon [We subjected] the wind, blowing forcefully, proceeding by his command toward the land which We had blessed. And We are ever, of all things, Knowing.

حْفِظِينَ لَهُمْ وَكُنَّا ذَٰلِكَ دُونَ عَمَلًا وَيَعْمَلُونَ لَهُۥ يَغُوصُونَ مَن ٱلشَّيَٰطِينِ وَمِن

21:82

Wa minash Shayaateeni mai yaghoosoona lahoo wa ya'maloona 'amalan doona zaalika wa kunna lahum haafizeen

SAHIH INTERNATIONAL:

And of the devils were those who dived for him and did work other than that. And We were of them a guardian.

The fact that Allah protects the *"devils"* helps us to identify who Allah really is. According to the Bible, it is the will of Jehovah to destroy Satan and the demons. And this will take place soon:

Romans 16:20: For his part, the God who gives peace will crush Satan under your feet shortly.

Muslims, you have a choice here. Do you want to serve a deity who conspires with the Devil and his demons or do you want to serve the true God who invites you to come under his protection from the Devil and his demons?

CHAPTER

XXIII

FOUR: WHY ALLAH CANNOT BE OUR
CREATOR

Four: Why Allah cannot be our Creator

The Qur'an teaches that the person who steals should have his hand cut off:

Surah 5:38: "As to the thief, Male or female, cut off his or her hands: a punishment by way of example, from God, for their crime: and God is exalted in power." (Yusuf Ali)

وَٱلسَّارِقُ وَٱلسَّارِقَةُ فَٱقْطَعُوٓا۟ أَيْدِيَهُمَا جَزَآءًۢ بِمَا كَسَبَا نَكَٰلًا مِّنَ ٱللَّهِ ۗ وَٱللَّهُ عَزِيزٌ حَكِيمٌ

Wassaariqu wassaariqatu faqta'oo aidiyahumaa jazaaa'am bimaa kasabaa nakaalam minal laah; wallaahu 'Azeezun hakeem

And the Hadith provides further clarification on this form of punishment:

Sahih Muslim, Book 017, Number 4175:

"A'isha reported that Allah's Messenger cut off the hand of a thief for a quarter of a dinar and upwards."

Sahih Muslim, Book 017, Number 4185:

"Abu Huraira reported Allah's Messenger as saying: 'let there be the curse of Allah upon a thief who steals an egg and his hand is cut off and steals a rope and his hand is cut off.'"

The above Hadiths prove that amputation was administered for even very trivial or minor thefts. In the following Hadith, a thief was brought to Muhammad and his hand was cut off. And on further orders from the Prophet, the hand of the thief was hung around his neck:

Sunan Abu Dawud, Book 38, Number 4397:

Narrated Fadalah ibn Ubayd: A thief was brought to the Apostle of Allah and his hand was cut off. Thereafter he commanded for it, and it was hung on his neck.

And the following Hadith reveals the extreme cruel nature of Allah's punishment:

Mishkat-ul-Masabih, Book II, Section 11, 1210-Theft, Hadith No. 127:

"It is narrated in Sharih Sunnat that Safwan-b-Umayyah came to Medina and slept in the mosque using his sheet as pillow. A thief came and stole his sheet. Safwan overtook him and came with him to the Messenger of Allah. Muhammad gave the order for the thief's hand to be cut off. Safwan said, "I did not wish it (that punishment); I give it (the sheet) to him as charity," upon which the Messenger of Allah asked, "Why didn't you (tell him) before you came with him?"

In other words, it is too late, and the man's hand must be cut off as required by Allah. The great Islamic historian, Al-Tabari, recorded an incident in which a woman expressed repentance, but the amputation was nevertheless administered.

Tafsir al-Tabari on Surah 5:38:

"A woman stole jeweler from some people who then brought her to The Prophet. He ordered that her right hand be cut off. The woman then asked him if there was room for repentance to which he replied, 'Today (that is after your hand is cut off) you will be pure from your sin like the day you were born.'"

Let us compare the above punishment of Allah for theft with the punishment that Jehovah commanded in the Bible. A comparative study will greatly aid us to identify which one of these two is the true Creator of mankind. Consider now how Jehovah dealt with the problem of theft. In the Bible, God gave specific laws whereby his people could deal with the problems of theft. We will cite just two examples out the many that the Bible specifies as punishments for the various forms of theft:

Exodus 22:1-4: "If a man steals a bull or a sheep and he slaughters or sells it, he is to compensate with five bulls for the bull and four sheep for the sheep ... If what he stole is found alive in his possession, whether it is a bull or a donkey or a sheep, he is to make double compensation. Leviticus 6:4-5: He must return the robbed thing which he has robbed or the extorted thing which he has taken by fraud or the thing in his charge which was put in his charge or the thing lost that he has found, or anything at all over which he might swear falsely, and he must make compensation for it in its full amount, and he will add to it a fifth of it. To the one whose it is he will give it on the day his guilt is proved."

According to the Law given to Moses, not only must the thief pay back the worth of whatever he stole but he must also compensate an additional amount to his victim as punishment for his theft. The true Creator of mankind never commanded any form of bodily damage as a punishment for property damage. He commanded bodily damage for bodily damage and property damage for property damage. The Creator knows that the worth of a human hand is above the worth of any property. Property was made for him. He was not made for property. This proves that the hand-cutting punishment in Islam originated from someone other than the Creator of the human hand. Furthermore, the Bible states:

Ephesians 4:28: "Let the one who steals steal no more; rather, let him do hard work, doing good work with his own hands, so that he may have something to share with someone in need."

Since amputation is never executed as a form of punishment for theft by Jehovah, repentant thieves are given a chance to redeem themselves. The reformed thief is admonished to do *"good work with his own hands"* so as to share something with someone in need. Under Islamic law, with their hands amputated, repentant thieves are not given the opportunity to be restored back as useful members of the community. In fact, the life-long disability resulting from Allah's punishment will impose great difficulty even for the repentant ones to seek employment. As such, they might be forced to steal again for their livelihood.

If we compare the teachings of the Qur'an with that of the Bible, we can see that the God who spoke in the Bible acts like a true Creator. As our Creator, Jehovah knows the true worth of the human hand. The deity who spoke to Muhammad exposes himself as an imposter. Let us now consider a real-life account in the Bible which will help us to recognize the underlying cause for the distinction between the laws of Jehovah and the laws of Allah. Two women came to King Solomon and they sought his judgment, each claiming that the living child belongs to her.

The First Woman explained: "This woman and I live in the same house. I gave birth to a boy and two days later she also gave birth to a baby boy. Then one night her baby died. But while I was asleep, she put her dead child next to me and took my baby. When I woke up and looked at the dead child, I saw that it was not mine."
At this the Other Woman said: "No! The living child is mine, and the dead one is hers!"
King Solomon said: "Bring me a sword."
So they brought him a sword. King Solomon then gave the order: "Cut the living child in two and give half to one woman and half to the other."
At this, the Real Mother who was filled with compassion for her son pleaded with Solomon: "Please, my lord, give her the living baby! Don't kill him!"
But the Other Woman said: "Neither I nor you shall have him. Cut him in two!"
Then King Solomon gave his ruling: "Give the living baby to the first woman. Do not kill him; she is his mother." (You can read the full account in 1 Kings 3:16-27).

How did King Solomon identify the true mother? He could see that the woman who did not want the child to be cut in two behaved like the true mother. She had the heart and compassion of a real mother. She would rather lose the baby and spare his life than lose him altogether.

It is the same with Jehovah our Creator. He displays the same feelings as the *"Real Mother"* because he is our Maker. As our Creator, he has tender compassion for us. He does not want to destroy something that is irreplaceable for something that could be easily replaced. As our Creator, he knows the true value of the human hand. In total contrast, Allah orders the precious irreplaceable hand to be amputated for even very trivial or minor thefts. This true-life account of these two mothers–one true and one false–serves to highlight the difference between Jehovah the Creator and Allah the imposter.

Muslims, we sincerely hope this account will aid you to identify your real Creator. And it is not Allah. This is another valid reason why you must leave Islam and become a Christian.

CHAPTER XXIV

FIVE: THE CREATOR OF DEATH

Five: The Creator of death

Muslims, the following Qur'anic verse is one of the most important verses in the Qur'an. It is one of the verses where Allah clearly reveals his identify to you. It is one of the verses that will help you to understand who you are really worshipping:

Surah 32:13: "If We had so willed, We could certainly have brought every soul its true guidance: but the Word from Me will come true, "I will fill Hell with Jinns and mankind all together." (Yusuf Ali)

أَجْمَعِي وَٱلنَّاسِ ٱلْجِنَّةِ مِنَ جَهَنَّمَ لَأَمْلَأَنَّ مِنِّى ٱلْقَوْلُ حَقَّ وَلَكِنْ هُدَلَهَا نَفْسٍ كُلَّ لَءَاتَيْنَا شِئْنَا وَلَوْ نَ

Wa law shi'naa la-aatainaa kulla nafsin hudaahaa wa laakin haqqal qawlu minnee la amla'anna jahannama minal jinnati wannaasi ajma'een

SAHIH INTERNATIONAL:

And if We had willed, We could have given every soul its guidance, but the word from Me will come into effect [that] "I will surely fill Hell with jinn and people all together.

The above Qur'anic verse reveals that Allah deliberately holds back guidance for the sole pleasure of filling Hell with mankind (and Jinns). How can Muslims submit to a deity who deliberately holds back guidance for the sole pleasure of fulfilling his predestined quota of the number of persons he desires to send there? This is grossly immoral. Without a doubt, this proves that Allah is a merciless and cruel deity.

It is important for Muslims to remember that in line with the teachings of Hell-fire in Islam, this would then mean a destination of unspeakable suffering in a fiery place of eternal torment for billions in the hereafter. Can Allah then really be the true God? This can only mean that the spirit that speaks until today in the Qur'an is neither divine nor godly but rather an ungodly demonic force that holds more than a billion Muslims captive. Is it any wonder then why Allah has no misgivings about predestining billions to a fiery Hell? In contrast to Allah, it is the earnest desire of Jehovah for sinners to repent from their sinful ways and gain everlasting life:

2 Peter 3:9: Jehovah is not slow concerning his promise, as some people consider slowness, but he is patient with you because he does not desire anyone to be destroyed but desires all to attain to repentance.

These are the hallmarks of a truly loving Creator. This loving attitude of Jehovah is further confirmed in the following Bible verses.

Ezekiel 18:21-23: "Now if someone wicked turns away from all the sins he has committed and keeps my statutes and does what is just and righteous, he will surely keep living. He will not die. None of the transgressions that he has committed will be held against him. He will keep living for doing what is righteous."

"Do I take any pleasure at all in the death of a wicked person?" declares the Sovereign Lord Jehovah. "Do I not prefer that he turn away from his evil ways and keep living?"

Jehovah God entreats the sinner to change his sinful course. Mercy is extended to a sinner who repents and leaves his sinful ways.

Isaiah 55:7: Let the wicked man leave his way. And the evil man his thoughts. Let him return to Jehovah, who will have mercy on him. To our God, for he will forgive in a large way.

Muslims should seriously reflect on this vital contrast between the merciful attitude of Jehovah and the utterly cruel trait of Allah. And Muslims should make a decision based on these vital differences between Allah and Jehovah.

One of the ninety-nine names of Allah is "Al-Mumit." Islamic lexicons explain the meaning of "Al-Mumit" in the following terms: "The Creator of Death," "The Slayer" or "The One who renders the living dead."

However, the Bible identifies the *Devil* as the one who brought *Death* to the human family:

Hebrews 2:14: "So that through his (Jesus) death he might bring to nothing the one having the means to cause death, that is, the Devil." And

John 8:44: "You are from your father the Devil, and you wish to do the desires of your father. That one was a murderer from the beginning."

Therefore, it is the *Devil* who is truly the *"Creator of Death."* Shockingly, this happens to be one of the names of Allah. This fact alone is sufficient to determine the real identity of Allah. In complete contrast to Allah, Jehovah is not *"The Creator of Death"* but the *"Source of Life."*

Psalms 36:9: "With you is the Source of life."

Revelation 4:11: "You are worthy, Jehovah our God, to receive the glory and the honor and the power, because you created all things, and because of your will they came into existence and were created."

Muslims, you need to know the truth about Allah. However, what is even more important than that is knowing the identity of the true God. Leaving Islam is only the first step in the right direction. To complete the journey, you need to return to the true God and worship Him.

CHAPTER XXV

SIX: ALLAH ADMITS HE IS SATAN

Six: Allah admits he is Satan

Muslims believe that Allah is the true God. And they also claim that the *Allah* who revealed the *Qur'an* and the *God* who revealed the *Torah* and the *Gospel* are one and the same. Nothing could be further from the truth. Christians know for a certainty that this is a preposterous lie. Therefore, this deceit needs to be exposed not for the advantage of the Christians but for the benefit of sincere Muslims. Muslims need to be shown who they are really worshipping. As to the identity of Allah, it is best that we use Islamic sources themselves to reveal who Allah really is. Using sources that are acceptable to Muslims will certainly be more effective than using external sources. Better still, we will let Allah himself disclose his real identity to the Muslims.

A woman who knew Muhammad intimately–as she was none other than his own aunt–said to him:

"Muhammad! I think your Satan has forsaken you, for I have not seen him with you for two or three nights!"

Well, how did Allah respond to this woman's representation of him as *Satan?* Did Allah feel insulted at being called *Satan?* Did Allah condemn the woman's blasphemous accusation against him? Shockingly, Allah did not voice a single complaint. His only reaction to the woman's criticism was his denial of having forsaken Muhammad. Allah's response to the woman's accusation is recorded in the following Qur'anic verses:

Surah 93:1-3: "I swear by the early hours of the day, And the night when it covers with darkness. Your Lord has not forsaken you, nor has He become displeased." (Shakir)

وَٱلضُّحَىٰ

93:1

Wad duhaa

SAHIH INTERNATIONAL:

By the morning brightness

سَجَىٰ إِذَا وَٱلَّيْلِ

93:2

Wal laili iza sajaa

SAHIH INTERNATIONAL:

And [by] the night when it covers with darkness,

قَلَىٰ وَمَا رَبُّكَ وَدَّعَكَ مَا

93:3

Ma wad da'aka rabbuka wa ma qalaa

SAHIH INTERNATIONAL:

Your Lord has not taken leave of you, [O Muhammad], nor has He detested [you].

In the above Qur'anic verses, Allah exposes himself as *Satan* in two very significant ways. He exposed himself not only by his failure to respond to the accusation that he is *Satan,* but more significantly by the way he replied to the accusation. By answering that he has not forsaken Muhammad, Allah clearly owns up to being that very *person* whom this woman accuses of forsaking Muhammad. And that is *Satan.* Therefore,

Allah confirms the woman's accusation that he is *Satan*. He owns up to being the very character that this woman associated him with. Allah accepted that he is who this woman identified him to be. Thereby, he exposed himself both by his silence to respond to the accusation that he is *Muhammad's Satan* and by taking the position of *Satan* when answering the accusation. Now read the full account of this enlightening event in the most authentic Hadith in the Muslim world. This Hadith provides the circumstances for the revealing of Surah 93:1-3.

Sahih Bukhari, Volume 6, Book 60, Number 475:

Narrated by Jundub bin Sufyan: Once Allah's Apostle became sick and could not offer his night prayer (Tahajjud) for two or three nights. Then a lady (the wife of Abu Lahab) came and said, "O Muhammad! I think that your Satan has forsaken you, for I have not seen him with you for two or three nights!" On that, Allah revealed:

"By the fore-noon, and by the night when it darkens, your Lord (O Muhammad) has neither forsaken you, nor hated you." (Surah 93.1-3).

Let us analyze this incident carefully. The wife of Abu Lahab openly expressed that *Muhammad's Satan has forsaken him*. And Allah responded by saying that he has not forsaken Muhammad. In fact, Allah inspired a Qur'anic verse reassuring Muhammad:

Surah 93:3: "Your Lord has not forsaken you." (Shakir)

Now, why would Allah inspire a Qur'anic verse saying that he has "*not forsaken*" Muhammad when the accusation of Abu Lahab's wife was specifically directed to *Satan?* Did not she expressly state that Muhammad's *Satan* had forsaken him? Why did Allah place himself in the shoes of *Satan?* Is this not an admission that he is *Satan?* By inspiring a Qur'anic verse to answer on behalf of *Satan,* is not Allah giving himself away as *Satan?* Let us put this in a much clearer format for our Muslim readers to understand:

Woman's accusation: "O Muhammad! I think that your Satan has forsaken you."

Allah's response: "Your Lord has not forsaken you."

Do Muslims need anything clearer than this to discern that Muhammad's Lord is *Satan?* Is this not a clear testimony in the

Qur'an that Allah is *Satan?* This is an irrefutable admission in the Qur'an that Allah is *Satan.* Allah responded instinctively without hesitation because that is who he truly is. Allah took issue with the women's remark that he has forsaken Muhammad but not with the more serious offense of being labeled as *Satan.* He finds nothing wrong in being identified as such. He did not voice a single word of objection against the woman's more serious offense of branding him as *Satan.*

Had Allah remained silent altogether, there would not be much to argue. However, since Allah viewed the incident serious enough to warrant a response in the Qur'an, why did he not respond to the more severe charge brought on against him by the woman? Well, one thing that is made absolutely clear in the Qur'an is that *Allah* alias *Satan* did not forsake Muhammad. Or is it *Satan* alias *Allah?* At times, even the most cautious serpent lets the truth slip out. This disclosure of the true identity of Allah in the Qur'an should not surprise us. The existence of many evil teachings in Islam is sufficient to reveal who Allah truly is. We will conclude this segment of the article by asking Muslims the following thought-provoking questions: Who would be happy when we sin? God or Satan? Now, consider the following Hadith very carefully:

Sahih Muslim, Book 37, Hadith Number 6622:

Abu Huraira reported Allah's Messenger having said: By Him in Whose Hand is my life, if you were not to commit sin, Allah would sweep you out of existence and He would replace you by those people who would commit sin and seek forgiveness from Allah, and He would have pardoned them.

Do we need to say more? Not only does Allah admit in the Qur'an that he is *Satan* but he also acts as one. Allah just admitted that he will destroy all those who do not sin. Can you fathom this absurdity? In Islam, sin leads to salvation and righteousness leads to destruction. It will be extremely wise for Muslims to leave Islam and become Christians.

CHAPTER XXVI

SEVEN: THE DISTINCTION BETWEEN JESUS AND MUHAMMAD

Seven: The distinction between Jesus and Muhammad

There are numerous differences between Jesus and Muhammad. However, in this article we will just concentrate on the distinction between the character of Jesus and the character of Muhammad. We will consider one example to help sincere Muslims see the vast difference between the character of Jesus and the character of Muhammad.

The following tragic account which is recorded in the Hadith testifies that Muhammad approved the killing of a pregnant mother when he was informed that she had criticized him.

Sunan Abu-Dawud, Book 38, Hadith Number 4348:

Narrated Abdullah Ibn Abbas: A blind man had a slave-mother who used to abuse the Prophet and disparage him. He forbade her but she did not stop. He rebuked her but she did not give up her habit. One night she began to slander the Prophet and abuse him. So he took a dagger, placed it on her belly, pressed it, and killed her. A child who came between her legs was smeared with the blood that was there. When the morning came, the Prophet was informed about it. He assembled the people and said: I adjure by Allah the man who has done this action and I adjure him by my right to him that he should stand up.

Jumping over the necks of the people and trembling the man stood up. He sat before the Prophet and said: Apostle of Allah! I am her master; she used to abuse you and disparage you. I forbade her, but she did not stop, and I rebuked her, but she did not abandon her habit. I have two sons like pearls from her, and she was my companion. Last night she began to abuse and disparage you. So I took a dagger, put it on her belly and pressed it till I killed her. Thereupon the Prophet said: Oh be witness, no retaliation is payable for her blood.

What cruelty! What injustice! Muhammad unjustly approved the killing of a pregnant mother and her unborn child just because the murderer said that she had insulted him. Will a true prophet of God condone the cold-blooded murder of a mother and her child? Does not the murder of an innocent child matter to him? A double murder has been committed and Muhammad did not even investigate to ascertain whether this murderer was lying to escape punishment. Muhammad's verdict was based solely on the murderer's word. Muhammad set an evil precedent. Muslims will now find it justifiable to kill anyone who insulted their Prophet. And Muslims are doing just that. Islamic records also show that another murder was committed against another woman who supposedly insulted Muhammad and he gave the same verdict:

Sunan Abu-Dawud Book 38, Hadith Number 4349:

Narrated Ali ibn AbuTalib: A Jewess used to abuse the Prophet (pbuh) and disparage him. A man strangled her till she died. The Apostle of Allah (pbuh) declared that no recompense was payable for her blood.

Muhammad left a legacy of evil for Muslims to follow. The abusive "Blasphemy Law" which is prevalent in many Islamic countries is a direct result of Muhammad's evil verdict. Today, this law is exploited to silence all those who criticize the Prophet of Islam. The authorization for all Muslims to act as divinely appointed executioners is clearly defined in the Qur'an:

Surah 4:89: They wish you would disbelieve as they disbelieved so you would be alike. So do not take from among them allies until they emigrate for the cause of Allah. But if they turn away, then seize them and kill them wherever you find them." (Sahih International)

سَوَآءً فَتَكُونُونَ كَفَرُواْ كَمَا تَكْفُرُونَ لَوْ وَدُّواْ
اللَّهِ سَبِيلِ فِى يُهَاجِرُواْ حَتَّىٰ أَوْلِيَآءَ مِنْهُمْ تَتَّخِذُواْ فَلَا
نَصِيرًا وَلَا وَلِيًّا مِنْهُمْ تَتَّخِذُواْ وَلَا وَجَدتُّمُوهُمْ حَيْثُ وَاقْتُلُوهُمْ فَخُذُوهُمْ تَوَلَّوْاْ فَإِن

Waddoo law takfuroona kamaa kafaroo fatakoonoona sawaaa'an falaa tattakhizoo minhum awliyaaa'a hattaa yuhaajiroo fee sabeelil laah; fa in tawallaw fa khuzoohum waqtuloohum haisu wajat tumoohum wa laa tattakhizoo minhum waliyyanw wa laa naseeraa

Let us now see the contrast in the character of Jesus. Let us evaluate how Jesus responded under an even more serious crime committed against him. See how he responded towards those who came to arrest him which finally led to his death by execution. Compare the malicious hatred of Muhammad with the outstanding quality of love displayed by Jesus Christ. When a great crowd with swords and clubs from the chief priests came to arrest Jesus, one of his disciples tried to defend him. Follow now the account of this incident in the Bible:

Matthew 26:51: With that, one of the companions of Jesus drew out his sword and struck the slave of the high priest and took off his ear. How did Jesus react?

Matthew 26:52-53: Then Jesus said to him: "Return your sword to its place, for all those who take up the sword will die by the sword. Jesus did not condone the violent action of his disciple just because it was carried out to protect him. In fact, he rebuked the disciple for his rash action. More than that, he lovingly healed the injured ear of the very man who came along with those who wanted to arrest him. Such is the love of Jesus Christ. Imagine how strongly Jesus would have reacted if his disciple had instead killed that man. If Jesus did not even approve the injuring of that man, would he condone the murdering of him? Never!

Luke 22:51: "And he touched the man's ear and healed him."

These are the hallmarks of a true Prophet of God. Christians are truly blessed for having Jesus as their Prophet. By his very example, he taught them the surpassing way of love. From the historical records of Islam itself, we can clearly see that Muhammad was an extremely cruel man. Great prophets of the true God such as Moses and Jesus displayed a completely different spirit than those manifested by Muhammad. Clearly, Muhammad does not qualify to be a prophet of the true God. Muslims should seriously consider whom they want to follow. Jesus or Muhammad? Interestingly, Jesus taught a simple way to test a prophet. He said that we can know a prophet by his fruits. Whether a prophet is true or false will be known by his works.

Matthew 7:15-20: "Watch out for false prophets that come to you disguised in sheep's clothing, but inside they are vicious wolves. You shall know them by their fruits. Do people gather grapes from thorns or figs from thistles? Likewise, every good tree produces fine fruit, but every rotten tree produces worthless fruit; a good tree cannot bear worthless fruit, neither can a rotten tree produce fine fruit. Every tree not producing fine fruit gets cut down and thrown into the fire. Really, then, by their fruits you will recognize those men."

What kind of fruits did the Prophet of Islam produce? Muhammad assassinated those who criticized him and executed those who escaped when he came to power. He was an extremely evil man. He justified murder in the name of Allah. His fruits were death and destruction. And we are not the ones saying this but Muhammad himself:

"The Prophet said, 'Hear me. By Him who holds Muhammad's life in his hand, I will bring you slaughter.'" (Ishaq: p.130; Tabari: VI:101)

We believe the evidences presented here is sufficient to touch the hearts of sincere Muslims and move them to leave Islam for Christianity.

CHAPTER XXVII

EIGHT: THE QURAN DISQUALIFIES MUHAMMAD'S PROPHETHOOD

Eight: The Quran disqualifies Muhammad's Prophethood

There are many convincing evidences to reject Muhammad's claim as a prophet of the true God. Ironically, one of the most compelling reasons can be found in the Qur'an itself. The Qur'an states that all prophets from the time of *Abraham* onwards will be established through his lineage. And the Qur'an qualifies this stated position of Abraham by adding that the *Prophethood* will thereafter continue exclusively through the lineage of *Isaac* and *Jacob*. Therefore, all prophets of the true God will henceforth be chosen only from among the *descendants* of *Isaac* and *Jacob*. Thus, the Qur'an disqualifies Muhammad as a prophet of the true God.

It may come as a shocking surprise for Muslims to learn that both the Holy Bible and the Qur'an disqualify Muhammad as a prophet of the true God. Read on to find out exactly how the Qur'an disqualifies Muhammad. If you are a Muslim reading this, the information presented here is of utmost importance and may help you to secure your eternal salvation. Centuries before the Qur'an came into existence, the Holy Bible speaks of the *"Covenant of Jehovah."* God made a *Covenant* with *Abraham, Isaac* and *Jacob*:

Exodus 2:24-25: "And God remembered his Covenant with Abraham, Isaac and Jacob. So God looked on the sons of Israel and God took notice."

2 Kings 13:23: "But Jehovah was gracious unto them and had compassion upon them for the sake of his of his Covenant with Abraham, Isaac and Jacob."

Psalms 105:7-10: "Jehovah is our God. His judgments are in the earth. He remembers his Covenant forever. The promise he made, to a thousand generations. The Covenant which he concluded with Abraham and his sworn statement to Isaac which he established as a statue even to Jacob. And as an Everlasting Covenant to Israel."

In recognition of this Covenant of Jehovah with Abraham, Isaac, and Jacob, the Qur'an also confirms that the Prophethood will remain in the lineage of Abraham, Isaac, and Jacob. Three different translations of Surah 29:27 is provided below:

Surah 29:27: And We bestowed upon Abraham (a son) Isaac and (a grandson) Jacob, and caused Prophethood and Revelation to continue among his progeny. (Shabbir)

And We bestowed on him Isaac and Jacob, and We established the Prophethood and the Scripture among his seed. (Pickthall)

And We granted him Ishaq and Yaqoub, and caused the Prophethood and the Book to remain in his seed. (Shakir)

While stating that the *Prophethood* will be established through the lineage of *Abraham*, the above Qur'anic verse specifically mentions *Isaac* and *Jacob* by name as the descendants through whom the *Prophethood* will continue thereafter. Therefore, the *Prophethood* will be established exclusively through the seeds of *Isaac* and *Jacob*. In other words, the *Prophethood* would be entrusted only to *Isaac* and *Jacob* and to their *descendants*.

That is why Allah confirmed that the Prophethood would "remain" in the lineage of Abraham through Isaac and Jacob. This means that anyone claiming to be a Prophet of the true God must be born in the "Prophetic Race" as specified in the Qur'an. They must be born in the lineage of Abraham, Isaac, and Jacob.

Since the Qur'an states that Prophethood would "remain" exclusively in the lineage of Isaac and Jacob, we must then ask whether Muhammad was a descendant of Isaac or Jacob. In other words, was he born in the Prophetic Race?

Muslims scholars claim that Muhammad was a descendant of Ishmael. But Ishmael is excluded completely in the *Prophetic lineage* of Surah 29:27. If Allah intends to include Ishmael, his name would be placed before *Isaac*, as he was older than *Isaac* by about fourteen years. But, Surah 29:27 completely omits any reference to Ishmael at the most critical moment when the *lineage* of the *Prophethood* was revealed in the Qur'an. The deliberate omission of Ishmael's name clearly serves to confirm that the *Prophetic lineage* will be established only through *Isaac*- not Ishmael. Furthermore, Muhammad could not be a descendant of both Ishmael and *Isaac* at the same instant since these two are step-brothers. Therefore, if Muhammad was a descendant of Ishmael, he cannot be a descendant of *Isaac*. Consider now the following Qur'anic verses:

Surah 19:49-50: When (Abraham) rejected his people and what they worshipped instead of God, We gave him Isaac and Jacob and made both of them Prophets. We granted them Our blessing and high renown. (Muhammad Sarwar)

نَبِيًّا جَعَلْنَا وَكُلًّا ۖ وَيَعْقُوبَ إِسْحَٰقَ لَهُ وَهَبْنَا اللَّهِ دُونِ مِن يَعْبُدُونَ وَمَا اعْتَزَلَهُمْ فَلَمَّا

19:49

Fa lam ma'tazalahum wa maa ya'budoona min doonil laahi wahabnaa lahoo is-haaqa wa ya'qoob; wa kullan ja'alnaa Nabiyyaa

SAHIH INTERNATIONAL:

So, when he had left them and those, they worshipped other than Allah, We gave him Isaac and Jacob, and each [of them] We made a prophet.

عَلِيًّا صِدْقٍ لِسَانَ لَهُمْ وَجَعَلْنَا رَّحْمَتِنَا مِّن لَهُم وَوَهَبْنَا

19:50

Wa wahabnaa lahum mirrahmatinaa wa ja'alnaa lahum lisaana sidqin 'aliyyaa (section 3)

SAHIH INTERNATIONAL:

And We gave them of Our mercy, and we made for them a reputation of high honor.

Once again, we notice the omission of Ishmael's name at a most significant moment. Ishmael's name was completely excluded while both *Isaac* and *Jacob* are named as the immediate successors of Abraham as the *Prophets of God.* The following Surahs not only confirm that the *"Children of Israel"* were given special preferences but they were also entrusted as recipients of the *Scripture* and the office of the *Prophethood.* The *"Children of Israel"* are the descendants of *Isaac* and *Jacob:*

Surah 2:47: "O Children of Israel! Remember My favour wherewith I favoured you and how I preferred you to all creatures." (Pickthall)

ٱلْعَٰلَمِينَ عَلَىٰ فَضَّلْتُكُمْ وَأَنِّي عَلَيْكُمْ أَنْعَمْتُ ٱلَّتِي نِعْمَتِيَ ٱذْكُرُوا۟ إِسْرَٰٓءِيلَ يَٰبَنِيَ

Yaa Baneee Israaa'eelaz kuroo ni'matiyal lateee an'amtu 'alaikum wa annee faddaltukum 'alal 'aalameen

Surah 45:16: And verily We gave the Scripture and the Command and the Prophethood, and provided them with good things and favoured them above all peoples. (Pickthall)

ٱلْعَٰ عَلَىٰ وَفَضَّلْنَٰهُمْ ٱلطَّيِّبَٰتِ مِّنَ وَرَزَقْنَٰهُم وَٱلنُّبُوَّةَ وَٱلْحُكْمَ ٱلْكِتَٰبَ إِسْرَٰٓءِيلَ بَنِىٓ ءَاتَيْنَا وَلَقَدْ لَمِينَ

Wa laqad aatainaa Baneee Israaa'eelal Kitaaba walhukma wan Nubuwwata wa razaqnaahum minat taiyibaati wa faddalnaahum;alal 'aalameen

Muhammad was not an Israelite but an Arab. Even though some Muslim scholars falsely claim that Muhammad was a descendant of Ishmael, it still does not qualify him as a true prophet since he is not a descendant of the *Prophetic Race.* Islam destroys its own credibility by admitting that Muhammad did not come from the *lineage* of the *Prophetic Race.*

Moreover, Muhammad was born into a family of pagan worshippers. Thus, Muhammad was a direct descendant of a pagan family long after the lineage of the Prophetic Race was firmly established. Renowned Arab Muslim scholar and historian, Hisham ibn al-Kalbi (737 C.E.–819 C.E.) disclosed this truth about

Muhammad's pagan origin in his esteemed work known as "Kitab al-Asnam" (The Book of Idols). On page 17, he stated:

'We have been told that the Apostle of Allah once mentioned al-Uzza saying, "I have offered a white sheep to al-'Uzza, while I was a follower of the religion of my people."'

Supporting this fact, the following Qur'anic verse admits that Muhammad was not acquainted with either Revelation or Faith before his alleged calling. Allah himself stated:

Surah 42:52: "And thus have We, by Our Command, sent inspiration to thee: you knew not before what was Revelation and what was Faith. (Yusuf Ali)

وَكَذَٰلِكَ أَوْحَيْنَآ إِلَيْكَ رُوحًا مِّنْ أَمْرِنَا
وَمَا كُنتَ تَدْرِى مَا ٱلْكِتَٰبُ وَلَا ٱلْإِيمَٰنُ وَلَٰكِن جَعَلْنَٰهُ نُورًا نَّهْدِى بِهِۦ مَن نَّشَآءُ مِنْ عِبَادِنَا
وَإِنَّكَ لَتَهْدِىٓ إِلَىٰ صِرَٰطٍ مُّسْتَقِيمٍ

Wa kazaalika awhainaaa ilaika roohan min amrinaa; maa kunta tadree mal Kitaabu wa lal eemaanu wa laakin ja'alnaahu nooran nahdee bihee man nashaaa'u min 'ibaadinaa; wa innaka latahdeee ilaaa Saraatin Mustaqeem

Al-'Uzza was one of the female deities worshipped by the *Quraysh Pagans.* While Muhammad was a direct descendant of pagan worshippers, both Moses and Jesus came from families who were devout worshippers of the true God. And both were born in the *Prophetic Race.* Jesus was a descendant of *Abraham* through the lineage of *Isaac* and *Jacob.* His genealogy is clearly recorded in the Bible linking him to *Abraham, Isaac* and *Jacob.* (Matthew 1:1-17) After choosing every single one of the *Prophets* from among the worshippers of the God of *Abraham, Isaac* and *Jacob,* would the true God now choose a pagan worshipper from a pagan family as his final prophet? We do not think so.

Muslims simply cannot qualify Muhammad as a true Prophet without disqualifying the words of Allah in Surah 29:27. If Muslims qualify Muhammad as a true *Prophet,* then Surah 29:27 becomes false. This would make the Qur'an false and disqualify it as the Word of God. On the other hand, if the Qur'an is true then Muhammad is automatically disqualified as a *Prophet* of the true God. Either way, Islam is false.

Therefore, if Muslims really value their eternal salvation, they must turn to the one who has the credentials of a true *Prophet.* Muslims must turn to Jesus. And this means leaving Islam. Islam stands and falls on the credentials of Muhammad. And Islam itself disqualifies him as a *Prophet* of the true God.

CHAPTER XXVIII

NINE: THE "STRAIGHT WAY" OF
SALVATION

Nine: The "straight Way" of Salvation

One of the Pillars of Islam is the *Daily Five Prayers*. And Muslims are taught to recite *Surah al-Fatiha* during these prayers which are performed at specific times of the day. This opening Surah in the Qur'an consists of seven verses imploring Allah for guidance. One of the verses beseeches Allah to show Muslims the *"Straight Way."*

Surah 1:6: Show us the Straight Way. (Yusuf Ali)

ٱهۡدِنَا ٱلصِّرَٰطَ ٱلۡمُسۡتَقِيمَ

Ihdinas-Siraatal-Mustaqeem
SAHIH INTERNATIONAL:
Guide us to the straight path –

As the above Qur'anic verse clearly demonstrates, the salvation of every single Muslim is very much dependent on discovering this *"Straight Way."* If Islam is truly the *"Straight Way"* as Muslims claim, then why is it necessary for Muslims to entreat Allah repeatedly on a daily basis throughout their entire life to show them the *"Straight Way"*? Even the faithful Muslims who are followers of Islam for decades are required to entreat Allah to show them the *"Straight Way."* Are they not already in the *"Straight Way"* as followers of Islam? To illustrate, if I am already living on the right street, would I be asking people to show me the right street?

Note carefully, the inspired prayer recorded in Surah 1:6 for Muslims to recite does not say, *"Help us remain in the Straight Way"* but *"Show us the Straight Way."* Is this not an admission that Islam is not the *"Straight Way"*? Furthermore, this inspired prayer in the Qur'an is exclusively written for those who are already Muslims and not for the non-Muslims. Centuries before the arrival of Muhammad, Jesus told his faithful followers:

John 14:6: "I am the Way and the Truth and the Life. No one comes to the Father except through me."

Jesus did not say, *"I am a Way"* but *"I am the Way."* Therefore, Jesus Christ is clearly testifying that he is the only way through whom one can gain salvation. In harmony with this truth, the following Qur'anic verse reveals an important qualification for Muslims to be in the *"Straight Way."*

Surah 43:61: And (Jesus) shall be a Sign for the coming of the Hour of Judgment: therefore, have no doubt about the (Hour), but follow you Me: This is a Straight Way. (Yusuf Ali)

مُسْتَقِيمٌ صِرَاطٌ هَٰذَا ۚ وَاتَّبِعُونِ بِهَا تَمْتَرُنَّ فَلَا لِلسَّاعَةِ لَعِلْمٌ وَإِنَّهُ

Wa innahoo la 'ilmun lis Saa'ati fa laa tamtarunna bihaa wattabi'oon; haazaa Siraatun Mustaqeem

SAHIH INTERNATIONAL:

And indeed, Jesus will be [a sign for] knowledge of the Hour, so be not in doubt of it, and follow Me. This is a straight path.

Verily (Jesus) is a Portent of the Hour. So be in no doubt concerning it and follow Me. This is the Straight Way. (Maududi)

In harmony with the teachings of Allah in the above Qur'anic verse, Muslims must recognize the fact that there is a vital link between the *"Straight Way"* and the coming of Jesus at the *"Hour of Judgment."* And the following Qur'anic verses reveal that obedience to Jesus is crucial for one to be in the *"Straight Way"* of salvation:

Surah 43:63-64: When Jesus came with Clear Signs, he said: "Now have I come to you with Wisdom, and in order to make clear to you some of the points on which you dispute: Therefore, fear God and obey me. For God, He is my Lord and your Lord: so worship you Him: This is a Straight Way." (Yusuf Ali)

وَلَمَّا جَآءَ عِيسَىٰ بِٱلْبَيِّنَـٰتِ قَالَ قَدْ جِئْتُكُم بِٱلْحِكْمَةِ وَلِأُبَيِّنَ لَكُم بَعْضَ ٱلَّذِى تَخْتَلِفُونَ فِيهِ فَٱتَّقُوا۟ ٱللَّهَ وَأَطِيعُونِ

43:63

Wa lammaa jaaa'a 'Eesaa bilbaiyinaati qaala qad ji'tukum bil Hikmati wa li-ubaiyina lakum ba'dal lazee takhtalifoona feehi fattaqul laaha wa atee'oon

SAHIH INTERNATIONAL:

And when Jesus brought clear proofs, he said, "I have come to you with wisdom and to make clear to you some of that over which you differ, so fear Allah and obey me.

إِنَّ ٱللَّهَ هُوَ رَبِّى وَرَبُّكُمْ فَٱعْبُدُوهُ ۚ هَـٰذَا صِرَٰطٌ مُّسْتَقِيمٌ

43:64

Innal laaha Huwa Rabbee wa Rabbukum fa'budooh; haaza Siraatum Mustaqeem

SAHIH INTERNATIONAL:

Indeed, Allah is my Lord and your Lord, so worship Him. This is a straight path."

Let us analyze the above Qur'anic verses carefully. These verses clearly teach that obedience to Jesus is an important precondition for one to remain in the *"Straight Way"* of salvation. This essential commitment requiring all true worshippers to be obedient to Jesus is also emphasized in another Qur'anic verse. In the following Qur'anic verse, Jesus states:

Surah 3:50: "I have come to you, to attest the Law which was before me. And to make lawful to you part of what was before forbidden to you; I have come to you with a Sign from your Lord. So fear God, and obey me." (Yusuf Ali)

وَمُصَدِّقًا لِّمَا بَيْنَ يَدَىَّ مِنَ ٱلتَّوْرَىٰةِ وَلِأُحِلَّ لَكُم بَعْضَ ٱلَّذِى حُرِّمَ عَلَيْكُمْ وَجِئْتُكُم بِـَٔايَةٍ مِّن رَّبِّكُمْ فَٱتَّقُوا۟ ٱللَّهَ وَأَطِيعُونِ

Wa musaddiqal limaa baina yadaiya minat Tawraati wa liuhilla lakum ba'dal lazee hurrima 'alaikum; wa ji'tukum bi Aayatim mir Rabbikum fattaqul laaha wa atee'oon

Some vital questions need to be raised here for our consideration. Is the requirement to obey Jesus still in force even after the arrival of Muhammad? And does the admonition to obey Jesus apply equally to Muslims? We will let the Qur'an answer these vital questions for us. Allah commanded Muhammad to make the following confessions regarding the extension of his authority as a Prophet of Allah. Listen to Muhammad:

Surah 72:21: Say: "Surely neither it is in my power to hurt you nor to bring you to the Right Way." (Maududi)

رَشَدًا وَلَا ضَرًّا لَكُمْ أَمْلِكُ لَآ إِنِّى قُلْ

Qul innee laaa amliku lakum darranw wa laa rashada

And

Surah 46:9: Say: "I am no new thing among the messengers of Allah, nor know I what will be done with me or with you. I do but follow that which is inspired in me, and I am but a plain warner." (Pickthall)

بِكُمْ وَلَا بِى يُفْعَلُ مَا أَدْرِى وَمَآ ٱلرُّسُلِ مِّنَ بِدْعًا كُنتُ مَا قُلْ
مُّبِينٌ نَذِيرٌ إِلَّا أَنَا۠ وَمَآ إِلَىَّ يُوحَىٰ مَا إِلَّا أَتَّبِعُ إِنْ ۖ

Qul maa kuntu bid'am minal Rusuli wa maaa adreee ma yuf'alu bee wa laa bikum in attabi'u illaa maa yoohaaa ilaiya wa maaa ana illaa nazeerum Mubeen.

As we can see, Muhammad is specifically addressing the Muslims in these Qur'anic verses. And these Qur'anic verses are simply testifying that Muslims cannot depend on Muhammad to guide them to the *"Straight Way"* of salvation. Muslims, please take note that your Prophet is clearly confessing that he cannot *"bring you to the Right Way."* To doubt this confession of Muhammad is to doubt the inspired message of Allah in the Qur'an. And Allah's message in the Qur'an is supposed to remain valid and true for all eternity. Consider now an experience that happened during the life-time of Muhammad. This account will aid you to have a better understanding of the issue under consideration:

Sahih Bukhari, Volume 5, Book 58, Number 266:
Narrated 'Um al-'Ala: "Uthman fell ill and I nursed him till he died, and we covered him with his clothes. Then the Prophet came to us. Addressing the dead body, I said, "O Abu As-Sa'ib, may Allah's Mercy be

on you! I bear witness that Allah has honored you." On that the Prophet said, "How do you know that Allah has honored him?" I replied, "I do not know. May my father and my mother be sacrificed for you, O Allah's Apostle! But who else is worthy of it if not Uthman?" He said, "As to him, by Allah, death has overtaken him, and I hope the best for him. By Allah, though I am the Apostle of Allah, yet I do not know what Allah will do to me."

Listen to another confession of Muhammad in the following Hadith:

Sahih Bukhari, Volume 4, Book 51, Number 16:

Narrated By Abu Huraira: When Allah revealed the Verse: "Warn your nearest kinsmen," Allah's Apostle got up and said, "O people of Quraish! Save yourselves from the Hellfire as I cannot save you from Allah's Punishment; O Bani Abd Manaf! I cannot save you from Allah's Punishment, O Safiya, the Aunt of Allah's Apostle! I cannot save you from Allah's Punishment; O Fatima bint Muhammad! Ask me anything from my wealth, but I cannot save you from Allah's Punishment."

The Prophet of Islam openly confessed to his followers that he is uncertain whether Allah will send him to Paradise or to Hell. These references should trouble any Muslim. Both the Qur'an and Hadith clearly testify that not only was Muhammad unsure of the salvation of his followers but he was also uncertain of his very own salvation. If Muhammad is uncertain about his very own salvation, can he then lead Muslims to the "*Straight Way*" of salvation?

We are not stating these facts to criticize but to alert Muslims of the dangers that their own Islamic sources reveal. When Islam fails to inspire hope in its very chosen Prophet, we can be certain it will disappoint its lesser adherents on the Day of Judgment. However, in contrast to this uncertainty regarding the future of Muhammad, the Qur'an bears witness to the salvation of Jesus with absolute certainty. It testifies to his glorious salvation of a heavenly life to be in the very presence of God for all eternity. Concerning Jesus, the Qur'an testifies:

Surah 4:158: "God raised him up to Himself. God is Majestic and All-wise." (Sarwar)

حَكِيمًا عَزِيزًا ٱللَّهُ وَكَانَ ۚ إِلَيْهِ ٱللَّهُ رَّفَعَهُ بَل

Bar rafa'ahul laahu ilayh; wa kaanal laahu 'Azeezan Hakeemaa

As we can see, Muhammad failed to inspire hope into the hearts of his followers. In contrast, reflect on the assurance that Jesus Christ gave his followers:

John 5:24: Most assuredly, I say to you, he who hears my word and believes in Him who sent me has everlasting life, and shall not come into judgment, but has passed from death into life.

And the Qur'an further testifies that the only thing which is absolutely certain for Muhammad and his followers is death:

Surah 39:30: "You Muhammad are destined to die and so are they. (Al-Muntakhab)

مَّيِّتُونَ وَإِنَّهُم مَّيِّتٌ إِنَّكَ

Innaka maiyitunw wa inna hum maiyitoon

Contrast the above outcome that Allah has in store for Muhammad and the Muslims with the hope that Jesus Christ extended to his true followers:

John 14:19: "Because I live, you will live also."

Both the Bible and the Qur'an testify that while Muhammad is dead, Jesus is alive! Let's go back to Surah 43:61. This Qur'anic verse clearly states that Jesus will be *"a Sign for the coming of the Hour of Judgment."* What does this actually mean? The following Hadith and the Tafsir which follows will enlighten Muslims on the meaning of this Qur'anic verse:

Sahih Bukhari, Volume 3, Number 656:

Narrated Abu Hurairah: Allah's Apostle said, "The Hour will not be established until the son of Mary (i.e. Jesus) descends amongst you as a just ruler."

Tafsir Ibn Abbas:

Verily in the coming of Jesus the son of Mary there is knowledge of the Hour, there is an indication of the coming of the Hour; it is also said that this means: his coming is a Sign of the advent of the Hour. (Tanwîr al-Miqbâs min Tafsîr Ibn 'Abbâs)

According to the Qur'an, the *"Hour of Judgment"* refers to the time of the end when God rewards the faithful and executes judgment on the wicked. Therefore, for Muslims to know the time and season of the *"Hour of Judgment,"* they must focus on Jesus–the source of the knowledge of the Hour.

Surah 43:61: And he ('Isa) is a source of knowledge of the Hour (the Day of Judgment). (Usmani)

مُسْتَقِيمٌ صِرَٰطٌ هَٰذَا ۚ وَٱتَّبِعُونِ بِهَا تَمْتَرُنَّ فَلَا لِّلسَّاعَةِ لَعِلْمٌ وَإِنَّهُۥ

Wa innahoo la 'ilmun lis Saa'ati fa laa tamtarunna bihaa wattabi'oon; haazaa Siraatun Mustaqeem

The salvation of Muslims is very much dependent on the outworking of the role of Jesus in God's divine purpose. Unless a Muslim becomes a follower of Jesus, he cannot attain salvation. Why do we say that with absolute conviction? It is because the Qur'an itself bears witness with absolute certainty to the salvation of the Christians:

Surah 3:55: "Behold! Allah said: 'O Jesus! I will take thee and raise thee to Myself and clear thee of the falsehood of those who blaspheme; I will make those who follow thee superior to those who disbelieve until the Day of Resurrection." (Yusuf Ali)

ٱتَّبَعُو ٱلَّذِينَ وَجَاعِلُ كَفَرُوا۟ ٱلَّذِينَ مِنَ وَمُطَهِّرُكَ إِلَىَّ وَرَافِعُكَ مُتَوَفِّيكَ إِنِّى يَٰعِيسَىٰٓ ٱللَّهُ قَالَ إِذْ

تَخْتَلِفُونَ فِيهِ كُنتُمْ فِيمَا بَيْنَكُمْ فَأَحْكُمُ مَرْجِعُكُمْ إِلَىَّ ثُمَّ ۚ ٱلْقِيَٰمَةِ يَوْمِ إِلَىٰ كَفَرُوا۟ ٱلَّذِينَ فَوْقَ كَ

Iz qaalal laahu yaa 'Eesaaa innee mutawaffeeka wa raafi'uka ilaiya wa mutah hiruka minal lazeena kafaroo wa jaa'ilul lazeenattaba ooka fawqal lazeena kafarooo ilaa Yawmil Qiyaamati summa ilaiya marji'ukum fa ahkumu bainakum feemaa kuntum feehi takhtaliifoon

This is a very profound statement in the Qur'an. It reveals the superiority of those who follow Jesus Christ. It does not say those who believe in Jesus will be made superior but those who actually follow him. The context of this Qur'anic verse shows that Allah spoke the above words to Jesus while he was still alive on the earth with his disciples. Thereafter, Jesus was raised to the Heavens. This event took place centuries before the birth of Islam. The followers of Jesus are known as Christians. It is important for Muslims to note that the above Qur'anic verse does not say that the Christians will be made *"superior"* until the arrival of Muhammad or until the arrival of the Qur'an but until the *"Day of Resurrection."*

The Day of Resurrection or *Qiyamah* will occur at the *"time of the end."* Therefore, from the time of the establishment of Christianity until the time of the end, true Christians will be made *"superior"* over the *"disbelievers."* Notice how the Qur'an makes a distinction between the *"disbelievers"* and the Christians. This contrast serves to identify Christians as true believers. From the founding of Christianity until today, true Christians have not and still do not submit to the teachings of the Qur'an. They only submit to the teachings of the Holy Bible. So how can Allah then exalt Christians and make them *"superior to those who disbelieve until the Day of Resurrection"* when they do not subscribe to the teachings of the Qur'an? The answer is obvious but not to Muslims. Muslims fail to realize that even according to the Qur'an, Christianity will remain as the true religion for all eternity.

The God of the true Christians is and has always been their heavenly Father, *Jehovah God.* It is not and has never been Allah. If true Christians are assured of salvation without Allah, without Muhammad, without Islam and without the Qur'an, then what are Muslims waiting for?

CHAPTER XXIX

TEN: FAIRY TALES IN THE QURAN

Ten: Fairy tales in the Quran

There are many fascinating *Fairy Tales* in the Qur'an. One *Fairy Tale* that touches the hearts of many pious Muslims is the amazing story of *"Muhammad's Adventure of the Seven Heavens"* on a flying steed with a human face. The Arabs affectionately refer to this story as *"Al-Miraj."* However, we will leave this intriguing tale for another time and concentrate on something closer to earth. We must admit that if not for the blood-spilling verses, the Qur'an would top *Grimm's Fairy Tales.* It will certainly be acclaimed as one of the best bed-time stories for children. One *Fairy Tale* that is sure to fascinate children will be the story of *"Allah in Wonderland."* Let's begin. *Once upon a time...*

There were gathered together unto Solomon his armies of the jinn and humankind, and of the birds, and they were set in battle order;

*till, when they reached the Valley of the Ants, an ant exclaimed: O ants!
Enter your dwellings lest Solomon and his armies crush you,
unperceiving. And Solomon smiled, laughing at her speech, and said:*

*My Lord, arouse me to be thankful for Thy favour wherewith
Thou hast favoured me and my parents, and to do good that shall be
pleasing unto Thee. – Surah 27:17-19 (Pickthall)*

يُوزَعُونَ فَهُمْ وَٱلطَّيْرِ وَٱلْإِنسِ ٱلْجِنِّ مِنَ جُنُودُهُ لِسُلَيْمَـٰنَ وَحُشِرَ

27:17

Wa hushira Sulaimaana junooduhoo minal jinni wal insi
wattairi fahum yooza'oon

SAHIH INTERNATIONAL:

*And gathered for Solomon were his soldiers of the jinn and men
and birds, and they were [marching] in rows.*

سُلَ يَحْطِمَنَّكُمْ لَا مَسَـٰكِنَكُمْ ٱدْخُلُوا ٱلنَّمْلُ يَـٰأَيُّهَا نَمْلَةٌ قَالَتْ ٱلنَّمْلِ وَادِ عَلَىٰ أَتَوْا إِذَآ حَتَّىٰٓ
يَشْعُرُونَ لَا وَهُمْ وَجُنُودُهُ يْمَـٰنُ

27:18

hattaaa izaaa ataw 'alaa waadin namli qaalat namlatuny
yaaa aiyuhan namlud khuloo masaakinakum laa yahtimannakum
Sulaimaanu wa junooduhoo wa hum laa yash'uroon

SAHIH INTERNATIONAL:

*Until, when they came upon the valley of the ants, an ant said,
"O ants, enter your dwellings that you not be crushed by Solomon and
his soldiers while they perceive not."*

وُلِدَ وَعَلَىٰ عَلَىَّ أَنْعَمْتَ ٱلَّتِىٓ نِعْمَتَكَ أَشْكُرَ أَنْ أَوْزِعْنِىَ رَبِّ وَقَالَ قَوْلِهَا مِّن ضَاحِكًا فَتَبَسَّمَ
ٱلصَّـٰلِحِينَ عِبَادِكَ فِى بِرَحْمَتِكَ وَأَدْخِلْنِى تَرْضَىٰهُ صَـٰلِحًا أَعْمَلَ وَأَنْ ئَ

27:19

Fatabassama daahikam min qawlihaa wa qaala Rabbi
awzi'nee an ashkura ni'mata kal lateee an'amta 'alaiya wa 'alaa
waalidaiya wa an a'mala saalihan tardaahu wa adkhilnee
birahmatika fee 'ibaadikas saaliheen

SAHIH INTERNATIONAL:

*So [Solomon] smiled, amused at her speech, and said, "My Lord,
enable me to be grateful for Your favor which You have bestowed upon
me and upon my parents and to do righteousness of which You approve.
And admit me by Your mercy into [the ranks of] Your righteous servants.*

Besides humans, the Qur'an claims that Solomon's army
included *"Jinns"* and *"Birds."* And to excite us even further, there
is also a *"Talking Ant"* in the Qur'an. This loving *Ant* cautions her
fellow-ants of any approaching dangers. The

vigilant *Ant* warns: *"O ants! Enter your dwellings lest Solomon and his armies crush you, unperceiving."* Of course, communicating such as this is only possible when a species has considerable thinking power and intelligence. And to converse such sophisticated information to other ants would require a language system comparable to human intelligence. But who cares? There is more.

Notice this *Ant* could actually distinguish between Solomon and his soldiers. It knows that one person among the many is special. And it knows his name is Solomon. This *Ant* even knows that Solomon is the commander of the armies since it uses the possessive pronoun *"his armies."* How did the *Ant* know all this? Was Solomon formally introduced to this *Ant* before? Now we have more than a *Talking Ant*. We have a *Talking Ant* with psychic powers. Furthermore, this *Ant* also knows the difference between intentional and unintentional behavior. It knows that Solomon's armies will not crush the ants *deliberately* but may do so *"unperceiving."* How did this *Ant* get all this information, as well as all the other details?

Also, how is it possible for Solomon to understand what the *Ant* was saying when ants do not have a language. Even if Muslims were to claim that Solomon was gifted with miraculous perception of the speech of ants, it is still not possible if there is no speech to perceive in the first place. But why spoil a good *Fairy Tale* with logic and sensible reasoning. If only Muslims are not blowing themselves up and killing us over these *Fairy Tales,* we can actually sit back and enjoy these amazing stories while sipping some coffee.

Wait a minute! The Qur'an also reveals about an amazing *"Talking Bird"* that praises and glorifies Allah. This fascinating *Bird* could even recite the Islamic creed: *"There is no god but Allah."* It could have either been born into a Muslim family or converted to Islam at some later stage. Was it circumcised as required by Islam? Well, Allah knows best. And this pious *Bird* tolerates no rivalry against Allah by those who worship others besides Allah. Having a solid foundation in the inspired Scriptures of Islam, this devout *Bird* understands that it is *Shaitan* who causes others to turn away from worshipping Allah.

Besides religious knowledge, it also knows some geography. It knows the names of the countries it visits. However, as a regular in Solomon's army, this *Bird* is also liable for punishment if it goes AWOL. It cannot risk flying from Jerusalem to Ethiopia without the official authorization of King Solomon. Rules are rules. Now read the amazing account of the *Hoopoe Bird*:

Surah 27:20-30: And he [Solomon] reviewed the birds, then said: How is it I see not the hoopoe or is it that he is of the absentees? I will most certainly punish him with a severe punishment, or kill him, or he shall bring to me a clear plea.

And he [the Hoopoe Bird] tarried not long, then said: I comprehend that which you do not comprehend and I have brought to you a sure information from Sheba. Surely I found a woman ruling over them, and she has been given abundance and she has a mighty throne: I found her and her people adoring the sun instead of Allah, and the Shaitan has made their deeds fair-seeming to them and thus turned them from the way, so they do not go aright That they do not make obeisance to Allah, Who brings forth what is hidden in the heavens and the earth and knows what you hide and what you make manifest: Allah, there is no god but He: He is the Lord of mighty power.

He [Solomon] said: We will see whether you have told the truth or whether you are of the liars: Take this my letter and hand it over to them, then turn away from them and see what answer they return.
She [Queen of Sheba] said: O chief! Surely an honorable letter has been delivered to me. Surely it is from Sulaiman [Solomon], and surely it is in the name of Allah, the Beneficent, the Merciful. (Sarwar)

Thanks to the missionary zeal of the *Hoopoe Bird* to spread the message of Allah far and wide, the Queen of Sheba finally submitted to Islam. And she lived happily ever after.

Coming back to reality, Muslims will be surprised to learn that the Qur'an itself admits that those who knew Muhammad recognized the fact that he was incorporating *"fables"* into the Qur'an. And these *"fables"* were familiar to them:

Surah 8:31: And when Our Revelation is recited to them they say, "We have heard all this before. We could say something like this if we wanted. This is nothing but ancient fables." (A. Haleem)

وَإِذَا تُتْلَىٰ عَلَيْهِمْ ءَايَـٰتُنَا قَالُوا۟ قَدْ سَمِعْنَا لَوْ نَشَآءُ لَقُلْنَا مِثْلَ هَـٰذَآ إِنْ ۚ هَـٰذَآ إِلَّآ أَسَـٰطِيرُ ٱلْأَوَّلِينَ

Wa izaa tutlaa 'alaihim Aayaatunaa qaaloo qad sami'naa law nashaaa'u laqulnaa misla haazaaa in haazaaa illaaa asaateerul awwaleen

Muslims should stop listening to false stories:
2 Timothy 4:3-4: For there will be a period of time when they will not put up with the wholesome teaching, but according to their own desires, they will surround themselves with teachers to have their ears tickled. They will turn away from listening to the truth and give attention to false stories.

A NOTE TO MUSLIMS

We have presented many compelling reasons in this book to help you make an evaluation of Islam. Nevertheless, they are by no means exhaustive. There are still many more reasons why Islam cannot be the religion of the true God. If you find this article offensive or even shocking, please check the Islamic references provided here on your own.   The article is intentionally written in an assertive manner so as to thaw you from the years of lies that you have been fed from infancy. Though this article may understandably upset or anger you, please remember that the ones telling such truths are in reality the best friends of the Muslims. While *Truth* may hurt, it is the *Lies* that will kill you. Your eternal salvation depends on knowing the *Truth* about your Creator.

Galatians 4:16: "Have I become your enemy because I tell you the truth?" - The Holy Bible

However, if your reluctance to accept Christianity is because of the teaching of Trinity, please be assured that the doctrine of the Trinity is not a Biblical teaching. The dogma of the Trinity does not exist in the Holy Bible. And the concept of the Trinity is against the teachings of Jesus. True Christians do not believe in the Trinity. When the nation of Israel received the Torah, Almighty God clearly revealed the following divine truth:

Deuteronomy 6:4: "Listen, O Israel: Jehovah our God is one Jehovah.

The Bible clearly states that God is one–not three in one. The Bible also makes it clear that Almighty God is a unique, single Being who has no equal:

Psalm 83:18: "You, whose name is Jehovah, you alone are the Most High over all the earth."

Isaiah 45:5: "I am Jehovah, and there is no one else. With the exception of me there is no God."

The Bible's original understanding of a single Supreme Being is firmly sustained in the teachings of Christianity. The inspired Scriptures that were given to the Christians strongly maintain the same divine standard of the Hebrew Scriptures that were given to the Jews:

Galatians 3:20: "God is only one."

1 Corinthians 8:6: For even though there are so-called gods, whether in heaven or on earth, just as there are many "gods" and many "lords," there is actually to us one God, the Father from whom all things are and we for him.

And Jesus Christ addressed his Father as *"the only true God."*

John 17:3: This means everlasting life, their coming to know you, the only true God, and the one whom you sent, Jesus Christ.
Jesus also made it absolutely clear that it is Jehovah alone we should worship:

Matthew 4:10: Jesus said to him: "Go away, Satan! For it is written: 'It is Jehovah your God you must worship, and it is to him alone you must render sacred service.

Dear Muslims, we sincerely hope the reasons provided in this article will move you to leave Islam. But more than that, we hope it will move you to search for the true God:

Isaiah 55:6: Search for Jehovah while he may be found. Call to him while he is near.
Shalom,

Dr. Maxwell Shimba

CONCLUSIONS
JESUS IS GOD IN THE QURAN

Jesus is God in the Qur'an

EXHIBIT ONE

This is a very important issue and everybody should know this fact. I studied the Qur'an and the Hadith and I will discuss this subject according to the Qur'an and the Holy Bible and we will find the truth that "Jesus is Allah according to the Qur'an."

Muslims always love to ask question but sorry to say they don't want to listen your answer. Muslims always think they are right and you are wrong! (Which is false). Therefore, if you don't have good idea about the Qur'an and the Holy Bible and any Muslim asks any question to you then I am sure it will strike like a hammer to your faith! One very minor question Muslims always asks, "Where Jesus said He is God?" I am sure so many of you heard this question.

Now I will show the Muslims in a very special way how we can prove them that Jesus said, 'I am the God' from their book and our book in the same time.

The God of Islam 'Allah' has 99 names. Each name of those is equal to other one. Which means there is no difference between the name of Allah or any of those 99 names. Allah is one of them and He is equal to all those names. No difference but equal. So, if Jesus claimed any of those names it means that Jesus is saying to Muslims that 'He is Muslims God too.'

So, I will tell you how many times Jesus said, 'I am God.' Which means Jesus is God to Muslims as well. There are so many verses in the Holy Bible but I picked only few verses from the Holy Bible.

I challenge all the Muslims in this Earth NOT to run away from this truth. Now my question to them, 'How can Muslims deny this truth?'

One of the names of God in Islam is AL-HAQ. Which means in Arabic 'The Truth.' Did Jesus say in the Holy Bible, "I am the Truth?' Yes. He said on John 14;9," I am the way and the truth and the life. No-one comes to the Father except through Me." The most important for Christians now that Jesus said, "He is the Truth." Always remember this truth.

Can any Muslim deny that is God's (Allah) another name is "The Truth" (AL-HAQ)? No. No one can deny this fact. Because this Truth in Islam is 'Allah'. AL is Arabic word and its English meaning is 'you talking about whom.' HAQ means Truth which in English we say 'I am the Truth'. In Arabic I am the 'AL-HAQ'. Can any Muslim deny that?

Another name for God of Islam is AL-BAETH. The Resurrection. Did Jesus say in the Gospel, "I am the Resurrection?" Yes. In the Gospel of John 11;25-26 Jesus says, "I am the Resurrection and the life. He who believes in Me will live, even though he dies; and who-ever lives and believes in Me will never die." When Muslims God 'Allah' is called 'AL-BEATH' which means resurrection, then it is clearly proven to all of us that Jesus Himself is Allah as Jesus says, "I am the Resurrection." In Arabic "I am the 'AL-BEATH.' There are not a single Muslim in this Earth can deny that. If any Muslim denies this truth, then he/she denies/reject 'Allah' as well because they deny the 99 names of Allah.

The God of Islam has two other names. "AL-AWAL" and "AL-AKHER." In English we say, "I am the Alfa-I am the Omega." (I am the First and I am the Last.) Isaiah 41;4 says, "I, the Lord-with the first of them and with the last-I am He." Also, the book of Revelation 22;13 says, "I am the Alpha and the Omega, the First and the Last, the Beginning and the End." Jesus is the AL-AWAL and Jesus is the AL-AKHER. Muslims there are no any option or excuse to refuse this truth. You have to accept Jesus as your "Allah."

One of the names of the God of Islam 'Allah' is the kings of King. In Arabic 'AL-MALEK.' The book of Revelation says on chapter 17 verse 14, "They will make war against the Lamb, but the Lamb will overcome them because He is Lord of lords and King of kings-and with Him will be His called, chosen and faithful followers."

One of the names of the God of Islam 'Allah' is the Guide-"AL-HADI." Which's English meaning is The Door/Gate. Did Jesus say that He is the Gate? Yes. In the Gospel of John 10;9 tells us Jesus said, "I am the gate; whoever enters through Me will be saved. He will come in and go out, and find pasture."

One of the names of the God of Islam 'Allah' is The Light which in Arabic is "Al-NUR." Did Jesus say that He is the Light or He is the AL-NUR? Yes. In the Gospel of John 8;12 says, "I am the Light of the world. He who follows Me shall not walk in darkness, but will have the light of life." All these verses are clearly proving that Jesus is Allah according to the Koran and no Muslims can deny this truth. (For readers references please check the Gospel of John. 10;9/15;1/6;35 and 10;11).

For this reason, I suggest you my dear Muslims make your decision now. Do not leave it for tomorrow. It may be too late. The door for repentance can be shut and you will live in everlasting regret and suffer punishment. Please do not try to knock the back door because you have to come through the front door and that door is Jesus Christ-AL-HADI.

EXHIBIT TWO

The Quran presents criteria to distinguish the true God from false gods.

Is He then Who creates like him who does not create? Do you not then mind?... And those whom they call on besides Allah have not created anything while they are themselves created; Dead (are they), not living, and they know not when they shall be raised. S. 16:17, 20-21 Shakir

And they have taken besides Him gods, who do not create anything while they are themselves created, and they control not for themselves any harm or profit, and they control not death nor life, nor raising (the dead) to life. S. 25:3 Shakir

These preceding passages state that:

1. The objects which others call upon besides God (i.e., whether other gods, angels, and/or individuals) have not created anything.
2. These objects cannot bring death, cause life, or resurrect.
3. These objects of worship are dead.
Which implies that:
1. God is the Creator.
2. God is the Source of Life.
3. God is ever-Living.

It is no secret that the Holy Bible states that the Lord Jesus created the cosmos and was called upon in worship by the first Christians:

"Through him all things were made; without him nothing was made that has been made... He was in the world, and though the world was made through him, the world did not recognize him." John 1:3, 10

"In Damascus there was a disciple named Ananias. The Lord called to him in a vision, 'Ananias!' 'Yes, Lord,' he answered. The Lord told him, 'Go to the house of Judas on Straight Street and ask for a man from Tarsus named Saul, for he is praying. In a vision he has seen a man named Ananias come and place his hands on him to restore his sight.' 'Lord,' Ananias answered, 'I have heard many reports about this man and all the harm he has done to your saints in Jerusalem. And he has come here with authority from the chief priests to arrest all who call on your name.' But the Lord said to Ananias, 'Go! This man is my chosen instrument to carry my name before the Gentiles and their kings and before the people of Israel. I will show him how much he must suffer for my name.' Then Ananias went to the house and entered it. Placing his hands on Saul, he said, 'Brother Saul, the Lord-Jesus, who appeared to you on the road as you were coming here--has sent me so that you may see again and be filled with the Holy Spirit'... All those who heard him were astonished and asked, 'Isn't he the man who raised havoc in Jerusalem among those who call on this name? And hasn't he come here to take them as prisoners to the chief priests?'" Acts 9:10-17, 21

"To the church of God in Corinth, to those sanctified in Christ Jesus and called to be holy, together with all those everywhere who call on the name of our Lord Jesus Christ-their Lord and ours:" 1 Corinthians 1:2

"He is the image of the invisible God, the firstborn over all creation. For BY HIM all things were created: things in heaven and on earth, visible and invisible, whether thrones or powers or rulers or authorities; all things were created BY HIM and FOR HIM. He is before all things, and IN HIM all things hold together. And he is the head of the body, the church; he is the beginning and the firstborn from among the dead, so that in everything he might have the supremacy." Colossians 1:15-18

"but in these last days he has spoken to us by his Son, whom he appointed heir of all things, and through whom he made the universe. The Son is the radiance of God's glory and the exact representation of his being, sustaining all things by his powerful word. After he had provided purification for sins, he sat down at the right hand of the Majesty in heaven... And again, when God brings his firstborn into the world, he says, 'Let all God's angels worship him'... But about the Son he says... 'In the beginning, O Lord, you laid the foundations of the earth, and the heavens are the work of your hands. They will perish, but you remain; they will all wear out like a garment. You will roll them up like a robe; like a garment they will be changed. But you remain the same, and your years will never end.'" Hebrews 1:2-3, 6, 8a, 10-12

According to the same Holy Bible, the Lord Jesus is alive forever and ever, having conquered death and ushering in glorious immortality:

"So do not be ashamed to testify about our Lord, or ashamed of me his prisoner. But join with me in suffering for the gospel, by the power of God, who has saved us and called us to a holy life-not because of anything we have done but because of his own purpose and grace. This grace was given us in Christ Jesus before the beginning of time, but it has now been revealed through the appearing of our Savior, Christ Jesus, who has destroyed death and has brought life and immortality to light through the gospel." 2 Timothy 1:8-10

"When I saw him, I fell at his feet as though dead. Then he placed his right hand on me and said: 'Do not be afraid. I am the First and the Last. I am the Living One; I was dead, and behold I am alive for ever and ever! And I hold the keys of death and Hades.'" Revelation 1:17-18

"To the angel of the church in Smyrna write: These are the words of him who is the First and the Last, who died and came to life again." Revelation 2:8

By conquering death, Christ demonstrated that he is truly the source of life for all:

"In him was life, and that life was the light of men." John 1:4

"For just as the Father raises the dead and gives them life, even so the Son gives life to whom he is pleased to give it... I tell you the truth, a time is coming and has now come when the dead will hear THE VOICE OF THE SON OF GOD and those who hear will live... Do not be amazed at this, for a time is coming when all who are in their graves will hear HIS VOICE and come out-those who have done good will rise to live, and those who have done evil will rise to be condemned." John 5:21, 25, 28-29

"Jesus said to her, 'I AM THE RESURRECTION AND THE LIFE. He who believes in me will live, even though he dies; and whoever lives and believes in me will never die. Do you believe this?' 'Yes, Lord,' she told him, 'I believe that you are the Christ, the Son of God, who was to come into the world.'" John 11:25-27

"Jesus answered, 'I am the way and the truth and THE LIFE. No one comes to the Father except through me.'" John 14:6

"But our citizenship is in heaven. And we eagerly await a Savior from there, the Lord Jesus Christ, who, by the power that enables him to bring everything under his control, will transform our lowly bodies so that they will be like his glorious body." Philippians 3:20-21

"For you died, and your life is now hidden with Christ in God. When Christ, who is your life, appears, then you also will appear with him in glory." Colossians 3:3-4

The Lord Jesus fits the criteria given in the Quran which demonstrates true Deity (i.e., the Creator, the Source of Life, and ever-Living). Christians are therefore justified in worshiping him as their sovereign Lord.

Now the Muslim will definitely object to our appeal to the Holy Bible on the grounds that it doesn't accurately reflect the life and teachings of the historical Jesus, and as such it cannot be used to prove that Jesus and his original followers truly believed that Christ was God.

It is not the object of this present paper to provide the evidence which establishes the historical veracity of the NT documents, or to demonstrate that the first followers of Christ confessed their belief in the absolute Deity of the Lord Jesus, or in his death and resurrection.

What we would like to do here is to show that even according to the testimony of the Quran, the Lord Jesus perfectly fulfills the criteria of being Deity.

"and he shall be a prophet to the people of Israel (saying), that I have come to you, with a sign from God, namely, that I will CREATE for you out of clay (annee AKHLUQU lakum mina ALTTEENI) as though it were the form of a bird, and I will blow thereon and it shall become a bird by God's permission; and I will heal the blind from birth, and lepers; and I will bring the dead to life by God's permission; and I will tell you what you eat and what ye store up in your houses. Verily, in that is a sign for you if ye be believers. S. 3:49 Palmer"

When God shall say, O Jesus son of Mary, remember my favor towards thee, and towards thy mother; when I strengthened thee with the holy spirit, that thou shouldest speak unto men in the cradle, and when thou wast grown up; and when I taught thee the scripture, and wisdom, and the law, and the gospel; and when thou didst CREATE of clay (wa-ith TAKHLUQU mina ALTTEENI) as it were the figure of a bird, by my permission, and didst breathe thereon, and it became a bird by my permission; and thou didst heal one blind from his birth, and the leper, by my permission; and when thou didst bring forth the dead [from their graves], by my permission; and when I with-held the children of Israel from [killing] thee, when thou hadst come unto them with evident [miracles], and such of them as believed not, said, this is nothing but manifest sorcery. S. 5:110 Sale

These two passages demonstrate that Christ has the breath of life and can create in exactly the same way God creates:

HE it is Who created you from clay (Huwa allathee KHALAQAKUM min TEENIN) and then HE decreed a term. And there is another term fixed with HIM. Yet you doubt. S. 6:2 Y. Ali

Behold, thy Lord said to the angels: "I am about to create man from clay (innee KHALIQUN basharan min TEENIN): When I have fashioned him (in due proportion) and breathed into him of My spirit, fall ye down in obeisance unto him." S. 38:71-72 Y. Ali.

Note the connection between God breathing his Spirit into man with Christ being strengthened with the Holy Spirit, breathing life into clay birds and resurrecting the dead. And also notice that Christ created a living bird from clay just as God created man from clay. These passages therefore teach that Christ had the same life-giving Spirit of God.

The Quran says by way of mocking the gods of the people:

"O mankind! A similitude has been coined, so listen to it (carefully): verily! Those on whom you call besides Allah cannot create (even) a fly, even though they combine together for the purpose. And if the fly snatched away a thing from them, they would have no power to release it from the fly. So weak are (both) the seeker and the sought." S. 22:73

Even though Jesus didn't create a fly, he did create a bird and breathed life into it just as Allah did to Adam!

In fact, according to one Salafi Muslim site the word for create (khalaqa) refers to creating something from nothing, an act which only God can perform:

Imam al-Bukhari reported in his Saheeh from Abu Sa`eed (may Allah be pleased with him) that the Prophet (Peace & Blessings of Allah be upon Him) said: "There is no created being but Allah created it." In Arabic, the word "khalaqa" means to make out of nothing, which is something that ONLY ALLAH CAN DO; it is impossible for anyone except Allah to do this. It also carries the meaning of decreeing or foreordaining. [**]

See Fath al-Bari Sharh Saheeh al-Bukhari, 13/390. (439: Evidence that only Allah is the Creator of life; bold and capital emphasis ours)

But this very same word is applied to Christ which means, at least according to the above position, that Jesus must be God! Note how this works out logically:

1. God alone can create out of nothing (i.e. the literal meaning of khalaqa).

2. Khalaqa is applied to Jesus.

3. Therefore, Jesus must be God according to Islam.

The Quran also implies that Christ is alive in heaven:

And when Allah said: O Isa, I am going to terminate the period of your stay (on earth) and cause you to ascend unto Me and purify you of those who disbelieve and make those who follow you above those who disbelieve to the day of resurrection; then to Me shall be your return, so I will decide between you concerning that in which you differed. S. 3:55 Shakir

That they said (in boast), "We killed Christ Jesus the son of Mary, the Apostle of God"; - but they killed him not, nor crucified him, but so it was made to appear to them, and those who differ therein are full of doubts, with no (certain) knowledge, but only conjecture to follow, for of a surety they killed him not:- Nay, God raised him up unto Himself; and God is Exalted in Power, Wise; - S. 4:157-158 Y. Ali

Orthodox Islam has generally understood these passages to mean that Christ was taken alive into heaven, into the very presence of God himself.

Moreover, specific Islamic narrations teach that Jesus will be an intercessor for his people:

... "Surely! Allah wrongs not even of the weight of an atom (or a smallest ant) but if there is any good (done) He doubles it." (4.40) The Prophet added, "Then THE PROPHETS and Angels and the believers will intercede, and (last of all) the Almighty (Allah) will say, 'Now remains My Intercession. He will then hold a handful of the Fire from which He will take out some people whose bodies have been burnt, and they will be thrown into a river at the entrance of Paradise, called the water of life. ..." (Sahih al-Bukhari, Volume 9, Book 93, Number 532s)

Ibn Kathir wrote in reference to Sura 3:45 that:

Held in honor in this world and in the Hereafter, and will be one of those who are near to Allah. Meaning, he will be a leader and honored by Allah in this life, because of the Law that Allah will reveal to him, sending down the Scripture to him, along with the other bounties that Allah will grant him with. `Isa will be honored in the Hereafter and will intercede with Allah, by His leave, on behalf of some people, just as is the case with his brethren the mighty Messengers of Allah, peace be upon them all. (Source)

The next text supports the interpretation that Jesus may intercede:

And We did not send before you any apostle but We revealed to him that there is no god but Me, therefore serve Me. And they say: The Beneficent God has taken to Himself a son. Glory be to Him. Nay! they are honored servants. They do not precede Him in speech and (only) according to His commandment do they act. He knows what is before them and what is behind them, and they do not intercede except for him whom He approves and for fear of Him they tremble. And whoever of them should say: Surely, I am a god besides Him, such a one do We recompense with hell; thus do, We recompense the unjust. S. 21:25-29 Shakir

This reference says that at least some of those honored servants who were wrongly worshiped as gods or considered children of God will indeed intercede. And since according to the Quran Jesus is an honored servant who was wrongly worshiped as God and as the Son of God this therefore means that he may well be one of those interceding.

But this directly conflicts with the following text:

And those whom they invoke besides God HAVE NO POWER OF INTERCESSION; - only he who bears witness to the Truth, and they know (him). If thou ask them, who created them, they will certainly say, God: How then are they deluded away (from the Truth)? (God has knowledge) of the (Prophet's) cry, "O my Lord! Truly these are people who will not believe!" S. 43:86-88

No intercessor will they have from those whom they made equal with Allah (partners i.e., their so-called associate gods), and they will (themselves) reject and deny their partners. S. 30:13 Hilali-Khan

The above references claim that those invoked by the unbelievers have no power to intercede. Jesus happens to be one of those very beings that so-called unbelieving Christians invoked and continue to invoke in their prayers. Thus, either Jesus can intercede which means that the Quran is wrong; or he cannot intercede which means that the Islamic tradition is wrong.

In light of the aforementioned citations, we are left with the conclusion that:

1. Jesus creates in the same way God creates.
2. Jesus gives life in the same way God gives life.
3. Jesus is alive in heaven.

Therefore, the Quran clearly shows that the Lord Jesus fits the description of God, fulfilling the very criteria which demonstrates that Christ is indeed very God of very God.

Yet, it is at this precise point that we have a contradiction within the Quran itself. There is no denying that the Quran rejects the Deity of Jesus (cf. 4:171; 5:17, 70-75; 9:30). But, as we just saw, the Quran attributes titles, qualities and functions to Christ which shows that he is indeed God. Other titles given to Christ which affirm his essential Deity include the Word of God and a Spirit from God (cf. 3:39, 45; 4:171).

A Muslim may say that Jesus was given the ability to create and give life by God, just as the passages themselves state. He didn't have this ability within himself. This response doesn't solve the contradiction, but only pushes it a step further.

Why would God grant Jesus the abilities and characteristics of Deity? Why is God permitting Jesus to perfectly fit the description and fulfill the criteria which places one within the category of God?

Second, the expression "by God's permission" doesn't necessarily mean that Christ was given abilities he did not already have. The statements can be understood in light of the biblical teaching that Christ did nothing on his own initiative, but did everything in perfect union with his Father's will. (cf. John 5:16-30)

In other words, the Quranic expression simply implies that Christ only exercised his divine prerogatives in accordance with the decree of God, never acting on his own behest or initiative. It need not deny that Christ always had these divine attributes and characteristics. This becomes all the more likely when we recall that the Quran describes Christ as God's Word and a Spirit proceeding from God, titles which point to Christ's divinity and pre-existence.

BIBLIOGRAPHY

Contemporary and Ancient Muslim Scholars
Interpretation and Background of Verses from the Qur'an:
1. Commentary of al-Baydawi, The Lights of Revelation, Dar Al Geel (The Generation)
2. Brief Commentary of Al Emam Al Tabarie, Dar Al Shorok (Sunrise)
3. Commentary of Al Galaleen, Al Azhar, supervision 1983
4. Commentary of Al Zama Khsharie, 4 volumes Al Kasshaf, Dar (The Arabic Book)
5. The Right in Qur'an's Science (Al Itkan) Al Seiewtie, Dar Al Torth (The Tradition) Abo-Al-Fadl
6. The Reasons of the Verses of the Qur'an (Asbab Al-Nuzul) Al Seiewtie, Nosair Library, Azhar scholars, supervision
7. Al Sahih Al Mosnad (The Reasons of Qur'anic Verses) Dar Al Arkam
8. Al Wahedy (The Reasons of Qur'anic Verses) including the Abrogator and the Abrogated verses concerning the law of Islam (Sharia)
9. The Bill of Legal Punishments, Azhar scholars
10. Ibn Taymiyya (36 volumes) Al Fatawy, Saudi Arabian scholars
11. The Ordinances (Akham) of the Qur'an, The Imam, Al-Shafi'i, Dar (The Scientific Books in 2 volumes)
12. The Sweetest (2 volumes) (Al Mohalla) Ibn Hazm (dozens of volumes), corrected version, Beirut, Lebanon
13. Zad-Al-Maad, Ibn Qayyim-al-Jawziyya, Library of 'Manara al-Isalmiyya 1984 and the 5th volume 1981, 2nd version
14. The Spirit of Islamic Religion - Afify Abdel Fatah, review Azhar scholars
15. The History of Islamic Legislation (shariaa) Dr. Ahmad Shalabi, 2nd version

16. Islamic Nation State - Taky Al Dean Akl Banahani, The Liberty Part, Al Kods (Israel)
17. The Main Issues (Kadaya) in Islam, Abdel Al Motal Al Seidi-Al Azhar University
18. The Shita and the Correction, Dr. Mosa Al Mosawy, 1978
19. The Opinions (Al Fatawy) 1-10, Mohamad Mutwaly Al Sharawy (Egypt)
20. You Ask and Islam Answers - Al Sharawy, Dar Al Muslim, 1982
21. Islam - A Dogma and A Law (Sharia) Al Imam Muhamad Shaltout (12 versions)
22. Islam in the Face of Modern Challenges, Abu al-ala al Mawdudi, 1983, 5th version)
23. The Rights of Non-Muslims in the Islamic State, Al Mawdudi
24. You Ask and Islam Answers, Abdul latif Mushtahari
25. Women of Paradise (1) Muhamad Ali Abul Alabbas, 1987, Qur'an's Library
26. The Revival of Religion's Science, Al Ghazali, Dar (The Knowledge) for printing and publishing, Beirut

Concerning the History of Islam/the Biography of Muhammad, His Disciples, His Relatives and Wives:

27. The Biography of the Apostle, Ibn Hisham, Dar Al Tawfikie Al Azhar
28. The Biography of Myhammad and the Wars (Maghazy) Ibn Isaac, Dr. Sohaul Zakkar, Dar Al Fekr
29. Al Rod Al Anf, Al Sohaily, Dar Al Fekr, 1971 30. The Biography of Muhammad, Al Halabbya, Dar (The Knowledge), Beirut
31. The History by Tabari, Dar (The Scientific Books), Beirut
32. The Biography of the Prophet, Ibn Kathir, Dar Al Knowledge, Beirut
33. The Beginning and the End, Ibn Kathir, Library of Maaref, Beirut
34. The Perfect in History, Ibn Al Athir, 1967, Dar Al Arabic Book
35. The History by Ibn Khaldon, Al Aaelmy, Beirut, 1971
36. The History of the Kholafa (Successor of Muhammad) Al Sweitie
37. The Prophetic Biography (Gawameh) Ibn Ham, Mecca Mokarrama
38. Al Gameh Kerawany, Islamic Tradition -17

39. The Light of Certainty "Nur Al Yaqin" Al Khodary, 24th version

40. The Life of Muhammad, Muhammad Husayn Haykal, Dar Al-Maaref, 17th version

41. Jurisprudence of Muhammad's Biography, Dr. Buti, Al Azhar, 7th version

42. Al Isaba (Life History of Muhammad's Friend) Ibn Hagar, Dar, The Arabid Book, Beirut

43. The Lion of the Forest (Asad Al Ghaba) Ibn Al Athir, Dar Al Shaab (People)

44. The History of the Arabic Nation, Dr. Abdul Fattah Shehata, Al Azhar, 1972

45. The Successor of the Prophet, Khalid Muhammad Khalid, Dar thabet. 1986

46. The Guided Caliphs, Dr. Abu Zeid Shalaby, Al Azhar, 1967

47. The Jurisprudence of Muhammad's Friends, Ibn Abbas, Abdel Aziz Al Shennawy, 1989

48. Explanation of Nahg Al Balagha, Ibn Al Hadid

49. Muhammad's Wives, Aisha Abdul Rahman

50. Muhammad's Daughters, Aisha Abdul Rahman, Dar The Arabic Book, Beirut (Bent Al Shati)

51. Ali and His Enemies, Dr. Nory Gafar, 1982, Beirut

52. Ali and His Sons, Taha Husain

53. The Big Division, Taha Husain

54. The Two Elders, Taha Husain

55. About the Biography of Muhammad, Taha Husain

56.. The Roots of Divisions in Islamic Parties, Hason Sadek, Madboly Library

57. Before the Fall, 1985, Dr. Farag Fouda

58. The Ignored (Neglected) Fact, 1986, Dr. Farag Fouda (NOTE: Dr. Fouda was killed by fanatic Muslims in 1992)

59. Three Books About Muhammad's Successors, Abu Bakr Omar and Ali, (Abbas Mahmoud Al Akkad).

(NOTE: Dr. Fouda, Taha and Al Akkad are not Muslim scholars, of course, but they depend totally upon all ancient Muslim scholars with accuracy and complete honesty and no Muslim scholar can object to that)

The Sayings of Muhammad (Sunnah) (NOTE: these are the most popular and important books among all Muslims.)
60. Sahih Bukhari
61. Sahih Muslim - Mawawy
62. Riyad As-Salihin
63. Hadith Qudsi